LORD DURHAM'S REPORT

CARLETON LIBRARY SERIES

The Carleton Library Series, funded by Carleton University under the
general editorship of the dean of the School of Graduate Studies and
Research, publishes books about Canadian economics, geography, history,
politics, society, and related subjects. It includes important new works as
well as reprints of classics in the fields. The editorial committee welcomes
manuscripts and suggestions, which should be sent to the dean of the School
of Graduate Studies and Research, Carleton University.

192 The Blacks in Canada: A History
(second edition)
Robin Winks

193 A Disciplined Intelligence
Critical Inquiry and Canadian
Thought in the Victorian Era
A.B. McKillop

194 Land, Power, and Economics
on the Frontier of Upper Canada
John Clarke

195 The Children of Aataentsic
A History of the Huron People
to 1660
Bruce G. Trigger

196 Silent Surrender
The Multinational Corporation in
Canada
Kari Levitt

197 Cree Narrative
Expressing the Personal Meanings
of Events
Richard J. Preston

198 The Dream of Nation
A Social and Intellectual History
of Quebec
Susan Mann

199 A Great Duty
Canadian Responses to Modern
Life and Mass Culture,
1939–1967
L.B. Kuffert

200 The Politics of Development
Forests, Mines, and Hydro-Electric
Power in Ontario, 1849–1941
H.V. Nelles

201 Watching Quebec: Selected Essays
Ramsay Cook

202 Land of the Midnight Sun
A History of the Yukon
*Ken S. Coates and William R.
Morrison*

203 The Canadian Quandary
Harry Johnson
(New edition)

204 Canada and the Cost of World
War II
The International Operation of the
Department of Finance, 1939–1947
Robert B. Bryce
Edited by Mathew Bellamy

205 Lament for a Nation
George Grant
(Anniversary edition)

206 Confederation Debates in the
Province of Canada, 1865
P.B. Waite
(New edition)

207 The History of Canadian Business,
1867–1914
R.T. Naylor

208 Lord Durham's Report
*Based on the Abridgement by
Gerald M. Craig*
(New edition)

NEW EDITION

Lord Durham's Report

AN ABRIDGEMENT OF
Report on the Affairs of British North America
BY LORD DURHAM

EDITED BY G.M. CRAIG
INTRODUCTIONS BY
G.M. CRAIG AND JANET AJZENSTAT
AFTERWORD BY GUY LAFOREST

Carleton Library Series 1, 208
McGill-Queen's University Press
Montreal & Kingston • London • Ithaca

© McGill-Queen's University Press 2007
ISBN: 978-0-7735-3000-3 (cloth)
ISBN: 978-0-7735-3001-0 (paper)

Legal deposit first quarter 2007
Bibliothèque nationale du Québec

Printed in Canada on acid-free paper.

McGill-Queen's University Press acknowledges the support of
the Canada Council for the Arts for our publishing program.
We also acknowledge the financial support of the Government
of Canada through the Book Publishing Industry Development
Program (BPIDP) for our publishing activities.

Canadian Cataloguing in Publication Data

Durham, John George Lambton, Earl of, 1792-1840
   Lord Durham's report: an abridgement of Report on the
affairs of British North America

   (Carleton library series; 1, 208)
   ISBN: 978-0-7735-3000-3 (bnd)
   ISBN: 978-0-7735-3001-0 (pbk)
   1. Canada – Politics and government – 1837-1838.   2. Canada –
History – Rebellion, 1837-1838.
   3. Ontario – Politics and government – 1791-1841.
   4. Quebec (Province) – Politics and government – 1791-1841.
   I. Craig, Gerald M.   II. Title.   III. Series

FC462.D87 1992   971.03'9   C92-090673-7
F1032.D87 1992

CONTENTS

INTRODUCTION TO THE 2006 EDITION   vii
Janet Ajzenstat

INTRODUCTION TO THE 1963 EDITION   xxxiii
G.M. Craig

LORD DURHAM'S COMMISSION   3

REPORT

Introductory   6

Lower Canada   10

Upper Canada   72

The Eastern Provinces and Newfoundland   102

Disposal of Public Lands   107

Emigration   118

General Review and Recommendations   124

AFTERWORD: LORD DURHAM, FRENCH CANADA,
AND QUEBEC   177
Guy Laforest

SUGGESTIONS FOR FURTHER READING   205

INDEX   209

INTRODUCTION TO THE 2006 EDITION

Every generation of Canadians reads the Durham Report, or learns of it. It was published in 1839 and has been in print ever since. It has given rise to innumerable scholarly discussions and articles and not a few books. In the 1840s, British North American reformers hailed it as the charter of free government because it promised the overthrow of the colonial oligarchies (the Family Compact, the Chateau Clique, and the "official parties" in the Maritime provinces). Twenty years later, the Fathers of Canadian Confederation found in it the model for a national legislature, the Parliament of the British North American union. In the last years of the nineteenth century and the first years of the twentieth, Englishmen turned to it for instructions on ruling the Empire's "senior Dominions"; in subsequent decades they found a prescription for the Commonwealth of Nations. It is the one text in Canada's political history that is routinely prefaced by the adjective, "famous." (We do not speak of the famous British North America Act, the famous Statute of Westminster, or the famous Canadian Charter of Rights and Freedoms.)

Consider this statement by C.P. Lucas, editor of the 1912 edition: "To all times and to all sorts and conditions of men [Lord Durham] has preached the doctrine, that for peoples, as for individuals, the one thing worth living for is to make, not to destroy, to build up, not to pull down: to unite small disjointed elements into a single whole; to reject absolutely and always the doctrine of *Divide et Impera*, because it is a sign of weakness, not of strength; to be strong and fear not; to speak unto the peoples of the earth that they go forward." Few commentators equal Lucas in enthusiasm, but some come close. In 1929 Durham's biographer, Chester New, describes the Report as "one of the few events of world-history of which one can say that this is the beginning of something absolutely new under the sun." He continues: "When the unique type of empire which it created has completely worked out its destiny, it will be time to venture a final estimate of [the Report's] significance." Introducing the edition of 1963, Gerald Craig advances an only somewhat more modest assessment: "no attempt to debunk or to deflate the great *Report* would be very successful. Despite all its shortcomings and defects it remains one of the most vigorous and perceptive expositions of the principles and practices of free government in the history of the English-speaking peoples."

The Report has had two "lives," so to speak. It treats two issues of perennial interest, distinct but ultimately connected. Each has been the subject of continuing debate and disagreement. First there is the matter of imperial rule and colonial liberation. Recall Chester New's suggestion that the Report created a "unique" type of empire. At the time New was writing it was commonly said that Durham proposed to give the British North Americans some of the freedoms associated with political independence – but only some of them – in order to forestall their bid for complete emancipation. The formula was described as unique because it called for strengthening the Empire by loosening imperial ties. But some of Durham's contemporaries tell a different story. They argue that he meant to give the British North Americans *all* the freedoms of independent nations, intending nothing less than colonial emancipation! Some of these early readers, chief among them Durham's ministerial colleagues in Britain, are appalled by the idea; Durham had been sent out to save the Empire, not to savage it. Others, like Nova Scotia's Joseph Howe, are elated. They rejoice in the idea of colonial autonomy and argue that in place of imperial rule Durham recommended, or foresaw, a new era of voluntary and effective cooperation among the former colonies, and between the former colonies and Britain. In short, some readers concluded that Durham had found a formula to bring democracy and global peace under one aegis, or perhaps I should say English-speaking peace, British peace. It was an idea to make the heart leap.

The second question of perennial interest, and the occasion of the second controversy, is whether Durham supposed that the exercise of "the principles and practices of free government," to use Craig's phrase, requires a population steeped in British "culture." Many passages in the Report suggest that he expected French Canadians to adopt not only the institutions of British democracy but also the culture, the social ways of life, typical of the Mother Country.

Gerald Craig reminds us – as if Canadians needed reminding – that the extraordinary praise for the Report is not unqualified. If it is often called famous, it is sometimes said to be "infamous." In the eyes of many, Craig among them, the Report's great defect is its suggestion that the French should assimilate to an English Canadian way of life. According to Craig, Durham was wrong on two counts. He was wrong to entertain the idea of assimilation (wrong from a moral standpoint, we might say), and wrong, hopelessly wrong, to suppose that uniting the provinces would accomplish this objective. Indeed, most Canadian scholars argue that after the union of Upper and Lower Canada in 1840, the French used the political institutions of the united province – the very institutions that Durham had recommended – to successfully defend the French Canadian way of life.

C.P. Lucas too had his doubts about Durham on French Canada. The empire that Lucas contemplated was composed of cultural groups, peoples, nationalities, ethnicities, religions, and races from every region of the globe. His question is whether Durham's apparent ignorance of culture's deep roots wrecked the formula for freedom and empire. Behind Lucas' doubts, and behind argument's like Craig's, a broader question lingers. Durham proposes the introduction of the constitutional principle we call responsible government, the principle that defines parliamentary systems. He intends the French Canadians to live with their English neighbours in a parliamentary democracy. Is he wrong to suppose that the practice of parliamentary democracy requires – or encourages – cultural homogeneity? Is it entirely wrong to suppose that liberal democracy, despite all hopes to the contrary, erodes particular cultures?

THE "STANDARD INTERPRETATION" (1929 TO THE PRESENT)

Today the issue of colonial emancipation is almost forgotten. Most Canadians reading the Report focus on the second great question, and most come to Gerald Craig's conclusion: the recommendation for responsible government is no doubt praiseworthy but Durham's expectation that the French Canadians would assimilate is, to put it briefly, offensive. As Chester New says: "[The] great weakness of the Report – all the more striking because it marked Durham's only failure in the sphere of political prophecy – is its treatment of the French-Canadians." Durham "came to Canada, with the prejudices of the British ruling class against the French-Canadians as a rebellious and contumacious race and an intense English feeling which sometimes closed the door to broader sympathies." His "woeful ignorance" of the variety of political opinion in the French population and his failure to respect French Canadian pride "marred what was in many respects a brilliant analysis of the situation in Lower Canada."

Craig follows New to the letter. "From the perspective of our own times," he argues, "the sections on the French Canadians appear to be the faultiest and the most misguided in the whole Report – the one great blot in an otherwise admirable and enlightened analysis." He adds in a well-known passage, "Lord Durham could not know as clearly in 1839 what we know today, that it is foolhardy and naïve to speak of breaking down the customs of a well-established and organized ethnic and cultural community."

The views submitted by New and Craig have become in this country what I call the "standard interpretation" of the Report: Durham was either prejudiced, as New argues, or merely ignorant, as Craig suggests. There have been a few squawks of protest from revisionist scholars (I am one), there are a few textbooks that break the pattern, but in the main the standard interpretation retains its clout. In English Canada, it is taken for granted. It has become a habit of mind.

As received wisdom it has done something, perhaps much, to shape relations between French and English Canadians. It undoubtedly gratifies English-speakers, especially those of "British stock." By expressing our disapproval of Durham on assimilation we say *mea culpa* for the sins of conquest and empire, and centuries of British snobbery. And we swear allegiance to liberal doctrines of cultural tolerance. But consider: the standard interpretation depicts French Canadians as "the other," to use a post-modern term, as a people not-like-us. It suggests, moreover, that Quebec's culture is static (it is "naïve to speak of breaking down the customs of a well-established and organized ethnic and cultural community"). And it hints at the idea that decisions about Quebec's future are up to "us," the English-speakers. However pleasant it may appear to Quebecers that, under the influence of the standard interpretation, English Canadians are led to regard Quebec as a distinctive society, it remains a fact that the interpretation conjures images of backwardness. It encourages the idea that French Canadians are hostile to change. At the time Gerald Craig was writing (the early 1960s) Quebec was in the process of transforming its economic and social institutions in radical fashion. But caught in the toils of the standard interpretation, Craig could not see the changes. Of course, English Canadians have never depended solely on the standard interpretation of Lord Durham's Report for their understanding of French-English relations. I wish merely to point out that the standard interpretation has injected a note of confusion. It has not made it easier for Canadians to define nationhood, nationality, and culture.

What *did* Durham mean to accomplish by the union of Upper and Lower Canada? He says outright that the British "race must ultimately prevail." The British must be "placed in the ascendant." Lower Canada must be "thoroughly assimilated to British ways and institutions." These passages and others like them leave a deep wound. I do not believe that anyone of French origin reading them will ever warm to Durham. One thing we can say, however, is that he did not envisage a static future for French Canada. Durham was a mover and shaker and he wanted the French to get a move on; he wanted them to advance into the sunny uplands of progress and prosperity. Indeed he thought they were already on the move: French Canadian businessmen and political elites were beginning to build a modern commercial society; they were interested in new technologies ("means of communication") and in social and constitutional reform. He makes it very clear, moreover, that some Englishmen and some British policies were impeding French Canadian ambitions. It suited Englishmen who had acquired seignories to keep their tenants down on the farm. It suited the English elites of Montreal to keep the French out of political office. Durham treats Englishmen with these views harshly. In this edition I have restored a passage cut by Craig in 1963, in which Durham argues that the French population favoured the overthrow of feudal tenure. See below, pages 17 to 19.

Nevertheless, we want to know whether he envisaged the eradication of the French Canadian "identity," that is, the French way of life. Indeed, what we really want to know is whether the adoption of modern political principles and business practices is compatible with maintenance of a distinctive identity and sense of cultural continuity. It will be easier to tackle this subject if we first look at the other great issue, the one of all-consuming importance for most of Durham's British commentators: would the prescription for democracy destroy the Empire? It may seem that we are taking a detour – a detour of approximately one hundred years – but long before it is over we will find that it has brought us back again to the issue of assimilation.

RESPONSIBLE GOVERNMENT AND EMPIRE (THE 1840s)

Responsible government promised self-government in the colonies: it promised, as I have said, at least a degree of independence from imperial control and perhaps a great deal of independence. But in 1839, understandably, the British Government had its doubts about emancipation. In June of that year, four months after the Report was published, Lord John Russell put this resolution before the British Parliament: "That while it is expedient to improve the composition of the Executive Council of Lower Canada, it is unadvisable to subject it to the responsibility demanded by the Legislative Assembly of that Province." It looked for a time as if the British Whigs would reject Durham's responsible government proposal.

Responsible government has two aspects. The first concerns the regime's head of state. In parliamentary democracies the governor or monarch represents the populace in its entirety; she also represents the *idea* of parliamentary democracy. But she does not govern: she must refrain from advocating specific policies and avoid party politics. As Frank MacKinnon puts it, the monarch *has* the powers of state but does not *wield* them. This aspect of responsible government is spelled out in the Constitution Act, 1867 (formerly called the British North America Act, 1867), in sections 9, 11, 12, and 13.

The second aspect of responsible government concerns the wielders. The monarch or governor is instructed by advisors, her "ministers," her "Cabinet" (in the colonies, the executive councillors); they wield the power. But – this is the crucial proviso – to maintain their right to *wield*, they must have the approval of the majority of the people's elected representatives in the lower chamber (in the colonies, the Legislative Assembly; today, the House of Commons) on measures of great importance, and especially on taxing and spending bills. The idea is perfectly familiar. Durham described it, we live with it today, and it is enshrined in the Constitution Act, 1867 in sections 53 and 54. (One hears it said that the Constitution Act, 1867 does not contain a reference to responsible government or a formula for it. I cannot understand how this false idea arose.)

The consequence is that those who are running the country or colony, the party elites in office, answer to the people's representatives in the popular chamber and thus to the electorate and the people at large. In Durham's words (in a passage referring to British practice), "When a ministry ceases to command a majority in Parliament on great questions of policy, its doom is immediately sealed; and it would appear to us as strange to attempt, for any time, to carry on a Government by means of ministers perpetually in a minority, as it would be to pass laws with a majority of votes against them." Once responsible government was established in the British North American colonies (for many of them, in 1848) the old oligarchs were shown the door. To use a slogan of the period, responsible government meant Power to the People – in a British system of parliamentary checks and balances. It is true that after 1848 the Colonial Office and Westminster Parliament still retained the right to look in on what was happening in the colonial legislatures and even to veto measures that would adversely affect British interests. But as a matter of fact Britain almost never interfered; on domestic matters, certainly, the colonists ran the show.

To repeat: under the old system the colonial Executive Council answered to the Governor and the Governor reported to the Colonial Office and thus to the Parliament of Westminster. The wielders of power in the colonies looked across the ocean to the centre of empire. (That was the theory; in practice their relative lack of accountability gave them a good many opportunities to do political favours for friends and family.) But now their heads were to be wrenched around and they would have to look to the interests of their constituents and the people of the province, on pain of losing office. What would keep them attuned to imperial matters? The question for Lord John Russell and others of like mind was whether the colonies would run away immediately or merely drift off over the course of the years.

A prominent Upper Canadian with views like Russell's was John Beverley Robinson. In *Canada and the Canada Bill* (1840) Robinson describes the operation of responsible government in the Westminster Parliament with greatest approval but opposes it for his own beloved province, arguing that its introduction would sever the imperial connection and thus deprive Upper Canada of British trade preferences and the security afforded by the British military presence. He is scathing on the subject of the meddlesome Lord Durham.

The classic defence of Durham on responsible government is found in a collection of four open letters to Lord John Russell published in the fall of 1839 by Nova Scotia's "tribune of the people," Joseph Howe. It is a superlative commentary: Howe is the colonial "Durham" par excellence. The letters range over many topics, but the burning issue between Howe and Russell can be stated in a sentence. Russell believed that political disagreements between the colonies and the home country would require formal procedures of resolution: on some questions, perhaps not many, the colonists would have to defer to Westminster. Howe did not accept the idea that disagreements would arise; he thus saw no need for formal procedures. In Howe's opinion, the introduction of responsible government would put an end to the major quarrels between colony and metropolis. And should petty difficulties make themselves known, "the good sense of all parties concerned may be safely trusted to avoid any violent or unpleasant collision."

Throughout, Howe claims to be speaking for Durham. Responsible government would end rebellion and promote an era of cooperation. Between the parliamentary nations, there would be accord. Among democracies, there is peace.

I would argue that Howe perfectly captures Durham's intention. Charles Buller and Edward Gibbon Wakefield, Durham's chief aides and researchers on the Canada tour, offer an interpretation very like Howe's. But later commentators disagree. It seems to these later readers inconceivable that an experienced political man like Durham would put his faith in feelings of mutuality and "good sense." They agree that Durham meant to save the Empire but they suggest that what he had in mind was a kind of imperial dualism, sometimes called "dyarchy," which would officially allocate some powers to the colonies and others – the crucial powers of control and compliance – to the British.

Chester New subscribes to the dyarchist interpretation: the vision of empire he calls "unique" is a form of dyarchy. But let us see for ourselves. Here is the crucial passage from the Report; it mentions "matters" of concern to the British, and it refers to British "control." "The matters, which so concern us, are very few. The constitution of the form of government, – the regulation of foreign relations, and of trade with the mother country, the other British Colonies, and foreign nations, – and the disposal of the public lands, are the only points of which the mother country requires a control." Gerald Craig comments: "Responsible government was the dynamic idea in the *Report*, but it must not be forgotten how severely the idea was qualified by Lord Durham. It would apply to what he called internal legislation, and he would withhold only those matters that concerned the relations of the colonies with the mother country." Durham argues that the "matters" of concern to Britain are few. Craig says that the "reserved areas, while only four in number, made up about three-quarters of the possible subjects for colonial legislation, and represented a more severe restriction on colonial legislative jurisdiction than the British government had been prepared to exact earlier in the decade."

Craig's interpretation has a superficial plausibility but it owes too much to New and to the dyarchists, men who were interested above all in discovering in the Report a formula for imperial rule in the Empire's heyday. Howe got the Report right: Durham did not regard the four "matters" as areas of conflict; his discussion was intended rather to forestall objections to the grant of responsible government and to reassure the Colonial Office that the emancipated colonies would *not* subvert British interests. Thus he argues that the colonists wanted a British constitution. There would be little or no quarrel about the first of the "reserved" items. On trade preferences and foreign affairs, including military assistance, the contention is similar: the interests of colonists and the British converged. Perhaps the most likely proposal to arouse controversary concerned "public lands." The British would be able to reach into the colonies to determine disposal of certain properties. But here too Durham sees no difficulties: the measure was intended to facilitate organized emigration from the home country and in Durham's opinion emigration from the homelands was something the colonists were desperate to encourage; thus he speaks of the measure's "reciprocal benefits." The fact is that Report is saturated with the idea of political independence and freedom. As we shall see, it is this idea of independence and freedom that appeals to Durham's French Canadian commentators.

In the imperial metropolis the talk about dyarchy's possibilities continued for decades and the Report was read and re-read. A new edition was published in 1902, the first since 1839, and reprinted in cheaper format in 1905; the first book on the Report was published in 1903, and the first biography of Durham in 1906. In 1912 Lucas published his three-volume edition, which includes his book-length introduction and an invaluable selection of the Report's appendixes and official dispatches, as well as Charles Buller's first-hand account.

EMPIRE AND "CULTURE":
THE 1890S TO THE 1930S

The early twentieth-century Empire was a huge enterprise, including the Dominions, India (an empire in its own right, the "Empire of India"), Crown Colonies, Chartered Companies, Protectorates, and Spheres of Influence. Administering it had become a great exercise in definition, the point of which was to determine who – what peoples, what "races" – are capable of self-government. In those heady years of British power, many concluded that while it is one thing to say that countries settled by Britons can rule themselves, it is another to suppose that "lesser breeds without the law," in Kipling's phrase, are competent. And Durham again was brought on board to support this position, or to elucidate it. Thus Lucas was prepared to countenance responsible government in the "sphere of settlement" (the "senior Dominions," like Canada), but not in the "sphere of rule."

Lucas and the "high imperialists," as I shall call them, are struggling with the idea of "culture." I mean by culture, way of life, the social mores of a particular population. The centrality of this notion in modern political and social thought is something I cannot do more than hint at here. It originates in the late eighteenth century as a reaction to the universalism of seventeenth-century thinkers such as John Locke. Locke argued that men and women, *whatever their country of origin, whatever their race or community, whatever their period in history*, are entitled to "life and liberty." More than this, men and women whatever their origin and time, whatever the conditions of their life, know themselves to be so entitled. The thesis revolutionized the politics of the seventeenth century and remains of crucial importance: it informs all modern rights codes, all demands for popular sovereignty, all pleas for national freedom. A glance at today's newspaper reveals its continuing impact. But if Locke is still influential, so too is the eighteenth-century reaction.

The "reactors," the Romantics as they are often called, contend that the most cherished characteristics of men and women, individually and as members of communities, are not captured by a doctrine of universalism. Individuals and communities are shaped by their particular experiences, by their origins, and history. History tells us who we are; *culture* gives us our "identity." Vast and gusty pronouncements about humankind and universal rights miss the point.

The high imperialists make a gesture in Locke's direction when they praise parliamentary institutions and assert the superiority of free government, the rule of law, and surety for individual liberty.

But they are deeply indebted to Romanticism and, above all, they are indebted to the Romantic idea that political institutions emerge from culture. They believe that culture runs deep: institutions are a by-product, epiphenomenal. Thus the imperialists suppose that England owed its parliamentary institutions and freedoms to its peculiar history, and they ask whether peoples without a history such as England's are destined to endure in perpetuity the rule of despots, rajas, and sheiks. Some imperialists are strict determinists: they accept the idea that inferior cultures are doomed to remain inferior. Others argue that culture can be changed. A population that has known only absolute rule can be encouraged to develop a culture of freedom. But those who adopt this line usually suggest that the development will take decades or centuries; hence the "white man's burden" with its obligation to rule in the interim and to educate for the future.

The high imperialists are caught between the Scylla of Locke's universalism and the Charybdis of "culture." All their thoughts on empire are informed by a deep contradiction. Locke encourages them to think that there are no naturally subordinate individuals or races and that absolute rule, even when tempered by good administration, even when undertaken on a promise of increased freedom in the future, is an offence against nature and nature's God. Their Romantic heritage argues that liberty in Locke's definition may *not* be natural; it may not be everyone's highest good. Thus time and again the business of Empire found the British praising the "English" institutions dear to Locke (parliamentary government, freedom, equality under the law) while imposing English forms of absolutism.

In the imperialists' scheme of things, the French Canadians were an anomaly. Lucas was convinced that non-Europeans could not participate in the British culture, or could participate only after long years of tutelage. Non-Europeans could and should be subjected to *rule*. But the French in Canada (and the Dutch in South Africa) were European "races." As Europeans they should *not* be ruled by a foreign power. And yet they were not of "British stock." Would the French in Canada be comfortable with British institutions? *Were* they comfortable? Though Lucas was writing seventy years after Durham and more than forty years after Confederation, he says almost nothing about the French Canadians of his own day, except to suggest that Durham's definition of liberalism was antiquated: "it seems curiously at variance with Liberalism, especially as Liberalism has been interpreted in later days." He adds, "modern life makes for greater courtesy and forbearance as between peoples and races."

Canadians like New and Craig, advocates of the standard interpretation, inherit the imperialists' quandary. Like their predecessors they are indebted to both Locke and the Romantics. Writing in 1972, Peter Burroughs argues that Durham's "attitude is not hard to explain ... knowledge concerning cultural differences between nations was still primitive." Supposedly, what Durham supremely did not know is that culture is primary and deep-rooted. Recall Craig: "Lord Durham could not know as clearly in 1839 what we know today, that it is foolhardy and naïve to speak of breaking down the customs of a well-established and organized ethnic and cultural community." Breaking down a culture is like "terra-forming," like hewing bedrock. So far the Canadian standard interpretation holds fast to the teachings of the former generation.

There is this difference. The imperialists, as I have suggested, favoured terra-forming: it might take generations to get results but as a job for the modern man (and even the modern woman), with all their advantages of wealth and education, it was a commendable undertaking. New, Craig, and Burroughs, in contrast, look on it as something akin to a crime against humanity. The high imperialists are still Whigs in their enthusiasm for adventure and change: their writings are alive with the nineteenth-century idea of progress. Even after World War I, Durham's British commentators are still Whiggish in this sense. They begin to dream of a great association of parliamentary peoples, the Commonwealth of Nations. The first sentence of Craig's Introduction reads: "Lord Durham's *Report* has come to occupy such a central place in the history of the Commonwealth of Nations that no apology is needed for making it readily available to students and readers." Statements like this are a reflection of the original imperial passion – though a pale one.

Taken all in all, the standard interpretation of the Report in Canada has a musty, conservative air. New, Craig, and Burroughs praise liberal freedoms but never confront Durham's contention that a people "left behind" in the march of progress is denied the freedom and the equality to which it is morally entitled. They see opposition between the proposals for responsible government and assimilation; they cannot see, or at any rate they do not explore, the idea that Durham believed the proposals interdependent.

WHERE ARE WE IN THE TWENTY-FIRST CENTURY?

Are we bounding into the future as a band of happy visionaries? One thing is clear: like the high imperialists and like adherents of the standard interpretation, we are divided souls. Insofar as we swear by universal codes of rights and democracy defined in terms of individual freedom, we are Lockeans. Insofar as we regard political institutions, including even bills of rights and liberal democracy, as the expression of historically situated cultures, we are Romantics. We ask whether it is appropriate to export to other parts of the globe, or to force on other parts, political institutions that originated in the West. And we have become markedly diffident about asserting the superiority of Western democracy. We wonder whether cultures in other regions will not give rise in the future to more benign institutions than ours, perhaps more democratic institutions, democratic in a different definition. We wonder whether in the past those regions had superior institutions that Westerners have carelessly or deliberately obliterated.

The standard interpretation is now at one remove from us. English-speakers still copy it into their textbooks, but I think that some no longer believe it. Most still accept Craig's rejection of assimilation, but some, perhaps many, have trouble appreciating his assessment of responsible government. (The Report "remains one of the most vigorous and perceptive expositions of the principles and practices of free government in the history of the English-speaking peoples.") Canadians today are in the process of forgetting why they once thought the parliamentary system admirable. We are losing confidence in the old English Constitution.

The process of forgetting had already begun in the 1960s and 1970s, when Craig and Burroughs were writing. As Jack Granatstein reminds us, historians were abandoning the study of constitutional law. Political scientists were abandoning the study of regimes. Craig and Burroughs themselves say little in defence of the substantive features of responsible government: they praise it but do not tell us why it is praiseworthy. As a nation we were embarking on what Peter Russell calls Canada's "constitutional odyssey," a project of "mega-constitutional" reform. Before the odyssey was over (it died an uneasy death in the national referendum of 1992, which voted down the package of constitutional reforms known as the Charlottetown Accord), it had convinced many that the political institutions of our past, the very institutions described in the Durham Report and enshrined in the Constitution Act, 1867, are inadequate for our purposes today and that our best hope for the future lies in creating new ones. But if we are to understand Durham on assimilation we must recapture, at least provisionally, the argument for parliamentary government. It is time to look – briefly – at the French Canadian commentators on the British Constitution from 1791.

THE FRENCH CANADIANS (1791 TO 1848)

The English Constitution came to French Canada as an imposition – or perhaps as a gift – and from the beginning the French had reason to examine it carefully. Remember the original question: are the institutions of liberal democracy compatible with maintenance of a distinctive identity and a sense of cultural continuity? The French Canadians of British North America, with a passionate sense of continuity and – as I shall show – a tradition of informed admiration for the British Constitution, may help us to "escape through the horns of the dilemma." The man to begin with is Pierre Bédard, the first leader of the majority party in the Legislative Assembly of Lower Canada.

When the British granted Lower Canada a representative legislature in 1791, the English in the province might well have supposed that it would be their task to teach the French how to conduct themselves in their new situation. Perhaps they happily anticipated a long period of tutelage. If so, they reckoned without Bédard. Trained in the classical manner of reading legal and philosophical texts, Bédard drew up for himself a course of study on

England. He read William Blackstone and Jean Louis de Lolme. He studied English history, especially the Civil War; he read the English Bill of Rights and related documents, and he followed current affairs in the debates of the Westminster Parliament. Among his English contemporaries he admired Edmund Burke and Charles James Fox. (Fox was also one of Durham's heroes.) In brief, he situated himself in the mainstream of Whiggish political thought, or perhaps we could allow ourselves to say that he inclined to the radical end of the Whig spectrum. Year after year he berated the British Governor, James Henry Craig, for withholding responsible government. (Bédard was the first person in British North America to recommend the principle of responsible government for adoption in the colonies and the first in the colonies, I believe, to describe it fully). He argued that as subjects of the British monarch, French Canadians should enjoy English rights and liberties in full measure and he made himself a positive nuisance. Durham, who was himself something of a Whig rebel, could have been his pupil.

From 1806 until 1810 (when the Governor seized his press and threw him and his associates in jail), Bédard published his program of reform and excerpts from his readings in his journal of political opinion, *Le Canadien*. He is perhaps Canada's best student of parliamentary government and a great journalist-teacher. The important thing for the argument here is that he derived from his readings the fundamental Lockean principle that there is no just government without the consent of the governed. He concluded that insofar as the Governor was attempting to deny the French Canadians equal rights, insofar as he was attempting to treat them as a subordinate people, he was violating the law of the British Constitution.

New suggests that Durham was woefully ignorant of the variety of constitutional opinion in Lower Canada. He might be right. Durham had been sent to discover the cause of the 1837 Rebellion and to pacify the colonies and it is understandable that he would give much of his attention to the leaders of the rebel party, especially in the lower province, men like Louis-Joseph Papineau. Before he left England he interviewed Papineau's agent in the British House of Commons, John Arthur Roebuck, and when he arrived in British North America he used Roebuck's notes and arguments as a guide to political sentiments in both Upper and Lower Canada. But Papineau and Roebuck were not friends of the British Constitution and responsible government: Papineau at this time was impatient with parliamentary checks and balances and with partisanship and the parliamentary game of political "ins" and "outs." In this essay I cannot spell out the quarrel between the constitutionalists and anti-constitutionalists that characterized the Canadas in the 1830s. It will be enough to say that Bédard and Durham are on the constitutionalist side: they are both indebted to Locke. But caught up in his attempt to explore the causes of the Rebellion Durham missed his natural allies. He paid too little attention to Bédard's great disciple, Etienne Parent. His focus on the Parti patriote was perhaps necessary but it had the consequence, just as New suggests, that he appears relatively ignorant of the tradition of support in Lower Canada for the British Constitution.

Recall the resolution in the Westminster Parliament on the occasion of Lord John Russell's speech of June 1839: "That while it is expedient to improve the composition of the Executive Council of Lower Canada, it is unadvisable to subject it to the responsibility demanded by the Legislative Assembly of that Province." Some French Canadians, among them Etienne Parent, were *demanding* responsible government. They did not see responsible government as a foreign imposition. They saw it as the source of liberation. That was Russell's understanding certainly and in his 1839 speech he was trying to find a way to make concessions without giving them the thing-in-itself.

After Bédard, Parent is Lower Canada's most perceptive student of constitutional law. Almost alone among Durham's contemporaries, almost alone among the commentators in every period, Parent treated with great seriousness Durham's contention that the assimilation of the French Canadians might be necessary if they were to enjoy the benefits of British freedom. As commentator on the Report, Parent is at least Joseph Howe's equal. Howe is a political man: he is thinking primarily about what the British and the colonists should do in the immediate aftermath of the Report. Though Parent undoubtedly influenced the course of political

events in his province, he is principally a theorist: there is something of the ivory tower about him; he is looking down the decades
and centuries. Howe has nothing to say on the subject of culture
and assimilation. Parent sees the many ramifications.

In the spring and summer of 1839, he published a translation of
the Report in instalments in *Le Canadien*, and then again in pam-
phlet form; his series of articles on the Report ran for months. He
had long admired the British constitution and had long endorsed
responsible government. He accepted the logic of Durham's
either/or: either self-government and assimilation or the continued
subordination of the French with the consequent attenuation of
freedom. He chose responsible government; he chose freedom and,
it appeared, he was prepared to pay the price. As Jacques Monet
says, Parent believed that "assimilation, though regrettable, would
not be too high a price, but 'une ouevre désirable à l'accomplisse-
ment de laquelle tout le monde doit travailler cordialement.'"

In the 15 May 1839 issue of *le Canadien* Parent wrote, "Nous
inviterons nos compatriotes à faire de nécessité vertu, à ne point
lutter contre le cours inflexible des événements." In the 23 Octo-
berissue, he said: "les canadiens-français n'ont plus rien à attendre
... pour leur nationalité. Que leur rest-il donc à faire dans leur pro-
pre intérêt et dans celui de leurs enfants, si ce n'est travailler eux-
mêmes de toutes leur forces à amener une assimilation qui brise la
barrière qui les sépare des populations que les environnent de
toutes parts." (Marcel-Pierre Hamel, editor of *Le Rapport de
Durham* [1948] says, "Etienne Parent, lui aussi, eut un terrible
moment de faiblesse.")

Parent took some comfort from the idea that the introduction of
responsible government and the union of Upper and Lower
Canada would encourage an alliance of the progressive elements in
the two provinces. Like many at the time, including Durham, he
anticipated cooperation between the French and English reformers. Thus he concluded that although the French nationality might
be submerged, something of its highest aims would be retained.

And yet he could not help thinking that there must be a way to
reconcile the two beloved "goods" – British freedom and the
French Canadian way of life. In later essays he begins to pull back
from his original decision to "pay the price." He looks for a com-

promise. He notes in this connection that the British administration had guaranteed rights of the French people, including rights that preserved their cultural distinctiveness, at the surrender in 1759 and in the Proclamation of 1763, the Quebec Act of 1774, and the Constitutional Act of 1791. Since he understood Durham to be arguing that responsible government would decrease political discontent in the colony and foster gratitude and appreciation of British institutions, thus strengthening the imperial connection, he is able to suggest that the introduction of responsible government would preserve at least some of the traditional guarantees of nationality.

Consider John Neilson's struggle with this dilemma. The editor of the *Gazette de Québec*, Neilson was as busy as Parent in the summer of 1839, superintending debate on the Report in French Canada. Like Parent he is passionately attached to both the French nationality and the British constitution. And like Parent again he believes that Durham had correctly described the choice before French Canadians. But Neilson puts nationality ahead of freedom and for this reason argues against responsible government. As Jacques Monet says, Neilson had a taste for the status quo. He believed that the representative institutions of the old Constitution of 1791 could be made to work adequately, if not perfectly, once the troublemakers of the 1837 Rebellion had been dealt with. He had as much confidence as Parent, or more, in the guarantees of particularity in the Acts of 1763, 1774, and 1791. But he did not agree with Parent that responsible government was compatible with the imperial connection: on this topic his argument resembles Lord John Russell's. Thus he had more than one reason to reject responsible government: it was inherently suspect and it would undermine imperial guarantees.

Parent has a second and more promising line of thought on freedom and nationality; he makes a second attempt to "escape through the horns." He fastens on the idea of federation, perhaps a union of the several British North American colonies, including the Maritime provinces – a scheme contemplated by Durham – in which Lower Canada would enjoy its own parliamentary institutions and would thus be in a position to maintain its distinctive social institutions. But the time was not ripe. Shortly after Durham embarked for his return to England (1 November 1838), the second Rebellion broke out. No British ministry was going to trust the French province with separate political institutions at that time. But I think we can say that Parent had seen the future. And a short generation later, all had changed.

THE VIEW FROM CONFEDERATION

Let me summarize the argument so far. Bédard argues that the British Constitution will not tolerate rule by the English "race." Parent sees – it is the dilemma that bedevils him – that the Constitution will not tolerate rule by the French "race." (It should be pointed out that in the mid-nineteenth century "race" did not necessarily include the idea of inherited characteristics. During the debates on Confederation in the Province of Canada George-Etienne Cartier speaks of the three great "races" in the United Kingdom. He means the English, Irish, and Scots. No one listening to Cartier took exception. Cartier refers to the French Canadians as a "race." The English Canadians were one "race" and the French were another.)

The British Constitution is meant to protect against rule by a permanent majority; it is designed to keep the political game going in the hope that majorities form and reform. Durham understood very well that the French Canadian party had been denied the right to political office and he proposed to correct the injustice. The introduction of responsible government would allow representatives of the French-speaking majority in Lower Canada to take their seats in the Executive Council. But he could not accept Papineau's formula. In Durham's opinion, to allow the French to govern without the checks and balances of the parliamentary system was merely to exchange one form of absolutism for another. Unconstrained rule by the French majority would soon become as intolerant as unconstrained rule by the Governors and their cronies. He concluded that what was needed was to get rid of factors that encouraged the identification of party with "race." When "race" intrudes, politics grinds to a halt, winners preen and posture, losers sulk, resentment grows by leaps and bounds, and violence threatens. His point in uniting the Canadas was to throw the

French and English political elites together so that they would appeal to the electorate on political and not on "racial" issues.

Durham calls his remedy, "British." Was it? Locke was an English philosopher, an exemplar of the early English Enlightenment. But remember Locke's insistence that his teaching applies universally. We might say that Durham was welcoming the French Canadians to "universalism." And we might note that they did not need his welcome: they had already thought matters through for themselves and seen the value of Locke's doctrine.

But our principal question remains unanswered. We still want to know whether universalism is implacably hostile to expressions of particularity. Must we, as the price of political justice and equality, banish completely all affection for national culture and origin? Today's communitarian thinkers argue that Locke's classical liberalism offers at best a prescription for unfeeling robots. They have a point! But the communitarians typically give too little recognition to the idea and the appeal of liberal justice. It is one of Parent's strengths that he does not underestimate liberalism's appeal. He sees *two* distinguishable "goods." The passionate and very human preference for particularity is one, dispassionate, even-handed justice is the other.

Looking back from the twenty-first century we may wonder what the fuss was about. Surely some program of multiculturalism or multi-nationalism does the trick! And indeed many liberal democracies depend on such programs and they work more or less well. In the nations that have welcomed immigrants, and especially – it is a curious fact – in the nations most heavily influenced by John Locke's individualism, we have found ways to allow particular loyalties considerable scope while defusing adverse effects. Remember Lucas' hopeful comment: "modern life makes for greater courtesy and forbearance as between peoples and races."

In my opinion the essential tension identified by Locke, Durham, Bédard, and Parent always remains. But there are devices for coping. Politics is a matter of compromise; even fundamental principles must be bent sometimes – a little – on occasion. The literature on this topic fills whole libraries; excellent contributions appear every year, not a few by Canadians. (A thorough study would begin with Locke's own writings on toleration.) In this essay I can only hint at how Durham's harsh logic, and Parent's reluctant acceptance of it, contributed to the development of Canadian toleration.

Consider the division of legislative powers in the Canadian federation as it was described in the legislative debates of the Confederation period. In a nutshell, the proposal was to allocate to the federal parliament issues of general concern to everyone in the federation without exception and to give the provincial parliaments the issues of nationality and particularity. At the federal level, we may say, Durham's formula was to obtain in all its rigour: in the Parliament of the united British North American colonies particularity would be ignored.

Of the many legislators who address this topic in the province of Canada and in the Atlantic provinces, I will cite three: George-Etienne Cartier, H.V. Langevin, and George Brown. They are speaking in the Legislative Assembly of the united province of Canada in support of the resolution on Confederation. The date is 1865. Cartier presents the division of powers as a means to preserve particularity: "Some parties ... pretended that it was impossible to carry out federation, on account of the differences of races and religions. Those who took this view of the question were in error. It was just the reverse. It was precisely on account of the variety of races, local interests, etc., that the federation system ought to be resorted to and would be found to work well." Langevin makes the same point: "Under the new system ... our interests in relation to race, religion and nationality ... will be better protected." But Langevin says more: in the legislature of the "general government" of the federation, "there will be no questions of race, nationality, religion, or locality, as this legislature will only be charged with the great, general questions which will interest alike the whole confederacy and not one locality only." And Langevin makes it clear, as perhaps Cartier does not, that the better protection for "interests in relation to race, religion and nationality" depends on the absolute exclusion of those interests from the federal Parliament.

George Brown reinforces Langevin's point. One-time leader of the Liberal party, in these debates he is allied with the Conservatives, Cartier and Langevin, in the party known as the Great Coalition: "Mr. Speaker, I am ... in favour of this scheme because it will bring to an end the sectional discord between Upper and Lower

Canada. It sweeps away the boundary line between the provinces so far as regards matters common to the whole people – it places all on an equal level – and the members of the federal legislature will meet at last as citizens of a common country. The questions that used to excite the most hostile feelings among us have been taken away from the general legislature and placed under the control of the local bodies. No man hereafter need be debarred from success in public life because his views, however popular in his own section, are unpopular in the other – for he will not have to deal with sectional questions; and the temptation to the government of the day to make capital out of local prejudices will be greatly lessened, if not altogether at an end."

To repeat: The contention is that the general legislature of the federation (soon to be known as the Parliament of Canada) will consider no question relating to "race." For that very reason it will command the allegiance of everyone, creating, out of the separate loyalties that dominated political debate before Confederation, one country. And it is because Confederation is to be one country in this sense that it can allow and protect expression of those separate loyalties at the provincial level. I hardly need to say that other speakers raise objections: many want to know what Cartier and his colleagues had to say about the "racial" minorities within the provinces. How would they fare? And I hardly need to say that the Canadian constitutional division of legislative powers has undergone many changes in the years since Confederation, some initiated by constitutional amendment, some brought about by the courts, and some, it appears, the more or less unanticipated result of ongoing political pressures. The elegant scheme defended by Cartier, Langevin, and Brown has been washed away. We have forgotten the scheme, we have forgotten the argument for it, and we have most certainly forgotten Lord Durham's role.

Janet Ajzenstat
October 2005

REFERENCES

Ajzenstat, Janet, Paul Romney, Ian Gentles, and William D. Gairdner, eds. 2003. *Canada's Founding Debates.* Toronto: University of Toronto Press.

Buller, Charles. 1840. "Responsible Government for the Colonies." In *Charles Buller and Responsible Government,* ed. E.M. Wrong. 1926. Oxford: The Clarendon Press.

Burroughs, Peter, ed. 1969. *The Colonial Reformers and Canada, 1830–1849; Selections from Documents and Publications of the Times.* Toronto: McClelland and Stewart (The Carleton Library).

De Lolme, Jean Louis. 1853. *The Constitution of England,* ed. John MacGregor. London: Henry G. Bohn. (The work was first published in French in 1770.)

Granatstein, Jack. 1998. *Who Killed Canadian History?* Toronto: HarperCollins.

Hamel, Marcel-Pierre, ed. and trans., 1948. *Le Rapport de Durham.* [Montréal]: Editions du Québec.

Howe, Joseph. 1839. Letters to Lord John Russell. In *Statutes, Treaties, and Documents of the Canadian Constitution, 1713–1929,* ed. W.P.M. Kennedy. 1930. Toronto: Oxford University Press.

Locke, John. 1690. *The Second Treatise of Government.* In *Two Treatises of Government,* ed. Peter Laslett. 1988. Cambridge: Cambridge University Press.

Locke, John. 1689. *A Letter Concerning Toleration,* ed. Patrick Romanell. 1950. Indianapolis: Bobbs-Merrill.

Lucas, C.P., ed. 1912. *Lord Durham's Report on the Affairs of British North America,* 3 vols. Oxford: The Clarendon Press.

Monet, Jacques. 1969. *The Last Cannon Shot: A Study of French-Canadian Nationalism, 1837–1850.* Toronto: University of Toronto Press.

New, Chester. 1929. "Introduction." In *Lord Durham's Mission to Canada an Abridgement of Lord Durham, A Biography of John George Lambton, First Earl of Durham by Chester New,* ed. H.W. McCready. 1963. Toronto: McClelland and Stewart (The Carleton Library).

Robinson, John Beverley. 1840. *Canada and the Canada Bill, Being an Examination of the Proposed Measure for the Future Government of Canada.* London: J. Hatchard and Son.

Russell, Lord John. 1839. "On Canadian Affairs." In *Statutes, Treaties, and Documents of the Canadian Constitution, 1713 -1929*, ed. W.P.M. Kennedy. 1930. Toronto: Oxford University Press.

Wakefield, Edward Gibbon. 1844. "Sir Charles Metcalfe in Canada." In *Charles Buller and Responsible Government*, ed. E.M. Wrong. 1926. Oxford: The Clarendon Press.

INTRODUCTION TO THE 1963 EDITION

Lord Durham's *Report* has come to occupy such a central place in the history of the Commonwealth of Nations that no apology is needed for making it readily available to students and readers, both inside and outside the schools and universities. Indeed, so much praise has been showered on the famous *Report* that it may come as a surprise to some to learn that when it appeared it was widely regarded as a partisan, opinionated, and inaccurate document and that even now, after the smoke of contemporary controversy has long since lifted, we can easily find glaring weaknesses of fact and argument in this noted and notorious state paper. Nevertheless, it is true that no attempt to debunk or to deflate the great *Report* would be very successful. Despite all its shortcomings and defects it remains one of the most vigorous and perceptive expositions of the principles and practice of free government in the history of the English-speaking peoples.

Thus the *Report* has come to have a significance and a relevance that far transcend the circumstances of its immediate origins. Yet, if we are to understand both the strong and the weak features of the document we must look back, however briefly, to those circumstances, for Lord Durham was not only uttering a testament of his political faith that he thought to be universally valid; he was also prescribing for a particular political problem.

That problem existed in the two provinces of Upper and Lower Canada, and much more ominously and immediately in the latter, where the legislative assembly had been suspended following the outbreak of rebellion in 1837. This rebellion, which had a much less serious counterpart in Upper Canada, had in turn been only

the last episode in a prolonged and increasingly acrimonious political conflict, a conflict that had seen the governor or lieutenant-
governor and the appointed executive and legislative councils
arrayed against the elected legislative assembly. In the upper
province the conflict had been intermittent, since the assembly had
as often been controlled by men in general sympathy with the government as by the opposition, and that had been especially true of
the year or so before the rebellion. Moreover, that uprising had
received support from only a fraction of the opposition. In the
lower province, however, the confrontation had been turbulent
and persistent: for more than fifteen years before 1837 a determined party of French-Canadian nationalists, joined by a few English-speaking associates, had controlled the Assembly and had
announced their intention of controlling the whole government.
The British government had sought to deflect these nationalists,
led by Louis Joseph Papineau, from their purpose by following a
policy of concession and conciliation, and had then abruptly
replaced this policy with a tougher one in the spring of 1837. The
upshot was the outbreak of a formidable uprising in the following
November, which shook Lower Canada to its foundations and
helped bring on the much smaller rising in the upper province.

These rebellions also shook the already wobbly Melbourne ministry in the mother country, and forced it to give Canadian affairs
much more attention than they usually received. Lord Melbourne's
answer to insistent demands that something be done about the
Canadas was to renew his plea to Lord Durham to take on the
government of these colonies and to make recommendations about
their future. Although he had refused this offer in the previous
summer, Lord Durham now felt that the crisis left him no choice
but to accept, especially since his commission would give him
unprecedented powers and authority to meet his heavy responsibilities. He gathered his staff about him and reached Quebec at the
end of May 1838.

Melbourne had turned to Durham because he needed a man of
the front rank for the post, and Durham was easily the most important British political figure – often thought of as a possible prime
minister – who had ever come out to Canada. Born in 1792 of one
of the oldest and richest families in the north of England, John

George Lambton from the start of his parliamentary career took his stand with the advanced Whigs, and had close ties with the Radicals. In 1830 "Radical Jack," who had become Baron Durham in 1828, entered the cabinet of his father-in-law, Lord Grey, and was at once in the thick of the fight for the Reform Bill. Indeed, he was its most pressing advocate in the government and shared with Lord John Russell the principal responsibility for drafting the measure. In 1833, however, ill-health forced this intense and ambitious man to resign from the cabinet, at which time he received an earldom. Two years later, he went to Russia as British ambassador, but a frail constitution again cut short his service.

The Melbourne government viewed Durham's return to England in 1837 with much trepidation. That government normally depended on the votes of a bloc of Radical members to maintain its precarious hold on office, yet the Radicals were both dissatisfied with Melbourne's failure to push for further reform and deeply alienated by the tough policy toward Lower Canada of the spring of 1837. If Durham joined the Radicals, and gave them a lead, the Whigs would almost certainly be turned out. Hence, it was essential for Melbourne to make overtures toward Durham. Yet the urbane and easy-going Melbourne shuddered at the thought of a cabinet colleague of such humourless intensity and so violent a temper. Thus Melbourne's urgent appeal to Durham, which would force the Radicals to hold their fire, arose much more out of the needs of British domestic politics than out of a concern to find the right man for Canada, although it happened to do just that.

The qualities that made Durham an uncomfortable colleague also made him an imperious governor who was quite prepared to stretch his already large powers. This aspect of his personality was revealed in many ways but most importantly in his decision to pardon the bulk of the prisoners accused of complicity in the rebellion, and to banish a few of the most serious offenders to Bermuda. There were sound political reasons for this decision, but it contained one or two legal flaws; in particular, Durham's commission did not extend to Bermuda. This flaw gave Durham's political opponents at home a stick with which to smite him, and they were quick to use it, especially Lord Brougham, once a close friend and now a bitter enemy. The din raised by the latter caused the Prime Minister to run for cover. Durham's ordinance was disallowed. To the Governor General in Canada this action made a mockery of Melbourne's promises of firm support and it came also as a vote of no-confidence. Durham decided at once that he had no choice but to resign, and after being in Canada just over five months he went home at the beginning of November. If communications had been faster his stay would presumably have been shorter. Contrary to the hopes and fears of many leading political figures, Durham made no effort to topple the Melbourne government upon his return. Instead, he and his staff devoted themselves without rest to the preparation of the *Report*, which was ready at the end of January 1839.

It was the crisis in Lower Canada, above all, that had brought Lord Durham across the Atlantic, and in his *Report* it was to this crisis that he turned at once after a brief introduction. His analysis of the problem was both trenchant and provocative. Before leaving home, he asserted, he had assumed that the contest was between a popular body contending for free government and an executive government upholding the Crown's prerogative. Instead, he found "two nations warring in the bosom of a single state ... a struggle, not of principles, but of races," and he then proceeded upon a lengthy discussion of the "deadly animosity that now separates the inhabitants of Lower Canada into the hostile divisions of French and English." He found the French Canadians to be at fault at almost every turn. To be sure, they had certain amiable personal qualities; but as a people they were backward and illiterate, clinging to outworn customs and institutions, unresponsive to the progressive tendencies of the age, and easy victims of the irresponsible demagogues who sprouted in their midst. Their leaders used control of the Assembly, not for valid ends, but to protect French-Canadian nationality "against the progressive intrusion of the English race." By contrast, the English minority was forward-looking and practical in outlook, concerned to advance the material development of the province, and understandably exasperated by French-Canadian opposition to all progressive measures. This exasperation had reached an intense stage with the outbreak of rebellion. Any solution for Lower Canada must take account of the determination of the English minority never again to tolerate French-Canadian control of the Assembly.

After his lengthy discussion of Lower Canada, which takes up nearly half the text of the *Report*, Lord Durham moved on to consider the condition of Upper Canada. Here there was no racial animosity as in the lower province, yet there was a rebellion to be explained, even though it had been a small one. In his treatment of Upper Canada, Lord Durham was at a considerable disadvantage, for he had been in the province for only eleven days, mainly at Niagara Falls. Nevertheless, he had no doubt about the prime cause of the political discontent that had been visible there for many years. It lay in a defective constitutional system that lodged irresponsible power in the hands of a small group of the lieutenant-governor's advisers, who were "linked together not only by common party interests, but by personalities." This "family compact" had a monopoly of offices, and it really ruled the province, for the lieutenant-governor usually yielded to it. Such a monopoly of power inevitably created an opposition, but this opposition, known as the reformers, discovered that even when they won a majority of the seats in the Assembly they could not implement their program. Hence the reformers, with a "practical good sense" that contrasted favourably with "the less prudent course of the French majority in the Assembly of Lower Canada," called for a change of constitutional practice that would make the executive council responsible to the Assembly. But the existing political discontent was greatly, and unnecessarily, heightened by the partisan administration of Sir Francis Bond Head, thus opening the way for the plot that led to rebellion.

The *Report*, after briefly examining affairs in the Atlantic provinces, proceeds to a thorough analysis of problems relating to land policy and immigration. Since this section reflected the views of a member of the staff, Edward Gibbon Wakefield, rather than of Lord Durham, and since the recommendations flowing from it were not acted upon, it might be argued that it could be omitted from an abridged edition of the *Report*. It has, in fact, been very considerably shortened in the text that follows, but many perceptive passages on the social and economic development of the provinces have been included.

Finally, after this lengthy discussion and analysis, Lord Durham came to his summing up and to his recommendations. British North America was afflicted with an "ill-contrived constitutional system" and suffered from "practical mismanagement" of its affairs at every turn. It was a condition that should not, and could not, continue; extensive and decisive measures were urgently needed. Urgency derived partly from the ingrained animosity of the races in Lower Canada, and partly from the proximity of the provinces to the United States. This latter factor was one to which reference is made on many pages of the *Report* and which affected its whole tone and direction. The English-speaking population of the provinces was acutely conscious of the material progress being made in the neighbouring states; unless they could see the prospect of an effective attack being made upon their own political and economic problems, they could not be expected to retain their British loyalty for an indefinite period. If things went on as they were, they might well find the American attraction too powerful to resist. As yet, however, their attachment to British allegiance continued to be strong, and there was still time for a solution that would bind them more closely to the mother country.

The solution was readily at hand – and here we come to the heart of Lord Durham's recommendations, and the reason for the enduring value of his *Report*. Like so many great ideas, it was extremely simple, not very original, indeed almost obvious. It lay in permitting the full and free operation of British institutions in the colonies, as at home. It lay in a constitutional reform that would establish "the foundation of an efficient and popular government, ensure harmony, in place of collision, between the various powers of the State, and bring the influence of a vigorous public opinion to bear on every detail of public affairs." Once this reform were made, colonial authorities could attack the many practical and concrete abuses and grievances; there was no need for Lord Durham or any other outsider to prescribe for these. In short, he argued that the British government must give up to the colonies the full authority to conduct their own internal affairs, and that it must be prepared to see those affairs administered by men in whom the representatives of the colonial electorate had confidence. Thus he argued for what has since become known as "responsible government," the cabinet system that was already in operation in Great Britain. In the colonies this principle would mean that the governor must draw his executive advisers from men who had the confidence of the majority in the Assembly, that he must be prepared to change his advisers when they lost the confidence of this majority, and that as long as they retained this confidence he must carry on the government, in all internal matters, according to their advice, despite differing views that he or the British government might have. If this principle were not accepted, wrote Durham, the colonies would surely be lost; if it were, their connection with the mother country would be permanent, and beneficial to both.

Responsible government was the dynamic idea in the *Report*, but it must not be forgotten how severely the idea was qualified by Lord Durham. It would apply to what he called internal legislation, and he would withhold only those matters that concerned the relations of the colonies with the mother country. These matters, he asserted, were very few: "the constitution of the form of government, – the regulation of foreign relations, and of trade with the mother country, the other British Colonies, and foreign nations, – and the disposal of the public lands." But these reserved areas, while only four in number, made up about three-quarters of the possible subjects for colonial legislation, and represented a more severe restriction on colonial legislative jurisdiction than the British government had been prepared to exact earlier in the decade. The grant of colonial self-government that Durham was prepared to make in 1839 was wholly genuine, but it was also extremely limited in scope. The limitations are not hard to explain. A broader grant of legislative competence would never have been accepted by the British government and parliament at this time. Nor would Durham have been in favour of it. As an ardent imperialist, he was concerned to avoid decentralization in the exercise of these vital legislative powers. Yet there is no reason to think that he would not have welcomed a gradual devolution as colonial legislatures and governments became more competent and more experienced under the schooling that responsible government would bring.

A second qualification was more fundamental, and more far-reaching in its implications and consequences. It was that the grant of responsible government could be made only to a legislature with an English-speaking majority. (Sometimes he spoke of the "English race," but apparently he considered it possible for other people to join this race, if English became their first language and if they became thoroughly imbued with an "English character.") Lord Durham has often been called a prophet of the modern Commonwealth, and with some reason; nevertheless, there is no warrant in his own utterances for believing that he would have favoured the grant of self-government to peoples who were not of British stock or who had not been thoroughly assimilated to British ways and institutions.

More particularly, of course, Lord Durham was not prepared to grant self-government to a legislature with a French-speaking majority. In the last section of the *Report* he continued and intensified the criticisms of the French Canadians that had marked the opening section on Lower Canada. This people was hopelessly inferior, and was doomed to be engulfed by the superior force and intelligence of the English-speaking majority in North America. Everything must be done to discourage the French Canadians from persisting in their "idle and narrow notion of a petty and visionary nationality." Any plan for the constitutional reform of the Canadian provinces must have imbedded in it the certainty that the French Canadians would be given an English character, that they would be amalgamated to the dominant race in North America. It should be noted that, according to his lights, Lord Durham did not seek to anglify the French Canadians out of harsh or vindictive motives. Considering the power and vigour of the English-speaking majority in North America, he did not believe that the French Canadians would ever be able to live on a level of equality with them. The French Canadians could not beat the majority; therefore, they should join it.

This line of reasoning led to the conclusion that the French Canadians must be subordinated to an English-speaking majority, in order that the process of assimilation and amalgamation might begin. This, in turn, meant intercolonial union. Lord Durham's strongest preference, for which he still had high hopes until he left Canada, was for a legislative union comprising the Canadas and the Maritime provinces, a union that would provide a very substantial English-speaking majority. But the Maritimes showed no enthusiasm for entering such a union, and Lord Durham realized that their consent would be gained, if at all, only after long and difficult negotiations. Yet the renewal of rebellion in Lower Canada in November 1838, as Durham returned home, showed the need for haste. Hence, the recommendation for union, as embodied in the *Report*, was for joining the two Canadas, leaving open the possibility of a broader legislative union at some time in the future. Dual union, although not an ideal answer, could be accomplished quickly and it would provide a working English-speaking majority, assuming that the English-speaking members all stuck together.

Responsible government and legislative union were the two outstanding recommendations in the *Report*, and they are the only two that can be reviewed in this brief introduction. But the reader of the text that follows will find that the *Report* contains many more striking and provocative observations and proposals on such matters as legislative procedure and administrative and judicial reform, municipal government, and the future relations of Canada and the United States. The passages on these and other subjects have helped to make the *Report* a document of enduring value and interest.

As was mentioned at the beginning, the *Report* was received by Lord Durham's contemporaries with more reservations than acclaim. Some doubted that it was his *Report* at all, and ascribed the bulk, if not all of it, to his staff, especially Wakefield and Charles Buller. (On this matter, see Chester New's biography of Lord Durham.) The same critics usually disliked its style; Lord Brougham said it read like a second-rate article in the Edinburgh Review; and it is true that it contained undiplomatic language that was needlessly offending, although this feature has enhanced its readability. Some Radicals were antagonized by the strictures on the French Canadians, while tories were incensed by criticisms of the Church of England's claims to the Clergy Reserves and by many other features of the *Report*. The Whig government, speaking through Lord John Russell, could not accept the doctrine of responsible government as set forth by Durham, although it was prepared to make certain piecemeal changes in colonial political practices. It did unite the two Canadas, although not in quite the form that Durham recommended, and it did adopt one or two of his practical and concrete suggestions.

The text of the *Report* reached Canada in the spring of 1839, and was soon widely reprinted in the newspapers. Here, too, the note of criticism was loud, and even strident. In Lower Canada the French Canadians were, of course, outraged by the low estimate placed upon their civilization and by the plan for lifting them to the level of the English race. The English-speaking minority in that province viewed these passages as ordinary common sense, and strongly approved the recommendation for union, which, after all, had been their own program for many years; but they were aghast at the proposal for responsible government, which would weaken and perhaps destroy their own political power. In Upper Canada conservatives and tories searched the *Report* in vain for anything with which they could agree. Committees of the Legislative Council and Assembly each submitted the *Report* to a severe and often telling review, stressing that the section on Upper Canada was full of factual inaccuracies and biased history, that the union would involve the people of the upper province in the bitter disputes of the lower, and that responsible government would allow the French-speaking majority of the one province to combine with the radical minority of the other to ride rough-shod over the loyal people of both. Only the reformers of Upper Canada were genuinely enthusiastic about the *Report*, for it gave powerful endorsement to their own program, responsible government, and the *Report* thus became a mighty weapon to be used against their conservative and tory opponents.

To carry the story further would be to recount the history of Canada for the following decade. Lord Durham himself died in 1840, and so did not live to see many things work out differently from his own hopes and expectations. Above all, he did not foresee, as the tories of Upper Canada did, that the French Canadians would join with the English-speaking reformers in an organized political party. It was this party that demonstrated that there was no alternative to responsible government, if Canada was to be governed peacefully and constitutionally within the British Empire, but it did it in such a way – by bi-racial co-operation – as to preclude the slightest movement toward Durham's other objective, the anglifying of the French Canadians. Thus, from the perspective of our own times, the sections on the French Canadians appear to be the faultiest and the most misguided in the whole *Report* – the one great blot in an otherwise admirable and enlightened analysis. Durham failed to see that Canadian development would have to be in the other direction: toward mutual respect and tolerance, towards the building of a nation based on a dual culture.

This adverse judgement on a major segment of the *Report* is now clear and irreversible, but we should also be concerned to understand as well as to judge. We should realize that no man of Lord Durham's time, who was as caught up as he was in the on-rushing material and political progress of the English-speaking peoples of the British Empire and the United States, could be expected to sympathize with an allegiance to conservative and traditional values. We should also note that Lord Durham could not know as clearly in 1839 what we know today, that it is foolhardy and naive to speak of breaking down the customs of a well-established and organized ethnic and cultural community; in the last century we have seen many such attempts fail that were much harsher and more determined than anything Lord Durham had in mind. Finally, many French Canadians of our own time would be the first to agree that in large part Lord Durham's strictures were as true as they were hard; in particular, that there was a need for more education and a more practical education. French-Canadian zeal in this matter may owe something to the dash of cold water in the *Report*.

If we turn to other aspects of the *Report*, it would not be hard to maintain the proposition that what was sound was not very new, and what was new was not very sound. The great proposal for responsible government was planted in Lord Durham's mind by Robert Baldwin, and it was an idea that was also well understood by reformers in Nova Scotia and New Brunswick. Durham's own refinement, the distinction between local and imperial matters, was of tactical value in 1839, but it was not very generous, and it began to break down almost at once. In particular, the whole elaborate scheme for imperial supervision of the public lands proved to be still-born. Finally, although Lord Durham had a remarkable vision of a British-American nationality, it was a rather near-sighted one that did not reach out to the prairies and the Pacific.

Any careful evaluation of Lord Durham's *Report* has to take account of these and other limitations, but it must also explain why it is still alive and not a musty and forgotten official document. On this score one may confidently allow the *Report* to speak for itself. Its vibrant and eloquent argument for the self-government of free men rises through all faulty insights and is as compelling and as vital today as when it first appeared.

The first official publication of Durham's *Report* was in the Parliamentary Papers for 1839 (the "blue books"), where the appendices and relevant dispatches were also printed. Portions of the text of the *Report* first saw the light of day in *The Times* of London and in several Canadian newspapers. The full text of the *Report* was also published in London, Toronto, and Montreal in 1839. These versions sufficed until the imperial revival led the Methuen publishing house of London to bring out a new edition, with an introductory note, in 1902, followed by a cheaper edition in 1905. Renewed interest in the *Report* culminated in the publication of an elaborate three-volume edition in 1912 (Oxford, Clarendon Press). Under the editorship of Sir Charles Lucas, the edition provided an introductory volume, the full text of the *Report* along with extensive explanatory notes, and a third volume of appendices and related dispatches. This remains the standard edition of the *Report*, and is still indispensable for a thorough study of the *Report*. In 1945 the Clarendon Press brought out an abridged version of the *Report*, with an extensive introduction by Sir Reginald Coupland. A French translation was published at Quebec in 1948, with an introduction and bibliography prepared by Marcel-Pierre Hamel.

Like Coupland's edition in its day, the purpose of the present edition is to make the enduring features of the *Report* available to the student and general reader at a modest price. This edition provides about three-quarters of the full text, and is somewhat fuller than Coupland's version, although the principles of selection are basically the same. In the main, the omitted portions consist of illustrative material and amplifying detail, and are indicated by the usual ellipses. The essential analysis of the state of the provinces, and the recommendations, are given in full.

GERALD M. CRAIG
March 1963

LORD DURHAM'S REPORT

COMMISSION

VICTORIA,
by the grace of God, of the United Kingdom of *Great Britain* and *Ireland* Queen, Defender of the Faith. TO Our right trusty and right well-beloved Cousin and Councillor, *John George* Earl of *Durham*, Knight Grand Cross of the Most Noble Order of the Bath, Greeting: WHEREAS, by five several Commissions under the Great Seal of Our United Kingdom of *Great Britain* and *Ireland*, We have constituted and appointed you, the said *John George Earl of Durham*, to be Our Captain General and Governor-in-Chief in and over each of Our Provinces of *Lower Canada*, *Upper Canada*, *Nova Scotia* and *New Brunswick*, and in and over Our Island of *Prince Edward*, in *North America*: And We have, by the said several Commissions, made provision for the administration of the government of Our said Provinces and of the said Island respectively, in the event of your absence, by authorizing the respective Lieutenant-Governors or Administrators of the Governments of the said Provinces and of the said Islands respectively, in that contingency, to exercise the powers by the said Commissions respectively granted to you: And whereas We have, by a Commission under the Great Seal of Our said United Kingdom of *Great Britain* and *Ireland*, constituted and appointed our trusty and well-beloved *Henry Prescott*, Esquire, Captain in Our Royal Navy, to be Our Governor and Commander-in-Chief in and over our Island of *Newfoundland* and its dependencies: And whereas there are at present certain weighty affairs to be adjusted in the said Provinces of *Lower* and *Upper Canada*: NOW KNOW YOU, THAT WE, reposing especial trust and confidence in the prudence, courage and loyalty

of you, the said *John George* Earl of *Durham*, have, of Our especial grace, certain knowledge, and mere motion, thought fit to constitute and appoint, and do hereby constitute and appoint you, the
said *John George* Earl of *Durham*, to be Our High Commissioner
for the adjustment of certain important questions depending in the
said Provinces of *Lower* and *Upper Canada* respecting the form
and future government of the said Provinces: And We do hereby
give and grant unto you, the said *John George* Earl of *Durham*, as
such High Commissioner as aforesaid, full power and authority in
Our name and in Our behalf, by all lawful ways and means, to
inquire into, and, as far as may be possible, to adjust all questions
depending in the said Provinces of *Lower* and *Upper Canada*, or
either of them, respecting the Form and Administration of the Civil
Government thereof respectively: And whereas, with a view to the
adjustment of such questions, We have deemed it expedient to
invest you with the further powers hereinafter mentioned: NOW
KNOW YOU, That WE do in like manner constitute and appoint you,
the said *John George* Earl of *Durham*, to be Our Governor General of all the said Provinces on the Continent of *North America*,
and of the said Islands of *Prince Edward* and *Newfoundland*: And
We do hereby require and command all Our Officers, Civil and
Military, and all other Inhabitants of Our said Provinces, and of
Our said Islands respectively, to be obedient, aiding and assisting
unto you, the said *John George* Earl of *Durham*, in the execution
of this Our Commission, and of the several powers and authorities
herein contained: Provided nevertheless, and We do hereby declare
Our pleasure to be, that in the execution of the powers hereby
vested in you, the said *John George* Earl of *Durham*, you do in all
things conform to such instructions as may from time to time be
addressed to you for your guidance by Us, under Our Sign Man-
ual and Signet, or by Our Order in Our Privy Council, or through
one of Our Principal Secretaries of State: Provided also, and We do
hereby declare Our pleasure to be, that nothing herein contained
shall extend, or be construed to extend, to revoke or to abrogate
the said Commission under the Great Seal of Our said United
Kingdom of *Great Britain* and *Ireland* appointing the said *Henry
Prescott* Governor and Commander-in-Chief of Our said Island of
Newfoundland, and its dependencies, as aforesaid: And We do

hereby declare, ordain and appoint that you, the said *John George* Earl of *Durham*, shall and may hold, execute and enjoy the said offices of High Commissioner and Governor General of Our said Provinces on the Continent of North America, and of the said Islands of *Prince Edward* and *Newfoundland*, as aforesaid, together with all and singular the powers and authorities hereby granted unto you for and during Our will and pleasure. In witness whereof, We have caused these Our Letters to be made Patent. Witness Ourself at Westminster, the Thirty-first day of March, in the First year of Our Reign.

By Writ of Privy Seal.
EDWARDS.

BRITISH NORTH AMERICA

REPORT

TO THE QUEEN'S
MOST EXCELLENT MAJESTY

MAY IT PLEASE YOUR MAJESTY,

YOUR MAJESTY, in entrusting me with the Government of the
Province of Lower Canada, during the critical period of the suspension of its constitution, was pleased, at the same time, to
impose on me a task of equal difficulty, and of far more permanent importance, by appointing me 'High Commissioner for the
adjustment of certain important questions depending in the
Provinces of Lower and Upper Canada, respecting the form and
future Government of the said Provinces'. To enable me to discharge this duty with the greater efficiency, I was invested, not
only with the title, but with the actual functions of Governor
General of all Your Majesty's North American Provinces; and my
instructions restricted my authority by none of those limitations
that had, in fact, deprived preceding Governors of Lower Canada
of all control over the other Provinces, which, nevertheless, it had
been the practice to render nominally subordinate to them. It was
in addition, therefore, to the exclusive management of the administrative business of an extensive and disturbed Province, to the
legislative duties that were accumulated on me during the
abeyance of its representative government, and to the constant
communications which I was compelled to maintain, not only
with the Lieutenant-Governors, but also with individual inhabitants of the other five Provinces, that I had to search into the
nature and extent of the questions, of which the adjustment is
requisite for the tranquillity of the Canadas; to set on foot various and extensive inquiries into the institutions and administration of those Provinces; and to devise such reforms in the system
of their government as might repair the mischief which had

already been done, and lay the foundations of order, tranquillity, and improvement.

The task of providing for the adjustment of questions affecting the very 'form and administration of Civil Government', was naturally limited to the two Provinces, in which the settlement of such questions had been rendered matter of urgent necessity, by the events that had in one seriously endangered, and in the other actually suspended, the working of the existing constitution. But though the necessity only reached thus far, the extension of my authority over all the British Provinces in North America, for the declared purpose of enabling me more effectually to adjust the constitutional questions then at issue in two of them, together with the specific instructions contained in Despatches from the Secretary of State, brought under my view the character and influence of the institutions established in all. I found in all these Provinces a form of government so nearly the same – institutions generally so similar, and occasionally so connected – and interests, feelings and habits so much in common, that it was obvious, at the first glance, that my conclusions would be formed without a proper use of the materials at my disposal, unless my inquiries were as extended as my power of making them. How inseparably connected I found the interests of Your Majesty's Provinces in North America, to what degree I met with common disorders, requiring common remedies, is an important topic, which it will be my duty to discuss very fully before closing this Report. My object at present is merely to explain the extent of the task imposed on me, and to point out the fact, that an inquiry originally directed only to two, has necessarily been extended over all Your Majesty's Provinces in North America.

While I found the field of inquiry thus large, and every day's experience and reflection impressed more deeply on my mind the importance of the decision which it would be my duty to suggest, it became equally clear that that decision, to be of any avail, must be prompt and final. I needed no personal observation to convince me of this; for the evils I had it in charge to remedy, are evils which no civilized community can long continue to bear. There is no class or section of Your Majesty's subjects in either of the Canadas, that does not suffer from both the existing disorder and the doubt which hangs over the future form and policy of the Government. While the present state of things is allowed to last, the actual inhabitants of these Provinces have no security for person or property, no enjoyment of what they possess, no stimulus to industry. The development of the vast resources of these extensive territories is arrested; and the population, which should be attracted to fill and fertilize them, is directed into foreign states. Every day during which a final and stable settlement is delayed, the condition of the Colonies becomes worse, the minds of men more exasperated, and the success of any scheme of adjustment more precarious.

I was aware of the necessity of promptitude in my decision on the most important of the questions committed to me at a very early period after my acceptance of the mission which Your Majesty was pleased to confide to me. Before leaving England, I assured Your Majesty's Ministers that the plan which I should suggest for the future government of the Canadas, should be in readiness by the commencement of the ensuing Session; and, though I had made provision that, under any circumstances, the measures which I might suggest should be explained and supported in Parliament by some person who would have had a share in the preparation of them, I added, that it was not improbable that I might deem it my paramount duty towards the Provinces entrusted to me to attend in my place in the House of Lords, for the purpose of explaining my own views, and supporting my own recommendations. My resignation of the office of Governor General has, therefore, in nowise precipitated my suggestion of the plan which appears to me best calculated to settle the future form and policy of government in the Canadas. It has prevented, certainly, my completing some inquiries which I had instituted, with a view of effecting practical reforms of essential, but still of subordinate importance. But with the chief of my duties as High Commissioner, that of suggesting the future constitution of these Colonies, that event has interfered in no way, except in so far as the circumstances which attended it occasioned an undue intrusion of extraneous business on the time which was left for the completion of my labours.

In truth, the administrative and legislative business which daily demanded my attention could, with difficulty, be discharged by the most unremitting labour on my own part, and on that of all those who accompanied me from England, or were employed by me in Canada.

It is in these circumstances, and under such disadvantages, that this Report has been prepared. I may not therefore present as extended and as complete a foundation as I could have wished, for those measures of vast and permanent importance which Parliament will find it necessary to adopt. But it will include the whole range of those subjects which it is essential should be brought under Your Majesty's view, and will prove that I have not rested content without fully developing the evils which lie at the root of the disorders of the North American Provinces, and at the same time suggesting remedies, which, to the best of my judgment, will provide an effectual cure.

The same reasons and the same obstacles have prevented me from annexing a greater amount of detail and illustration, which, under more favourable circumstances, it would have been incumbent on me to collect, for the purpose of rendering clear and familiar to every mind, every particular of the state of things, on which little correct, and much false information has hitherto been current in this country. I cannot, therefore, but deeply regret that such a drawback on its efficacy should have been a necessary consequence of the circumstances under which the Report has been prepared. I still hope that the materials collected by me, though not as ample as I could have desired, will, nevertheless, be found sufficient for enabling the Imperial Legislature to form a sound decision on the important interests which are involved in the result of its deliberations.

These interests are indeed of great magnitude; and on the course which Your Majesty and Your Parliament may adopt, with respect to the North American Colonies, will depend the future destinies, not only of the million and a half of Your Majesty's subjects who at present inhabit those Provinces, but of that vast population which those ample and fertile territories are fit and destined hereafter to support. No portion of the American Continent possesses greater natural resources for the maintenance of large and flourishing communities. An almost boundless range of the richest soil still remains unsettled, and may be rendered available for the purposes of agriculture. The wealth of inexhaustible forests of the best timber in America, and of extensive regions of the most valuable minerals, have as yet been scarcely touched. Along the whole line of sea-coast, around each island, and in every river, are to be found the greatest and richest fisheries in the world. The best fuel and the most abundant water-power are available for the coarser manufactures, for which an easy and certain market will be found. Trade with other continents is favoured by the possession of a large number of safe and spacious harbours; long, deep and numerous rivers, and vast inland seas, supply the means of easy intercourse; and the structure of the country generally affords the utmost facility for every species of communication by land. Unbounded materials of agricultural, commercial and manufacturing industry are there: it depends upon the present decision of the Imperial Legislature to determine for whose benefit they are to be rendered available. The country which has founded and maintained these Colonies at a vast expense of blood and treasure, may justly expect its compensation in turning their unappropriated resources to the account of its own redundant population; they are the rightful patrimony of the English people, the ample appanage which God and Nature have set aside in the New World for those whose lot has assigned them but insufficient portions in the Old. Under wise and free institutions, these great advantages may yet be secured to Your Majesty's subjects; and a connexion secured by the link of kindred origin and mutual benefits may continue to bind to the British Empire the ample territories of its North American Provinces, and the large and flourishing population by which they will assuredly be filled.

LOWER CANADA

The prominent place which the dissensions of Lower Canada had, for some years, occupied in the eyes of the Imperial Legislature, the alarming state of disorder indicated or occasioned by the recent insurrection, and the paramount necessity of my applying my earliest efforts to the re-establishment of free and regular government in that particular Colony, in which it was then wholly suspended, necessarily directed my first inquiries to the Province of which the local government was vested in my hands. The suspension of the constitution gave me an essential advantage over my predecessors in the conduct of my inquiries; it not merely relieved me from the burthen of constant discussions with the legislative bodies, but it enabled me to turn my attention from the alleged, to the real grievances of the Province; to leave on one side those matters of temporary contest, which accident, or the interests and passions of parties, had elevated into undue importance; and, without reference to the representations of the disputants, to endeavour to make myself master of the real condition of the people, and the real causes of dissatisfaction or suffering. It was also a great advantage to me in one respect, that the ordinary business of the government of the Province was combined with the functions of my inquiry. The routine of every day's administrative business brought strongly and familiarly before me the working of the institutions on which I was called to judge. The condition of the people, the system by which they were governed, were thus rendered familiar to me, and I soon became satisfied that I must search in the very composition of society, and in the fundamental institutions of government, for the causes of the constant and extensive disorder which I witnessed.

The lengthened and various discussions which had for some years been carried on between the contending parties in the Colony, and the representations which had been circulated at home, had produced in mine, as in most minds in England, a very erroneous view of the parties at issue in Lower Canada. The quarrel which I was sent for the purpose of healing, had been a quarrel between the executive Government and the popular branch of the legislature. The latter body had, apparently, been contending for popular rights and free government. The executive Government had been defending the prerogative of the Crown, and the institutions which, in accordance with the principles of the British Constitution, had been established as checks on the unbridled exercise of popular power. Though, during the dispute, indications had been given of the existence of dissensions yet deeper and more formidable than any which arose from simply political causes, I had still, in common with most of my countrymen, imagined that the original and constant source of the evil was to be found in the defects of the political institutions of the Provinces; that a reform of the constitution, or perhaps merely the introduction of a sounder practice into the administration of the government, would remove an causes of contest and complaint. This opinion was strengthened by the well-known fact, that the political dissensions which had produced their most formidable results in this Province, had assumed a similar, though milder, form in the neighbouring Colonies; and that the tranquillity of each of the North American Provinces was subject to constant disturbance from collision between the executive and the representatives of the people. The constitutions of these Colonies, the official characters and positions of the contending parties, the avowed subjects of dispute, and the general principles asserted on each side, were so similar, that I could not but concur in the very general opinion, that the common quarrel was the result of some common defect in the almost identical institutions of these Provinces. I looked on it as a dispute analogous to those with which history and experience have made us so familiar in Europe, – a dispute between a people demanding an extension of popular privileges, on the one hand, and an executive, on the other, defending the powers which it conceived necessary for the maintenance of order. I supposed that my principal business would be that of determining how far each party might be in the right, or which was in the wrong; of devising some means of removing the defects which had occasioned the collision; and of restoring such a balance of the constitutional powers as might secure the free and peaceful working of the machine of government.

In a Dispatch which I addressed to Your Majesty's Principal Secretary of State for the Colonies on the 9th of August last,[1] I detailed, with great minuteness, the impressions which had been produced on my mind by the state of things which existed in Lower Canada: I acknowledged that the experience derived from my residence in the Province had completely changed my view of the relative influence of the causes which had been assigned for the existing disorders. I had not, indeed, been brought to believe that the institutions of Lower Canada were less defective than I had originally presumed them to be. From the peculiar circumstances

1 Printed in Sir C.P. Lucas, ed., *Lord Durham's Report on the Affairs of British North America*, 3 vols. (Oxford, 1912), III, 319-31.

in which I was placed, I was enabled to make such effectual observations as convinced me that there had existed in the constitution of the Province, in the balance of political powers, in the spirit and practice of administration in every department of the Government, defects that were quite sufficient to account for a great degree of mismanagement and dissatisfaction. The same observation had also impressed on me the conviction, that, for the peculiar and disastrous dissensions of this Province, there existed a far deeper and far more efficient cause, – a cause which penetrated beneath its political institutions into its social state, – a cause which no reform of constitution or laws, that should leave the elements of society unaltered, could remove; but which must be removed, ere any success could be expected in any attempt to remedy the many evils of this unhappy Province. I expected to find a contest between a government and a people: I found two nations warring in the bosom of a single state: I found a struggle, not of principles, but of races; and I perceived that it would be idle to attempt any amelioration of laws or institutions until we could first succeed in terminating the deadly animosity that now separates the inhabitants of Lower Canada into the hostile divisions of French and English.

It would be vain for me to expect that any description I can give will impress on Your Majesty such a view of the animosity of these races as my personal experience in Lower Canada has forced on me. Our happy immunity from any feelings of national hostility, renders it difficult for us to comprehend the intensity of the hatred which the difference of language, of laws, and of manners, creates between those who inhabit the same village, and are citizens of the same state. We are ready to believe that the real motive of the quarrel is something else; and that the difference of race has slightly and occasionally aggravated dissensions, which we attribute to some more usual cause. Experience of a state of society, so unhappily divided as that of Lower Canada, leads to an exactly contrary opinion. The national feud forces itself on the very senses, irresistibly and palpably, as the origin or the essence of every dispute which divides the community; we discover that dissensions, which appear to have another origin, are but forms of this constant and all-pervading quarrel; and that every contest is one of French and English in the outset, or becomes so ere it has run its course.

The political discontents, for which the vicious system of government has given too much cause, have for a long time concealed or modified the influence of the national quarrel. It has been argued, that origin can have but little effect in dividing the country, inasmuch as individuals of each race have constantly been enlisted together on the side of Government, or been found united in leading the Assembly to assail its alleged abuses; that the names of some of the prominent leaders of the rebellion mark their English, while those of some of the most unpopular supporters of the Government denote their French, origin; and that the representatives, if not of an actual majority (as has occasionally been asserted), at any rate of a large proportion of the purely English population, have been found constantly voting with the majority of the Assembly against what is called the British party. Temporary and local causes have, no doubt, to a certain extent, produced such results. The national hostility has not assumed its permanent influence till of late years, nor has it exhibited itself every where at once. While it displayed itself long ago in the cities of Quebec and Montreal, where the leaders and masses of the rival races most speedily came into collision, the inhabitants of the eastern townships, who were removed from all personal contact with the French, and those of the district below Quebec, who experienced little interference from the English, continued to a very late period to entertain comparatively friendly feelings towards those of the opposite races. But this is a distinction which has unfortunately, year after year, been exhibiting itself more strongly, and diffusing itself more widely. One by one the ancient English leaders of the Assembly have fallen off from the majority, and attached themselves to the party which supported the British Government against it. Every election from the townships added to the English minority. On the other hand, year after year, in spite of the various influences which a government can exercise, and of which no people in the world are more susceptible than the French Canadians; in spite of the additional motives of prudence and patriotism which deter timid or calm men from acting with a party, obviously endangering the public tranquillity by the violence of its conduct, the number of French Canadians, on whom the Government could rely, has been narrowed by the influence of those associations which have drawn them into the ranks of their kindred. The insurrection of 1837 completed the division. Since the resort to arms the two races have been distinctly and completely arrayed against each other. No portion of the English population was backward in taking arms in defence of the Government; with a single exception, no portion of the Canadian population was allowed to do so, even where it was asserted by some that their loyalty inclined them thereto. The exasperation thus generated has extended over the whole of each race. The most just and sensible of the English, those whose politics had always been most liberal, those who had always advocated the most moderate policy in the provincial disputes, seem from that moment to have taken their part against the French as resolutely, if not as fiercely, as the rest of their countrymen, and to have joined in the determination never again to submit to a French majority. A few exceptions mark the existence, rather than militate against the truth of the general rule of national hostility. A few of the French, distinguished by moderate and enlarged views, still condemn the narrow national prejudices and ruinous violence of their countrymen, while they equally resist what they consider the violent and unjust pretensions of a minority, and endeavour to form a middle party between the two extremes. A large part of the Catholic clergy, a few of the principal proprietors of the seigniorial families, and some of those who are influenced by ancient connexions of party, support the Government against revolutionary violence. A very few persons of English origin (not more, perhaps, than fifty out of the whole number) still continue to act with the party which they originally espoused. Those who affect to form a middle party exercise no influence on the contending extremes; and those who side with the nation from which their birth distinguishes them, are regarded by their countrymen with aggravated hatred, as renegades from their race; while they obtain but little of the real affection, confidence or esteem of those whom they have joined.

The grounds of quarrel which are commonly alleged, appear, on investigation, to have little to do with its real cause; and the inquirer, who has imagined that the public demonstrations or professions of the parties have put him in possession of their real motives and designs, is surprised to find, upon nearer observation, how much he has been deceived by the false colours under which they have been in the habit of fighting. It is not, indeed, surprising, that each party should, in this instance, have practised more than the usual frauds of language, by which factions, in every country, seek to secure the sympathy of other communities. A quarrel based on the mere ground of national animosity, appears so revolting to the notions of good sense and charity prevalent in the civilized world, that the parties who feel such a passion the most strongly, and indulge it the most openly, are at great pains to class themselves under any denominations but those which would correctly designate their objects and feelings. The French Canadians have attempted to shroud their hostility to the influence of English emigration, and the introduction of British institutions, under the guise of warfare against the Government and its supporters, whom they represented to be a small knot of corrupt and insolent dependents; being a majority, they have invoked the principles of popular control and democracy, and appealed with no little effect to the sympathy of liberal politicians in every quarter of the world. The English, finding their opponents in collision with the Government, have raised the cry of loyalty and attachment to British connexion, and denounced the republican designs of the French, whom they designate, or rather used to designate, by the appellation of Radicals. Thus the French have been viewed as a democratic party, contending for reform; and the English as a conservative minority, protecting the menaced connexion with the British Crown, and the supreme authority of the Empire. There is truth in this notion in so far as respects the means by which each party sought to carry its own views of Government into effect. The French majority asserted the most democratic doctrines of the rights of a numerical majority. The English minority availed itself of the protection of the prerogative, and allied itself with all those of the colonial institutions which enabled the few to resist the will of the many. But when we look to the objects of each party, the analogy to our own politics seems to be lost, if not actually reversed; the French appear to have used their democratic arms for conservative purposes, rather than those of liberal and enlightened movement; and the sympathies of the friends of reform are naturally enlisted on the side of sound amelioration which the English minority in vain attempted to introduce into the antiquated laws of the Province.

Yet even on the questions which had been most recently the prominent matters of dispute between the two parties, it is difficult to believe that the hostility of the races was the effect, and not the cause, of the pertinacity with which the desired reforms were pressed or resisted.

The English complained of the Assembly's refusal to establish Registry Offices, and to commute the feudal tenures: and yet it was among the ablest and most influential leaders of the English that I found some of the opponents of both the proposed reforms. The leaders of the French were anxious to disclaim any hostility to these reforms themselves. Many of them represented the reluctance which the Assembly had exhibited to entertain these questions, as a result of the extraordinary influence which Mr. Papineau exercised over that body; his opposition was accounted for by some peculiar prejudices of education and professional practice, in which he was said to find little concurrence among his countrymen; it was stated that even his influence would not have prevented these questions from being very favourably entertained by the Assembly, had it ever met again; and I received assurances of a friendly disposition towards them, which I must say were very much at variance with the reluctance which the leading men of the party showed to any co-operation with me in the attempts which I subsequently made to carry these very objects into effect. At the same time while the leading men of the French party thus rendered themselves liable to the imputation of a timid or narrow-minded opposition to these improvements, the mass of the French population, who are immediate sufferers by the abuses of the seignorial system, exhibited, in every possible shape, their hostility to the state of things which their leaders had so obstinately maintained. There is every reason to believe that a great number of the peasants who fought at St. Denis and St. Charles, imagined that the principal result of success would be the overthrow of tithes and feudal burthens; and in the declaration of independence which Dr. Robert Nelson issued, two of the objects of the insurrection were stated to be the abolition of feudal tenures and the establishment of Registry

Offices.* When I observe these inconsistencies of conduct among the opponents and supporters of these reforms; when I consider that their attainment was prevented by means of the *censitaires*, the very persons most interested in their success, and that they were not more eagerly demanded by the wealthier of the English, than by the artisans and labourers of that race whose individual interests would hardly have derived much direct benefit from their success, I cannot but think that many, both of the supporters and of the opponents, cared less for the measures themselves, than for the handle which the agitation of them gave to their national hostility; that the Assembly resisted these changes chiefly because the English desired them; and that the eagerness with which many of the English urged them was stimulated by finding them opposed by the French.

Nor did I find the spirit which animated each party at all more coincident with the representations current in this country, than their objects appeared, when tried by English, or rather European ideas of reforming legislation. An utterly uneducated and singularly inert population, implicitly obeying leaders who ruled them by the influence of a blind confidence and narrow national prejudices, accorded very little with the resemblance which had been discovered to that high-spirited democracy which effected the American Revolution. Still less could I discover in the English population those slavish tools of a narrow official clique, or a few purse-proud merchants, which their opponents had described them as being. I have found the main body of the English population,

---

* Among the few petitions, except those of mere compliment, which I received from French Canadians, were three or four for the abolition and commutation of the feudal tenures. But the most remarkable was one which was presented from the inhabitants of the county of Saguenay, and supported by Mr. Charles Drolet, late M.P.P. for that county. The petitioners, who represented themselves as suffering under a degree of distress of which the existence is too deplorably certain, prayed to be allowed to settle on the wild lands at the head of the Saguenay. They expressed their willingness to take the lands on any conditions which the Government might propose, but they prayed that it should not be granted on the feudal tenure.

consisting of hardy farmers and humble mechanics, composing a very independent, not very manageable, and, sometimes a rather turbulent, democracy. Though constantly professing a somewhat extravagant loyalty and high prerogative doctrines, I found them very determined on maintaining in their own persons a great respect for popular rights, and singularly ready to enforce their wishes by the strongest means of constitutional pressure on the Government. Between them and the Canadians I found the strongest hostility; and that hostility was, as might be expected, most strongly developed among the humblest and rudest of the body. Between them and the small knot of officials, whose influence has been represented as so formidable, I found no sympathy whatever; and it must be said, in justice to this body of officials, who have been so much assailed as the enemies of the Canadian people, that however little I can excuse the injurious influence of that system of administration, which they were called upon to carry into execution, the members of the oldest and most powerful official families were, of all the English in the country, those in whom I generally found most sympathy with, and kindly feeling towards, the French population. I could not therefore believe that this animosity was only that subsisting between an official oligarchy and a people; and again, I was brought to a conviction that the contest, which had been represented as a contest of classes, was, in fact, a contest of races.

However unwilling we may be to attribute the disorders of a country connected with us to a cause so fatal to its tranquillity, and one which it seems so difficult to remove, no very long or laboured consideration of the relative characters and position of these races is needed for convincing us of their invincible hostility towards each other. It is scarcely possible to conceive descendants of any of the great European nations more unlike each other in character and temperament, more totally separated from each other by language, laws, and modes of life, or placed in circumstances more calculated to produce mutual misunderstanding, jealousy and hatred. To conceive the incompatibility of the two races in Canada, it is not enough that we should picture to ourselves a community composed of equal proportions of French and English. We must bear in mind what kind of French and English they are that are brought in contact, and in what proportions they meet.

The institutions of France, during the period of the colonization of Canada, were, perhaps, more than those of any other European nation, calculated to repress the intelligence and freedom of the great mass of the people. These institutions followed the Canadian colonist across the Atlantic. The same central, ill-organized, unimproving and repressive despotism extended over him. Not merely was he allowed no voice in the government of his Province, or the choice of his rulers, but he was not even permitted to associate with his neighbours for the regulation of those municipal affairs, which the central authority neglected under the pretext of managing. He obtained his land on a tenure singularly calculated to promote his immediate comfort, and to check his desire to better his condition; he was placed at once in a life of constant and unvarying labour, of great material comfort, and feudal dependence. The ecclesiastical authority to which he had been accustomed established its institutions around him, and the priest continued to exercise over him his ancient influence. No general provision was made for education; and, as its necessity was not appreciated, the colonist made no attempt to repair the negligence of his government. It need not surprise us that, under such circumstances, a race of men habituated to the incessant labour of a rude and unskilled agriculture, and habitually fond of social enjoyments, congregated together in rural communities, occupying portions of the wholly unappropriated soil, sufficient to provide each family with material comforts, far beyond their ancient means, or almost their conceptions; that they made little advance beyond the first progress in comfort, which the bounty of the soil absolutely forced upon them; that under the same institutions they remained the same uninstructed, inactive, unprogressive people. Along the alluvial banks of the St. Lawrence, and its tributaries, they have cleared two or three strips of land, cultivated them in the worst method of small farming, and established a series of continuous villages, which give the country of the seigniories the appearance of a never-ending street. Besides the cities which were the seats of government, no towns were established; the rude manufactures of the country were, and still are, carried on in the cottage by the family of the habitant; and an insignificant proportion of the population derived their subsistence from the scarcely discernible commerce of the Province. Whatever energy existed among the population was employed in the fur trade, and the occupations of hunting, which they and their descendants have carried beyond the Rocky Mountains, and still, in great measure, monopolize in the whole valley of the Mississippi. The mass of the community exhibited in the New World the characteristics of the peasantry of Europe. Society was dense; and even the wants and the poverty which the pressure of population occasions in the Old World, became not to be wholly unknown. They clung to ancient prejudices, ancient customs and ancient laws, not from any strong sense of their beneficial effects, but with the unreasoning tenacity of an uneducated and unprogressive people. Nor were they wanting in the virtues of a simple and industrious life, or in those which common consent attributes to the nation from which they spring. The temptations which, in other states of society, lead to offences against property, and the passions which prompt to violence, were little known among them. They are mild and kindly, frugal, industrious and honest, very sociable, cheerful and hospitable, and distinguished for a courtesy and real politeness, which pervades every class of society. The conquest has changed them but little. The higher classes, and the inhabitants of the towns, have adopted some English customs and feelings; but the continued negligence of the British Government left the mass of the people without any of the institutions which would have elevated them in freedom and civilization. It has left them without the education and without the institutions of local self-government, that would have assimilated their character and habits, in the easiest and best way, to those of the Empire of which they became a part. They remain an old and stationary society, in a new and progressive world. In all essentials they are still French; but French in every respect dissimilar to those of France in the present day. They resemble rather the French of the provinces under the old régime.

I cannot pass over this subject without calling particular attention to a peculiarity in the social condition of this people, of which the important bearing on the troubles of Lower Canada has never, in my opinion, been properly estimated. The circumstances of a new and unsettled country, the operation of the French laws of inheritance, and the absence of any means of accumulation, by commerce or manufactures, have produced a remarkable equality of properties and conditions. A few seigniorial families possess large, though not often very valuable properties; the class entirely dependent on wages is very small; the bulk of the population is composed of the hard-working yeomanry of the country districts, commonly called *habitants*, and their connexions engaged in other occupations. It is impossible to exaggerate the want of education among the habitants; no means of instruction have ever been provided for them, and they are almost universally destitute of the qualifications even of reading and writing. It came to my knowledge that out of a great number of boys and girls assembled at the schoolhouse door of St. Thomas, all but three admitted, on inquiry, that they could not read. Yet the children of this large parish attend school regularly, and actually make use of books. They hold the catechism book in their hand, as if they were reading, while they only repeat its contents, which they know by rote. The common assertion, however, that all classes of the Canadians are equally ignorant, is perfectly erroneous; for I know of no people among whom a larger provision exists for the higher kinds of elementary education, or among whom such education is really extended to a larger proportion of the population. The piety and benevolence of the early possessors of the country founded, in the seminaries that exist in different parts of the Province, institutions, of which the funds and activity have long been directed to the promotion of education. Seminaries and colleges have been, by these bodies, established in the cities, and in other central points. The education given in these establishments greatly resembles the kind given in the English public schools, though it is rather more varied. It is entirely in the hands of the Catholic clergy. The number of pupils in these establishments is estimated altogether at about a thousand; and they turn out every year, as far as I could ascertain, between two and three hundred young men thus educated. Almost all of these are members of the family of some habitant, whom the possession of greater quickness than his brothers has induced the father or the curate of the parish to select and send to the seminary. These young men possessing a degree of information immeasurably superior to that of their families, are naturally averse to what they regard as descending to the humble occupations of their parents. A few become priests; but as the military and naval professions are closed against the colonist, the greater part can only find a position suited to their notions of their own qualifications in the learned professions of advocate, notary and surgeon. As from this cause these professions are greatly overstocked, we find every village in Lower Canada filled with notaries and surgeons, with little practice to occupy their attention, and living among their own families, or at any rate among exactly the same class. Thus the persons of most education in every village belong to the same families, and the same original station in life, as the illiterate habitants whom I have described. They are connected with them by all the associations of early youth, and the ties of blood. The most perfect equality always marks their intercourse, and the superior in education is separated by no barrier of manners, or pride, or distinct interests, from the singularly ignorant peasantry by which he is surrounded. He combines, therefore, the influences of superior knowledge and social equality, and wields a power over the mass, which I do not believe that the educated class of any other portion of the world possess. To this singular state of things I attribute the extraordinary influence of the Canadian demagogues. The most uninstructed population any where trusted with political power, is thus placed in the hands of a small body of instructed persons, in whom it reposes the confidence which nothing but such domestic connexion, and such community of interest could generate. Over the class of persons by whom the peasantry are thus led, the Government has not acquired, or ever laboured to acquire, influence; its members have been thrown into opposition by the system of exclusion, long prevalent in the colony; and it is by their agency that the leaders of the Assembly have been enabled hitherto to move as one mass, in whatever direction they thought proper, the simple and ductile population of the country. The entire neglect of education by the Government has thus, more than any other cause, contributed to render this people ungovernable, and to invest the agitator with the power, which he wields against the laws and the public tranquillity.

Among this people, the progress of emigration has of late years introduced an English population, exhibiting the characteristics with which we are familiar, as those of the most enterprising of every class of our countrymen. The circumstances of the early colonial administration excluded the native Canadian from power, and vested all offices of trust and emolument in the hands of strangers of English origin. The highest posts in the law were confided to the same class of persons. The functionaries of the civil government, together with the officers of the army, composed a kind of privileged class, occupying the first place in the community, and excluding the higher class of the natives from society, as well as from the government of their own country. It was not till within a very few years, as was testified by persons who had seen much of the country, that this society of civil and military functionaries ceased to exhibit towards the higher order of Canadians an exclusiveness of demeanour, which was more revolting to a sensitive and polite people than the monopoly of power and profit; nor was this national favouritism discontinued, until after repeated complaints and an angry contest, which had excited passions that concession could not allay. The races had become enemies ere a tardy justice was extorted; and even then the Government discovered a mode of distributing its patronage among the Canadians, which was quite as offensive to that people as their previous exclusion.

It was not long after the conquest, that another and larger class of English settlers began to enter the Province. English capital was attracted to Canada by the vast quantity and valuable nature of the exportable produce of the country, and the great facilities for commerce, presented by the natural means of internal intercourse. The ancient trade of the country was conducted on a much larger and more profitable scale; and new branches of industry were explored. The active and regular habits of the English capitalist drove out of all the more profitable kinds of industry their inert and careless competitors of the French race; but in respect of the greater part (almost the whole) of the commerce and manufactures of the country, the English cannot be said to have encroached on the French; for, in fact, they created employments and profits which had not previously existed. A few of the ancient race smarted under the loss occasioned by the success of English competition; but all felt yet more acutely the gradual increase of a class of strangers in whose hands the wealth of the country appeared to centre, and whose expenditure and influence eclipsed those of the class which had previously occupied the first position in the country. Nor was the intrusion of the English limited to commercial enterprises. By degrees, large portions of land were occupied by them; nor did they confine themselves to the unsettled and distant country of the townships. The wealthy capitalist invested his money in the purchase of seigniorial properties; and it is estimated, that at the present moment full half of the more valuable seigniories are actually owned by English proprietors. The seigniorial tenure is one so little adapted to our notions of proprietary rights, that the new seignior, without any consciousness or intention of injustice, in many instances exercised his rights in a manner which would appear perfectly fair in this country, but which the Canadian settler reasonably regarded as oppressive. The English purchaser found an equally unexpected and just cause of complaint in that uncertainty of the laws, which rendered his possession of property precarious, and in those incidents of the tenure which rendered its alienation or improvement difficult. But an irritation, greater than that occasioned by the transfer of the large properties, was caused by the competition of the English with the French farmer. The English farmer carried with him the experience and habits of the most improved agriculture in the world. He settled himself in the townships bordering on the seigniories, and brought a fresh soil and improved cultivation to compete with the worn-out and slovenly farm of the habitant. He often took the very farm which the Canadian settler had abandoned, and, by superior management, made that a source of profit which had only impoverished his predecessor. The ascendancy which an unjust favouritism had contributed to give to the English race in the government and the legal profession, their own superior energy, skill and capital secured to them in every branch of industry. They have developed the resources of the country; they have constructed or improved its means of communication; they have created its internal and foreign commerce. The entire wholesale, and a large portion of the retail trade of the Province, with the most profitable and flourishing farms, are now in the hands of this numerical minority of the population.

In Lower Canada the mere working class which depends on wages, though proportionally large in comparison with that to be found in any other portion of the American continent, is, according to our ideas, very small. Competition between persons of different origin in this class, has not exhibited itself till very recently, and is, even now, almost confined to the cities. The large mass of the labouring population are French in the employ of English capitalists. The more skilled class of artisans are generally English; but in the general run of the more laborious employments, the French Canadians fully hold their ground against English rivalry. The emigration which took place a few years ago, brought in a class which entered into more direct competition with the French in some kinds of employment in the towns; but the individuals affected by this competition were not very many. I do not believe that the animosity which exists between the working classes of the two origins is the necessary result of a collision of interests, or of a jealousy of the superior success of English labour. But national prejudices naturally exercise the greatest influence over the most uneducated; the difference of language is less easily overcome; the differences of manners and customs less easily appreciated. The labourers, whom the emigration introduced, contained a number of very ignorant, turbulent and demoralized persons, whose conduct and manners alike revolted the well-ordered and courteous natives of the same class. The working men naturally ranged themselves on the side of the educated and wealthy of their own countrymen. When once engaged in the conflict, their passions were less restrained by education and prudence; and the national hostility now rages most fiercely between those whose interests in reality bring them the least in collision.

The two races thus distinct have been brought into the same community, under circumstances which rendered their contact inevitably productive of collision. The difference of language from the first kept them asunder. It is not any where a virtue of the English race to look with complacency on any manners, customs or laws which appear strange to them; accustomed to form a high estimate of their own superiority, they take no pains to conceal from others their contempt and intolerance of their usages. They found the French Canadians filled with an equal amount of national pride; a sensitive, but inactive pride, which disposes that people not to resent insult, but rather to keep aloof from those who would keep them under. The French could not but feel the superiority of English enterprise; they could not shut their eyes to their success in every undertaking in which they came into contact, and to the constant superiority which they were acquiring. They looked upon their rivals with alarm, with jealousy, and finally with hatred. The English repaid them with a scorn, which soon also assumed the same form of hatred. The French complained of the arrogance and injustice of the English; the English accused the French of the vices of a weak and conquered people, and charged them with meanness and perfidy. The entire mistrust which the two races have thus learned to conceive of each other's intentions, induces them to put the worst construction on the most innocent conduct; to judge every word, every act, and every intention unfairly; to attribute the most odious designs, and reject every overture of kindness or fairness, as covering secret designs of treachery and malignity.

Religion formed no bond of intercourse and union. It is, indeed, an admirable feature of Canadian society, that it is entirely devoid of any religious dissensions. Sectarian intolerance is not merely not avowed, but it hardly seems to influence men's feelings. But though the prudence and liberality of both parties has prevented this fruitful source of animosity from embittering their quarrels, the difference of religion has in fact tended to keep them asunder. Their priests have been distinct; they have not met even in the same church.

No common education has served to remove and soften the differences of origin and language. The associations of youth, the sports of childhood, and the studies by which the character of manhood is modified, are distinct and totally different. In Montreal and Quebec there are English schools and French schools; the children in these are accustomed to fight nation against nation, and the quarrels that arise among boys in the streets usually exhibit a division into English on one side, and French on the other.

As they are taught apart, so are their studies different. The literature with which each is the most conversant, is that of the peculiar language of each; and all the ideas which men derive from books, come to each of them from perfectly different sources. The difference of language in this respect produces effects quite apart from those which it has on the mere intercourse of the two races. Those who have reflected on the powerful influence of language on thought, will perceive in how different a manner people who speak in different languages are apt to think; and those who are familiar with the literature of France, know that the same opinion will be expressed by an English and French writer of the present day, not merely in different words, but in a style so different as to mark utterly different habits of thought. This difference is very striking in Lower Canada; it exists not merely in the books of most influence and repute, which are of course those of the great writers of France and England, and by which the minds of the respective races are formed, but it is observable in the writings which now issue from the colonial press. The articles in the newspapers of each race, are written in a style as widely different as those of France and England at present; and the arguments which convince the one, are calculated to appear utterly unintelligible to the other.

This difference of language produces misconceptions yet more fatal even than those which it occasions with respect to opinions; it aggravates the national animosities, by representing all the events of the day in utterly different lights. The political misrepresentation of facts is one of the incidents of a free press in every free country; but in nations in which all speak the same language, those who receive a misrepresentation from one side, have generally some means of learning the truth from the other. In Lower Canada, however, where the French and English papers represent adverse opinions, and where no large portion of the community can read both languages with ease, those who receive the misrepresentation are rarely able to avail themselves of the means of correction. It is difficult to conceive the perversity with which misrepresentations are habitually made, and the gross delusions which find currency among the people; they thus live in a world of misconceptions, in which each party is set against the other not only by diversity of feelings and opinions, but by an actual belief in an utterly different set of facts.

The differences thus early occasioned by education and language, are in no wise softened by the intercourse of after-life; their business and occupations do not bring the two races into friendly contact and co-operation, but only present them to each other in occasional rivalry. . . .

The hostility which thus pervades society, was some time growing before it became of prominent importance in the politics of the Province. It was inevitable that such social feelings must end in a deadly political strife. The French regarded with jealousy the influence in politics of a daily increasing body of the strangers, whom they so much disliked and dreaded; the wealthy English were offended at finding that their property gave them no influence over their French dependents, who were acting under the guidance of leaders of their own race; and the farmers and traders of the same race were not long before they began to bear with impatience their utter political nullity in the midst of the majority of a population, whose ignorance they contemned, and whose political views and conduct seemed utterly at variance with their own notions of the principles and practice of self-government. The superior political and practical intelligence of the English cannot be, for a moment, disputed. The great mass of the Canadian population, who cannot read or write, and have found in few of the institutions of their country, even the elements of political education, were obviously inferior to the English settlers, of whom a large proportion had received a considerable amount of education, and had been trained in their own country, to take a part in public business of one kind or another. With respect to the more educated classes, the superiority is not so general or apparent; indeed from all the information that I could collect, I incline to think that the greater amount of refinement, of speculative thought, and of the knowledge that books can give, is, with some brilliant exceptions, to be found among the French. But I have no hesitation in stating, even more decidedly, that the circumstances in which the English have been placed in Lower Canada, acting on their original political education, have endowed the leaders of that population with much of that practical sagacity, tact, and energy in politics, in which I must say, that the bad institutions of the Colony have, in my opinion, rendered the leaders of the French deplorably deficient. That a race which felt itself thus superior in political activity and intelligence, should submit with patience to the rule of a majority which it could not respect, was impossible. At what time and from what particular cause the hostility between such a majority and such a minority, which was sure sooner or later to break out, actually became of paramount importance, it is difficult to say. The hostility between the Assembly and the British Government had long given a tendency to attacks, on the part of the popular leaders, on the nation to which that government belonged. It is said that the appeals to the national pride and animosities of the French, became more direct and general on the occasion of the abortive attempt to re-unite Upper and Lower Canada in 1822, which the leaders of the Assembly viewed or represented as a blow aimed at the institutions of their Province. The anger of the English was excited by the denunciations of themselves, which, subsequently to this period, they were in the habit of hearing. They had possibly some little sympathy with the members of the provincial government of their own race; and their feelings were, probably, yet more strongly excited in favour of the connexion of the Colony with Great Britain, which the proceedings of the Assembly appeared to endanger. But the abuses existing under the provincial government, gave such inducements to remain in opposition to it, that the representatives of each race continued for a long time to act together against it. And as the bulk of the English population in the townships and on the Ottawa were brought into very little personal contact with the French, I am inclined to think that it might have been some time longer, ere the disputes of origin would have assumed an importance paramount to all others, had not the Assembly come into collision with the whole English population by its policy with respect to internal improvements, and to the old and defective laws, which operated as a bar to the alienation of land, and to the formation of associations for commercial purposes.

   The English population, an immigrant and enterprising population, looked on the American Provinces as a vast field for settlement and speculation, and in the common spirit of the Anglo-Saxon inhabitants of that continent, regarded it as the chief business of the Government, to promote, by all possible use of its legislative and administrative powers, the increase of population and the accumulation of property; they found the laws of real property exceedingly adverse to the easy alienation of land, which is, in a new country, absolutely essential to its settlement and improvement; they found the greatest deficiency in the internal communications of the country, and the utter want of local self-government rendered it necessary for them to apply to the Assembly for every road or bridge, or other public work that was needed; they wished to form themselves into companies for the establishment of banks, and the construction of railroads and canals, and to obtain the powers necessary for the completion of such works with funds of their own. And as the first requisite for the improvement of the country, they desired that a large proportion of the revenue should be applied to the completion of that great series of public works, by which it was proposed to render the Saint Lawrence and the Ottawa navigable throughout their whole extent.

Without going so far as to accuse the Assembly of a deliberate design to check the settlement and improvement of Lower Canada, it cannot be denied that they looked with considerable jealousy and dislike on the increase and prosperity of what they regarded as a foreign and hostile race; they looked on the Province as the patrimony of their own race; they viewed it not as a country to be settled, but as one already settled; and instead of legislating in the American spirit, and first providing for the future population of the Province, their primary care was, in the spirit of legislation which prevails in the old world, to guard the interests and feelings of the present race of inhabitants, to whom they considered the new-comers as subordinate; they refused to increase the burthens of the country by imposing taxes to meet the expenditure required for improvement, and they also refused to direct to that object any of the funds previously devoted to other purposes. The improvement of the harbour of Montreal was suspended, from a political antipathy to a leading English merchant who had been the most active of the Commissioners, and by whom it had been conducted with the most admirable success. It is but just to say that some of the works which the Assembly authorized and encouraged were undertaken on a scale of due moderation, and satisfactorily perfected and brought into operation. Others, especially the great communications which I have mentioned above, the Assembly showed a great reluctance to promote or even to permit. It is true that there was considerable foundation for their objections to the plan on which the Legislature of Upper Canada had commenced some of these works, and to the mode in which it had carried them on; but the English complained, that instead of profiting by the experience which they might have derived from this source, the Assembly seemed only to make its objections a pretext for doing nothing. The applications for banks, railroads and canals were laid on one side until some general measures could be adopted with regard to such undertakings; but the general measures thus promised were never passed, and the particular enterprises in question were prevented. The adoption of a registry was refused on the alleged ground of its inconsistency with the French institutions of the Province, and no measure to attain this desirable end, in a less obnoxious mode, was prepared by the leaders of the Assembly. The feudal tenure was supported, as a mild and just provision for the settlement of a new country; a kind of assurance given by a Committee of the Assembly, that some steps should be taken to remove the most injurious incidents of the seigniorial tenure, produced no practical results; and the enterprises of the English were still thwarted by the obnoxious laws of the country. In all these decisions of the Assembly, in its discussions, and in the apparent motives of its conduct, the English population perceived traces of a desire to repress the influx and the success of their race. A measure for imposing a tax on emigrants, though recommended by the Home Government, and warranted by the policy of those neighbouring states, which give the greatest encouragement to immigration, was argued on such grounds in the Assembly, that it was not unjustly regarded as indicative of an intention to exclude any further accession to the English population; and the industry of the English was thus retarded by this conduct of the Assembly. Some districts, particularly that of the Eastern Townships, where the French race has no footing, were seriously injured by the refusal of necessary improvements; and the English inhabitants generally regarded the policy of the Assembly as a plan for preventing any further emigration to the Province, of stopping the growth of English wealth, and of rendering precarious the English property already invested or acquired in Lower Canada.

The Assembly of which they thus complained, and of which they entertained apprehensions so serious, was at the same time in collision with the executive Government. The party in power, and which, by means of the Legislative Council, kept the Assembly in check, gladly availed itself of the discontents of this powerful and energetic minority, offered it its protection, and undertook the furtherance of its views; and thus was cemented the singular alliance between the English population and the Colonial officials, who combined from perfectly different motives, and with perfectly different objects, against a common enemy. The English desired reform and liberal measures from the Assembly, which refused them, while it was urging other reforms and demanding other liberal measures from the executive Government. The Assembly complained of the oppressive use of the power of the executive; the English complained that they, a minority, suffered under the oppressive use to which power was turned by the French majority. Thus a bold and intelligent democracy was impelled, by its impatience for liberal measures, joined to its national antipathies, to make common cause with a government which was at issue with the majority on the question of popular rights. The actual conflict commenced by a collision between the executive and the French majority; and, as the English population rallied round the Government, supported its pretensions, and designated themselves by the appellation of 'loyal', the causes of the quarrel were naturally supposed to be much more simple than they really were; and the extent of the division which existed among the inhabitants of Lower Canada, the number and nature of the combatants arrayed on each side, and the irremediable nature of the dispute, were concealed from the public view.

The treasonable attempt of the French party to carry its political objects into effect by an appeal to arms, brought these hostile races into general and armed collision. I will not dwell on the melancholy scenes exhibited in the progress of the contest, or the fierce passions which held an unchecked sway during the insurrection, or immediately after its suppression. It is not difficult to conceive how greatly the evils, which I have described as previously existing, have been aggravated by the war; how terror and revenge nourished, in each portion of the population, a bitter and irreconcileable hatred to each other, and to the institutions of the country. The French population, who had for some time exercised a great and increasing power through the medium of the House of Assembly, found their hopes unexpectedly prostrated in the dust. The physical force which they had vaunted was called into action, and proved to be utterly inefficient. The hope of recovering their previous ascendancy under a constitution, similar to that suspended, almost ceased to exist. Removed from all actual share in the government of their country, they brood in sullen silence over the memory of their fallen countrymen, of their burnt villages, of their ruined property, of their extinguished ascendancy, and of their humbled nationality. To the Government and the English they ascribe these wrongs, and nourish against both an indiscriminating and eternal

animosity. Nor have the English inhabitants forgotten in their triumph the terror with which they suddenly saw themselves surrounded by an insurgent majority, and the incidents which alone
appeared to save them from the unchecked domination of their
antagonists. They find themselves still a minority in the midst of a
hostile and organized people; apprehensions of secret conspiracies
and sanguinary designs haunt them unceasingly, and their only
hope of safety is supposed to rest on systematically terrifying and
disabling the French, and in preventing a majority of that race from
ever again being predominant in any portion of the legislature of
the Province. I describe in strong terms the feelings which appear to
me to animate each portion of the population; and the picture
which I draw represents a state of things so little familiar to the personal experience of the people of this country, that many will probably regard it as the work of mere imagination; but I feel confident
that the accuracy and moderation of my description will be
acknowledged by all who have seen the state of society in Lower
Canada during the last year. Nor do I exaggerate the inevitable con-
stancy any more than the intensity of this animosity. Never again
will the present generation of French Canadians yield a loyal submission to a British Government; never again will the English population tolerate the authority of a House of Assembly, in which the
French shall possess or even approximate to a majority.

Nor is it simply the working of representative government which
is placed out of question by the present disposition of the two
races; every institution which requires for its efficiency a confidence in the mass of the people, or co-operation between its
classes, is practically in abeyance in Lower Canada. The militia, on
which the main defence of the Province against external enemies,
and the discharge of many of the functions of internal police have
hitherto depended, is completely disorganized. A muster of that
force would, in some districts, be the occasion for quarrels
between the races, and in the greater part of the country the
attempting to arm or employ it would be merely arming the enemies of the Government. The course of justice is entirely
obstructed by the same cause; a just decision in any political case
is not to be relied upon; even the judicial bench is, in the opinion
of both races, divided into two hostile sections of French and English, from neither of which is justice expected by the mass of the

hostile party. The partiality of grand and petty juries is a matter of certainty; each race relies on the vote of its countrymen to save it harmless from the law, and the mode of challenging allows of such an exclusion of the hostile party that the French offender may make sure of, and the English hope for a favourable jury, and a consequent acquittal. . . .

In such a state of feelings the course of civil government is hopelessly suspended. No confidence can be felt in the stability of any existing institution, or the security of person and property. It cannot occasion surprise that this state of things should have destroyed the tranquillity and happiness of families; that it should have depreciated the value of property, and that it should have arrested the improvement and settlement of the country. The alarming decline of the value of landed property was attested to me by some of the principal proprietors of the Province. The continual and progressive decrease of the revenue, though in some degree attributable to other causes, indicates a diminution of the wealth of the country. The staple export trade of the Province, the timber trade, has not suffered; but instead of exporting grain, the Province is now obliged to import for its own consumption. The influx of emigrants, once so considerable, has very greatly diminished. In 1832 the number of emigrants who landed at the port of Quebec amounted to 52,000; in 1837 it had fallen to a few more than 22,000; and in 1838 it did not amount to 5,000. Insecurity begins to be so strongly felt by the loyal inhabitants of the seigniories, that many of them are compelled, by fear or necessity, to quit their occupations, and seek refuge in the cities. If the present state of things continues, the most enterprising and wealthy capitalists of the Province will thus in a short time be driven from the seats of their present industry.

Nor does there appear to be the slightest chance of putting an end to this animosity during the present generation. Passions inflamed during so long a period cannot speedily be calmed. The state of education which I have previously described as placing the peasantry entirely at the mercy of agitators, the total absence of any class of persons, or any organization of authority that could counteract this mischievous influence, and the serious decline in the district of Montreal of the influence of the clergy, concur in rendering it absolutely impossible for the Government to produce any better state of feeling among the French population. It is even impossible to impress on a people so circumstanced the salutary dread of the power of Great Britain, which the presence of a large military force in the Province might be expected to produce. I have been informed by witnesses so numerous and so trustworthy, that I cannot doubt the correctness of their statements, that the peasantry were generally ignorant of the large amount of force which was sent into their country last year. The newspapers that circulate among them had informed them that Great Britain had no troops to send out; that in order to produce an impression on the minds of the country people, the same regiments were marched backwards and forwards in different directions, and represented as additional arrivals from home. This explanation was promulgated among the people by the agitators of each village; and I have no doubt that the mass of the habitants really believed that the Government was endeavouring to impose on them by this species of fraud. It is a population with whom the authority has no means of contact or explanation. It is difficult even to ascertain what amount of influence the ancient leaders of the French party continue to possess. The name of Mr. Papineau is still cherished by the people; and the idea is current that, at the appointed time, he will return, at the head of an immense army, and re-establish 'La Nation Canadienne'. But there is great reason to doubt whether his name be not used as a mere watchword; whether the people are not in fact running entirely counter to his counsels and policy; and whether they are not really under the guidance of separate petty agitators, who have no plan but that of a senseless and reckless determination to show in every way their hostility to the British Government and English race. Their ultimate designs and hopes are equally unintelligible. Some vague expectation of absolute independence still seems to delude them. The national vanity, which is a remarkable ingredient in their character induces many to flatter themselves with the idea of a Canadian Republic; the sounder information of others has led them to perceive that a separation from Great Britain must be followed by a junction with the great Confederation on their southern frontier. But they seem apparently reckless of the consequences, provided they can wreak their vengeance on the English. There is no people against which early associations and every conceivable difference of manners and opinions, have implanted in the Canadian mind a more ancient and rooted national antipathy than that which they feel against the people of the United States. Their more discerning leaders feel that their chances of preserving their nationality would be greatly diminished by an incorporation with the United States; and recent symptoms of Anti-Catholic feeling in New England, well known to the Canadian population, have generated a very general belief that their religion, which even they do not accuse the British party of assailing, would find little favour or respect from their neighbours. Yet none even of these considerations weigh against their present all-absorbing hatred of the English; and I am persuaded that they would purchase vengeance and a momentary triumph, by the aid of any enemies, or submission to any yoke. This provisional but complete cessation of their ancient antipathy to the Americans, is now admitted even by those who most strongly denied it during the last spring, and who then asserted that an American war would as completely unite the whole population against the common enemy, as it did in 1813. My subsequent experience leaves no doubt in my mind that the views which were contained in my Dispatch of the 9th of August are perfectly correct; and that an invading American army might rely on the co-operation of almost the entire French population of Lower Canada.

In the Dispatch above referred to I also described the state of feeling among the English population, nor can I encourage a hope that that portion of the community is at all more inclined to any settlement of the present quarrel that would leave any share of power to the hostile race. Circumstances having thrown the English into the ranks of the Government, and the folly of their opponents having placed them, on the other hand, in a state of permanent collision with it, the former possess the advantage of having the force of Government, and the authority of the laws on their side in the present stage of the contest. Their exertions during the recent troubles have contributed to maintain the supremacy of the law, and the continuance of the connexion with Great Britain; but it would in my opinion be dangerous to rely on the continuance of such a state of feeling as now prevails among them, in the event of a different policy being adopted by the Imperial Government. Indeed the prevalent sentiment among them is one of anything but satisfaction with the course which has been long pursued, with reference to Lower Canada, by the British Legislature and Executive. The calmer view, which distant spectators are enabled to take of the conduct of the two parties, and the disposition which is evinced to make a fair adjustment of the contending claims, appear iniquitous and injurious in the eyes of men who think that they alone have any claim to the favour of that Government by which they alone have stood fast. They complain loudly and bitterly of the whole course pursued by the Imperial Government, with respect to the quarrel of the two races, as having being founded on an utter ignorance or disregard of the real question at issue, as having fostered the mischievous pretensions of French nationality, and as having by the vacillation and inconsistency which marked it, discouraged loyalty and fomented rebellion. Every measure of clemency or even justice towards their opponents they regard with jealousy, as indicating a disposition towards that conciliatory policy which is the subject of their angry recollection; for they feel that being a minority, any return to the due course of constitutional government would again subject them to a French majority; and to this I am persuaded they would never peaceably submit. They do not hesitate to say that they will not tolerate much longer the being made the sport of parties at home, and that if the mother country forgets what is due to the loyal and enterprising men of her own race, they must protect themselves. In the significant language of one of their own ablest advocates, they assert that 'Lower Canada must be *English*, at the expense, if necessary, of not being *British*.'

I have, in Dispatches of a later date than that to which I have had occasion so frequently to refer, called the attention of the Home Government to the growth of this alarming state of feeling among the English population. The course of the late troubles, and the assistance which the French insurgents derived from some citizens of the United States, have caused a most intense exasperation among the Canadian loyalists against the American Government and people. Their papers have teemed with the most unmeasured denunciations of the good faith of the authorities, of the character and morality of the people, and of the political institutions of the United States. Yet, under this surface of hostility, it is easy to detect a strong under current of an exactly contrary feeling. As the general opinion of the American people became more apparent during the course of the last year, the English of Lower Canada were surprised to find how strong, in spite of the first burst of sympathy, with a people supposed to be struggling for independence, was the real sympathy of their republican neighbours with the great objects of the minority. Without abandoning their attachment to their mother country, they have begun, as men in a state of uncertainty are apt to do, to calculate the probable consequences of a separation, if it should unfortunately occur, and be followed by an incorporation with the United States. In spite of the shock which it would occasion their feelings, they undoubtedly think that they should find some compensation in the promotion of their interests; they believe that the influx of American emigration would speedily place the English race in a majority; they talk frequently and loudly of what has occurred in Louisiana, where, by means which they utterly misrepresent, the end nevertheless of securing an English predominance over a French population, has undoubtedly been attained; they assert very confidently that the Americans would make a very speedy and decisive settlement of the pretensions of the French; and they believe, that after the first shock of an entirely new political state had been got over, they and their posterity would share in that amazing progress, and that great material prosperity, which every day's experience shows them is the lot of the people of the United States. I do not believe that such a feeling has yet sapped their strong allegiance to the British empire; but their allegiance is founded on their deep-rooted attachment to British as distinguished from French institutions. And if they find that that authority which they have maintained against its recent assailants, is to be exerted in such a manner as to subject them again to what they call a French dominion, I feel perfectly confident that they would attempt to avert the result, by courting, on any terms, an union with an Anglo-Saxon people. Such is the lamentable and hazardous state of things produced by the conflict of races which has so long divided the Province of Lower Canada, and which has assumed the formidable and irreconcileable character which I have depicted. In describing the nature of this conflict, I have specified the causes in which it originated; and though I have mentioned the conduct and constitution of the Colonial

Government as modifying the character of the struggle, I have not attributed to political causes a state of things which would, I believe, under any political institutions have resulted from the very composition of society. A jealousy between two races, so long habituated to regard each other with hereditary enmity, and so differing in habits, in language and in laws, would have been inevitable under any form of government. That liberal institutions and a prudent policy might have changed the character of the struggle I have no doubt; but they could not have prevented it; they could only have softened its character, and brought it more speedily a more decisive and peaceful conclusion. Unhappily, however, the system of government pursued in Lower Canada has been based on the policy of perpetuating that very separation of the races, and encouraging these very notions of conflicting nationalities which it ought to have been the first and chief care of Government to check and extinguish. From the period of the conquest to the present time, the conduct of the Government has aggravated the evil, and the origin of the present extreme disorder may be found in the institutions by which the character of the colony was determined.

There are two modes by which a government may deal with a conquered territory. The first course open to it is that of respecting the rights and nationality of the actual occupants; of recognizing the existing laws, and preserving established institutions; of giving no encouragement to the influx of the conquering people, and, without attempting any change in the elements of the community, merely incorporating the Province under the general authority of the central Government. The second is that of treating the conquered territory as one open to the conquerors, of encouraging their influx, of regarding the conquered race as entirely subordinate, and of endeavouring as speedily and as rapidly as possible to assimilate the character and institutions of its new subjects to those of the great body of its empire. In the case of an old and long-settled country, in which the land is appropriated, in which little room is left for colonization, and in which the race of the actual occupants must continue to constitute the bulk of the future population of the province, policy as well as humanity render the well-being of the conquered people the first care of a just government, and recommend the adoption of the first-mentioned system; but in a new and unsettled country, a provident legislator would regard as his first object the interests not of the few individuals who happen at the moment to inhabit a portion of the soil, but those of that comparatively vast population by which he may reasonably expect that it will be filled; he would form his plans with a view of attracting and nourishing that future population, and he would therefore establish those institutions which would be most acceptable to the race by which he hoped to colonize the country. The course which I have described as best suited to an old and settled country, would have been impossible in the American continent, unless the conquering state meant to renounce the immediate use of the unsettled lands of the Province; and in this case such a course would have been additionally unadvisable, unless the British Government were prepared to abandon to the scanty population of French whom it found in Lower Canada, not merely the possession of the vast extent of rich soil which that Province contains, but also the mouth of the St. Lawrence, and all the facilities for trade which the entrance of that great river commands.

In the first regulations adopted by the British Government for the settlement of the Canadas, in the Proclamation of 1763, and the Commission of the Governor-in-Chief of the Province of Quebec, in the offers by which officers and soldiers of the British army, and settlers from the other North American Provinces, were tempted to accept grants of land in the Canadas, we perceive very clear indications of an intention of adopting the second and the wiser of the two systems. Unfortunately, however, the conquest of Canada was almost immediately followed by the commencement of those discontents which ended in the independence of the United Provinces. From that period, the colonial policy of this country appears to have undergone a complete change. To prevent the further dismemberment of the Empire became the primary object with our statesmen; and an especial anxiety was exhibited to adopt every expedient which appeared calculated to prevent the remaining North American Colonies from following the example of successful revolt. Unfortunately the distinct national character of the French inhabitants of Canada, and their ancient hostility to the people of New England, presented the easiest and most obvious line of demarcation. To isolate the inhabitants of the British from those of the revolted Colonies, became the policy of the Government; and the nationality of the French Canadians was therefore cultivated, as a means of perpetual and entire separation from their neighbours. It seems also to have been considered the policy of the British Government to govern its colonies by means of division, and to break them down as much as possible into petty isolated communities, incapable of combination, and possessing no sufficient strength for individual resistance to the Empire. Indications of such designs are to be found in many of the acts of the British Government with respect to its North American Colonies. In 1775 instructions were sent from England, directing that all grants of land within the Province of Quebec, then comprising Upper and Lower Canada, were to be made in fief and seigniory; and even the grants to the refugee loyalists, and officers and privates of the colonial corps, promised in 1786, were ordered to be made on the same tenure. In no instance was it more singularly exhibited than in the condition annexed to the grants of land in Prince Edward's Island, by which it was stipulated that the Island was to be settled by 'foreign Protestants'; as if they were to be foreign in order to separate them from the people of New England, and Protestants in order to keep them apart from the Canadian and Acadian Catholics. It was part of the same policy to separate the French of Canada from the British emigrants, and to conciliate the former by the retention of their language, laws, and religious institutions. For this purpose Canada was afterwards divided into two Provinces, the settled portion being allotted to the French, and the unsettled being destined to become the seat of British colonization. Thus, instead of availing itself of the means which the extent and nature of the Province afforded for the gradual introduction of such an English population into its various parts as might have easily placed the French in a minority, the Government deliberately constituted the French into a majority, and recognized and strengthened their indistinct national character. Had the sounder policy of making the Province English, in all its institutions, been adopted from the first, and steadily persevered in, the French would probably have been speedily outnumbered, and the beneficial operation of the free institutions of England would never have been impeded by the animosities of origin.

Not only, however, did the Government adopt the unwise course of dividing Canada, and forming in one of its divisions a French community, speaking the French language, and retaining French institutions, but it did not even carry this consistently into effect; for at the same time provision was made for encouraging the emigration of English into the very Province which was said to be assigned to the French. Even the French institutions were not extended over the whole of Lower Canada. The civil law of France, as a whole, and the legal provision for the Catholic clergy were limited to the portion of the country then settled by the French, and comprised in the seigniories; though some provision was made for the formation of new seigniories, almost the whole of the then unsettled portion of the Province was formed into townships, in which the law of England was partially established, and the Protestant religion alone endowed. Thus two populations of hostile origin and different characters, were brought into juxtaposition under a common government, but under different institutions; each was taught to cherish its own language, laws and habits, and each, at the same time, if it moved beyond its original limits, was brought under different institutions, and associated with a different people. The unenterprising character of the French population, and, above all, its attachment to its church (for the enlargement of which, in proportion to the increase or diffusion of the Catholic population, very inadequate provision was made) have produced the effect of confining it within its ancient limits. But the English were attracted into the seigniories, and especially into the cities, by the facilities of commerce afforded by the great rivers. To have effectually given the policy of retaining French institutions and a French population in Lower Canada a fair chance of success, no other institutions should have been allowed, and no other race should have received any encouragement to settle therein. The Province should have been set apart to be wholly French, if it was not to be rendered completely English. The attempt to encourage English emigration into a community, of which the French character was still to be preserved, was an error which planted the seeds of a contest of races in the very constitution of the Colony; this was an error, I mean, even on the assumption that it was possible to exclude the English race from French

Canada. But it was quite impossible to exclude the English race from any part of the North American continent. It will be acknowledged by every one who has observed the progress of Anglo-Saxon colonization in America, that sooner or later the English race was sure to predominate even numerically in Lower Canada, as they predominate already, by their superior knowledge, energy, enterprise and wealth. The error, therefore, to which the present contest must be attributed, is the vain endeavour to preserve a French Canadian nationality in the midst of Anglo-American colonies and states.

That contest has arisen by degrees. The scanty number of the English who settled in Lower Canada during the earlier period of our possession, put out of the question any ideas of rivalry between the races. Indeed, until the popular principles of English institutions were brought effectually into operation, the paramount authority of the Government left little room for dispute among any but the few who contended for its favours. It was not until the English had established a vast trade and accumulated considerable wealth, until a great part of the landed property of the Province was vested in their hands, until a large English population was found in the cities, had scattered itself over large portions of the country, and had formed considerable communities in the townships, and not until the development of representative government had placed substantial power in the hands of the people, that that people divided itself into races, arrayed against each other in intense and enduring animosity.

The errors of the Government did not cease with that, to which I have attributed the origin of this animosity. The defects of the colonial constitution necessarily brought the executive Government into collision with the people; and the disputes of the Government and the people called into action the animosities of race; nor has the policy of the Government obviated the evils inherent in the constitution of the Colony, and the composition of society. It has done nothing to repair its original error, by making the Province English. Occupied in a continued conflict with the Assembly, successive Governors and their councils have overlooked, in great measure, the real importance of the feud of origin; and the Imperial Government, far removed from opportunities of personal observation of the peculiar state of society, has shaped its policy so as to aggravate the disorder. In some instances it has actually conceded the mischievous pretensions of nationality, in order to evade popular claims; as in attempting to divide the Legislative Council, and the patronage of Government, equally between the two races, in order to avoid the demands for an elective Council, and a responsible Executive: sometimes it has, for a while, pursued the opposite course. A policy founded on imperfect information, and conducted by continually changing hands, has exhibited to the Colony a system of vacillation which was in fact no system at all. The alternate concessions to the contending races have only irritated both, impaired the authority of Government, and, by keeping alive the hopes of a French Canadian nationality, counteracted the influences which might, ere this, have brought the quarrel to its natural and necessary termination. It is impossible to determine precisely the respective effects of the social and political causes. The struggle between the Government and the Assembly, has aggravated the animosities of race; and the animosities of race have rendered the political difference irreconcileable. No remedy can be efficient that does not operate upon both evils. At the root of the disorders of Lower Canada, lies the conflict of the two races, which compose its population; until this is settled, no good government is practicable; for whether the political institutions be reformed or left unchanged, whether the powers of the Government be entrusted to the majority or the minority, we may rest assured, that while the hostility of the races continues, whichever of them is entrusted with power, will use it for partial purposes.

I have described the contest between the French and English races in Lower Canada with minuteness, because it was my wish to produce a complete and general conviction of the prominent importance of that struggle, when we are taking into consideration the causes of those disorders which have so grievously afflicted the Province. I have not, however, during the course of my preceding remarks, been able to avoid alluding to other causes, which have greatly contributed to occasion the existing state of things; and I have specified among these the defects of the constitution, and the errors arising out of the system of government. It is, indeed, impossible to believe that the assigned causes of the struggle between the

Government and the majority have had no effect, even though we may believe that they have had much less than the contending parties imagined. It is impossible to observe the great similarity of the constitutions established in all our North American Provinces, and the striking tendency of all to terminate in pretty nearly the same result, without entertaining a belief that some defect in the form of government, and some erroneous principle of administration, have been common to all; the hostility of the races being palpably insufficient to account for all the evils which have affected Lower Canada, inasmuch as nearly the same results have been exhibited among the homogeneous population of the other provinces. It is but too evident that Lower Canada, or the two Canadas, have not alone exhibited repeated conflicts between the Executive and the popular branches of the legislature. The representative body of Upper Canada was before the late election, hostile to the policy of the Government; the most serious discontents have only recently been calmed in Prince Edward's Island and New Brunswick; the Government is still, I believe, in a minority in the Lower House in Nova Scotia; and the dissensions of Newfoundland are hardly less violent than those of the Canadas. It may fairly be said, that the natural state of government in all these Colonies is that of collision between the Executive and the representative body. In all of them the administration of public affairs is habitually confided to those who do not co-operate harmoniously with the popular branch of the legislature; and the Government is constantly proposing measures which the majority of the Assembly reject, and refusing its assent to bills which that body has passed.

A state of things, so different from the working of any successful experiment of representative government, appears to indicate a deviation from sound constitutional principles or practice. Though occasional collisions between the Crown and the House of Commons have occurred in this country since the establishment of our constitution at the Revolution of 1688, they have been rare and transient. A state of frequent and lasting collisions appears almost identical with one of convulsion and anarchy; and its occurrence in any country is calculated to perplex us as to the mode in which any government can be carried on therein, without an entire evasion of popular control. But, when we examine into the system of government in these colonies, it would almost seem as if the object of those by whom it was established had been the combining of apparently popular institutions with an utter absence of all efficient control of the people over their rulers. Representative assemblies were established on the basis of a very wide, and, in some cases, almost universal suffrage; the annual meeting of these bodies was secured by positive enactment, and their apparent attributes were locally nearly as extensive as those of the English House of Commons. At the same time the Crown almost entirely relied on its territorial resources, and on duties imposed by Imperial Acts, prior to the introduction of the representative system, for carrying on the government, without securing the assent of the representative body either to its policy or to the persons by whom that policy was to be administered.

It was not until some years after the commencement of the present century that the population of Lower Canada began to understand the representative system which had been extended to them, and that the Assembly evinced any inclination to make use of its powers. Immediately, however, upon its so doing, it found how limited those powers were, and entered upon a struggle to obtain the authority which analogy pointed out as inherent in a representative assembly. Its freedom of speech immediately brought it into collision with the Governor; and the practical working of the Assembly commenced by its principal leaders being thrown into prison. In course of time, however, the Government was induced, by its necessities, to accept the Assembly's offer to raise an additional revenue by fresh taxes; and the Assembly thus acquired a certain control over the levying and appropriation of a portion of the public revenue. From that time, until the final abandonment in 1832 of every portion of the reserved revenue, excepting the casual and territorial funds, an unceasing contest was carried on, in which the Assembly, making use of every power which it gained, for the purpose of gaining more, acquired, step by step, an entire control over the whole revenue of the country.

I pass thus briefly over the events which have heretofore been considered the principal features of the Canadian controversy, because, as the contest has ended in the concession of the financial demands of the Assembly, and the admission by the Government of the impropriety of attempting to withhold any portion of the public revenues from its control, that contest can now be regarded as of no importance, except as accounting for the exasperation and suspicion which survived it. Nor am I inclined to think that the disputes which subsequently occurred are to be attributed entirely to the operation of mere angry feelings. A substantial cause of contest yet remained. The Assembly, after it had obtained entire control over the public revenues, still found itself deprived of all voice in the choice or even designation of the persons in whose administration of affairs it could feel confidence. All the administrative power of Government remained entirely free from its influence; and though Mr. Papineau appears by his own conduct to have deprived himself of that influence in the Government which he might have acquired, I must attribute the refusal of a civil list to the determination of the Assembly not to give up its only means of subjecting the functionaries of Government to any responsibility.

The powers for which the Assembly contended, appear in both instances to be such as it was perfectly justified in demanding. It is difficult to conceive what could have been their theory of government who imagined that in any colony of England a body invested with the name and character of a representative Assembly, could be deprived of any of those powers which, in the opinion of Englishmen, are inherent in a popular legislature. It was a vain delusion to imagine that by mere limitations in the Constitutional Act, or an exclusive system of government, a body, strong in the consciousness of wielding the public opinion of the majority, could regard certain portions of the provincial revenues as sacred from its control, could confine itself to the mere business of making laws, and look on as a passive or indifferent spectator, while those laws were carried into effect or evaded, and the whole business of the country was conducted by men, in whose intentions or capacity it had not the slightest confidence. Yet such was the limitation placed on the authority of the Assembly of Lower Canada; it might refuse or pass laws, vote or withhold supplies, but it could exercise no influence on the nominations of a single servant of the Crown. The Executive Council, the law officers, and whatever heads of departments are known to the administrative system of the Province, were placed in power, without any regard to the wishes of the people or their representatives; nor indeed are there wanting instances in which a mere hostility to the majority of the Assembly elevated the most incompetent persons to posts of honour and trust. However decidedly the Assembly might condemn the policy of the Government, the persons who had advised that policy, retained their offices and their power of giving bad advice. If a law was passed after repeated conflicts, it had to be carried into effect by those who had most strenuously opposed it. The wisdom of adopting the true principle of representative government and facilitating the management of public affairs, by entrusting it to the persons who have the confidence of the representative body, has never been recognized in the government of the North American Colonies. All the officers of government were independent of the Assembly; and that body which had nothing to say to their appointment, was left to get on as it best might, with a set of public functionaries, whose paramount feeling may not unfairly be said to have been one of hostility to itself.

A body of holders of office thus constituted, without reference to the people or their representatives, must in fact, from the very nature of colonial government, acquire the entire direction of the affairs of the Province. A Governor, arriving in a colony in which he almost invariably has had no previous acquaintance with the state of parties, or the character of individuals, is compelled to throw himself almost entirely upon those whom he finds placed in the position of his official advisers. His first acts must necessarily be performed, and his first appointments made, at their suggestion. And as these first acts and appointments give a character to his policy, he is generally brought thereby into immediate collision with the other parties in the country, and thrown into more complete dependence upon the official party and its friends. Thus, a Governor of Lower Canada has almost always been brought into collision with the Assembly, which his advisers regard as their enemy. In the course of the contest in which he was thus involved, the provocations which he received from the Assembly, and the light in which their conduct was represented by those who alone had any access to him, naturally imbued him with many of their antipathies; his position compelled him to seek the support of some party against the Assembly; and his feelings and his necessities thus combined to induce him to bestow his patronage and to shape his measures to promote the interests of the party on which he was obliged to lean. Thus, every successive year consolidated and enlarged the strength of the ruling party. Fortified by family connexion, and the common interest felt by all who held, and all who desired, subordinate offices, that party was thus erected into a solid and permanent power, controlled by no responsibility, subject to no serious change, exercising over the whole government of the Province an authority utterly independent of the people and its representatives, and possessing the only means of influencing either the Government at home, or the colonial representative of the Crown.

This entire separation of the legislative and executive powers of a State, is the natural error of governments desirous of being free from the check of representative institutions. Since the Revolution of 1688, the stability of the English constitution has been secured by that wise principle of our Government which has vested the direction of the national policy, and the distribution of patronage, in the leaders of the Parliamentary majority. However partial the Monarch might be to particular ministers, or however he might have personally committed himself to their policy, he has invariably been constrained to abandon both, as soon as the opinion of the people has been irrevocably pronounced against them through the medium of the House of Commons. The practice of carrying on a representative government on a different principle, seems to be the rock on which the continental imitations of the British Constitution have invariably split; and the French Revolution of 1830 was the necessary result of an attempt to uphold a ministry with which no Parliament could be got to act in concert. It is difficult to understand how any English statesmen could have imagined that representative and irresponsible government could be successfully combined. There seems, indeed, to be an idea, that the character of representative institutions ought to be thus modified in colonies; that it is an incident of colonial dependence that the officers of government should be nominated by the Crown, without any reference to the wishes of the community, whose interests are entrusted to their keeping. It has never been very clearly explained what are the imperial interests, which require this complete nullification of representative government. But if there be such a necessity, it is quite clear that a representative government in a colony must be a mockery, and a source of confusion. For those who support this system have never yet been able to devise, or to exhibit in the practical working of colonial government, any means for making so complete an abrogation of political influence palatable to the representative body. It is not difficult to apply the case to our own country. Let it be imagined that at a general election the opposition were to return 500 out of 658 members of the House of Commons, and that the whole policy of the ministry should be condemned, and every Bill introduced by it, rejected by this immense majority. Let it be supposed that the Crown should consider it a point of honour and duty to retain a ministry so condemned and so thwarted; that repeated dissolutions should in no way increase, but should even diminish, the ministerial minority, and that the only result which could be obtained by such a development of the force of the opposition, were not the slightest change in the policy of the ministry, not the removal of a single minister, but simply the election of a Speaker of the politics of the majority; and, I think, it will not be difficult to imagine the fate of such a system of government. Yet such was the system, such literally was the course of events in Lower Canada, and such in character, though not quite in degree, was the spectacle exhibited in Upper Canada, and, at one time or another, in everyone of the North American Colonies. To suppose that such a system would work well there, implies a belief that the French Canadians have enjoyed representative institutions for half a century, without acquiring any of the characteristics of a free people; that Englishmen renounce every political opinion and feeling when they enter a colony, or that the spirit of Anglo-Saxon freedom is utterly changed and weakened among those who are transplanted across the Atlantic.

It appears, therefore, that the opposition of the Assembly to the Government was the unavoidable result of a system which stinted the popular branch of the legislature of the necessary privileges of a representative body, and produced thereby a long series of attempts on the part of that body to acquire control over the administration of the Province. I say all this without reference to the ultimate aim of the Assembly, which I have before described as being the maintenance of a Canadian nationality against the progressive intrusion of the English race. Having no responsible ministers to deal with, it entered upon that system of long inquiries by means of its committees, which brought the whole action of the executive immediately under its purview, and transgressed our notions of the proper limits of Parliamentary interference. Having no influence in the choice of any public functionary, no power to procure the removal of such as were obnoxious to it merely on political grounds, and seeing almost every office of the Colony filled by persons in whom it had no confidence, it entered on that vicious course of assailing its prominent opponents individually, and disqualifying them for the public service, by making them the subjects of inquiries and consequent impeachments, not always conducted with even the appearance of a due regard to justice; and when nothing else could attain its end of altering the policy or the composition of the colonial government, it had recourse to that *ultima ratio* of representative power to which the more prudent forbearance of the Crown has never driven the House of Commons in England, and endeavoured to disable the whole machine of Government by a general refusal of the supplies.

It was an unhappy consequence of the system which I have been describing, that it relieved the popular leaders of all the responsibilities of opposition. A member of opposition in this country acts and speaks with the contingency of becoming a minister constantly before his eyes, and he feels, therefore, the necessity of proposing no course, and of asserting no principles, on which he would not be prepared to conduct the Government, if he were immediately offered it. But the colonial demagogue bids high for popularity without the fear of future exposure. Hopelessly excluded from power, he expresses the wildest opinions, and appeals to the most mischievous passions of the people, without any apprehension of having his sincerity or prudence hereafter tested, by being placed in a position to carry his views into effect; and thus the prominent places in the ranks of opposition are occupied for the most part by men of strong passions, and merely declamatory powers, who think but little of reforming the abuses which serve them as topics for exciting discontent.

The collision with the executive Government necessarily brought on one with the Legislative Council. The composition of this body, which has been so much the subject of discussion both here and in the Colony, must certainly be admitted to have been such as could give it no weight with the people, or with the representative body, on which it was meant to be a check. The majority was always composed of members of the party which conducted the executive Government; the clerks of each Council were members of the other; and, in fact, the Legislative Council was practically hardly any thing but a veto in the hands of public functionaries on all the acts of that popular branch of the legislature in which they were always in a minority. This veto they used without much scruple. I am far from concurring in the censure which the Assembly and its advocates have attempted to cast on the acts of the Legislative Council. I have no hesitation in saying that many of the Bills which it is most severely blamed for rejecting, were Bills which it could not have passed without a dereliction of its duty to the constitution, the connexion with Great Britain, and the whole English population of the Colony. If there is any censure to be passed on its general conduct, it is for having confined itself to the merely negative and defensive duties of a legislative body; for having too frequently contented itself with merely defeating objectionable methods of obtaining desirable ends, without completing its duty by proposing measures, which would have achieved the good in view without the mixture of evil. The national animosities which pervaded the legislation of the Assembly, and its thorough want of legislative skill or respect for constitutional principles, rendered almost all its Bills obnoxious to the objections made by the Legislative Council; and the serious evil which their enactment would have occasioned, convinces me that the Colony has reason to congratulate itself on the existence of an institution which possessed and used the power of stopping a course of legislation that, if successful, would have sacrificed every British interest, and overthrown every guarantee of order and national liberty. It is not difficult for us to judge thus calmly of the respective merits of these distant parties; but it must have been a great and deep-rooted respect for the constitution and composition of the Legislative Council, that could have induced the representatives of a great majority to submit with patience to the impediment thus placed in their way by a few individuals. But the Legislative Council was neither theoretically unobjectionable, nor personally esteemed by the Assembly; its opposition appeared to that body but another form of official hostility, and it was inevitable that the Assembly should, sooner or later, make those assaults on the constitution of the Legislative Council which, by the singular want of judgment and temper with which they were conducted, ended in the destruction of the provincial constitution.

From the commencement, therefore, to the end of the disputes which mark the whole Parliamentary history of Lower Canada, I look on the conduct of the Assembly as a constant warfare with the executive, for the purpose of obtaining the powers inherent in a representative body by the very nature of representative government. It was to accomplish this purpose, that it used every means in its power; but it must be censured for having, in pursuit of this object, perverted its powers of legislation, and disturbed the whole working of the constitution. It made the business of legislation, and the practical improvement of the country, subordinate to its struggle for power; and, being denied its legitimate privileges, it endeavoured to extend its authority in modes totally incompatible with the principles of constitutional liberty. . . .

It is melancholy to think of the opportunities of good legislation which were sacrificed in this mere contest for power. No country in the world ever demanded from a paternal government, or patriotic representatives, more unceasing and vigorous reforms, both of its laws and its administrative system. Lower Canada had, when we received it at the conquest, two institutions, which alone preserved the semblance of order and civilization in the community, – the Catholic church and the militia, which was so constituted and used, as partially to supply the want of better civil institutions. The beneficial influence of the Catholic church has been cramped and weakened; the militia is now annihilated, and years must elapse ere it can be revived and used to any good purpose. Lower Canada remains without municipal institutions of local self-government, which are the foundations of Anglo-Saxon freedom and civilization; nor is their absence compensated by any thing like the centralization of France. The most defective judicial institutions remain unreformed. Alone, among the nations that have sprung from the French, Lower Canada remains under the unchanged civil laws of ancient France. Alone, among the nations of the American Continent, it is without a public system of education. Nor has it, in other respects, caught the spirit of American progress. While the Assembly was wasting the surplus revenues of the Province in jobs for the increase of patronage, and in petty peddling in parochial business, it left untouched those vast and easy means of communication which deserved, and would have repaid the application of the provincial revenues. The state of New York made its own St. Lawrence from Lake Erie to the Hudson, while the Government of Lower Canada could not achieve, or even attempt, the few miles of canal and dredging which would have rendered its mighty rivers navigable almost to their sources. The time which should have been devoted to wise legislation, was spent in a contest for power between the executive and the people, which a wise executive would have stopped at the outset, by submitting to a legitimate responsibility, and which a wise people would have ceased to press when it had virtually attained its end. This collision, and the defective constitution were, in conjunction with the quarrel of the races, the causes of the mischiefs which I have detailed. It will be a ground, I trust, of permanent congratulation, that the contest terminated in the destruction of the impracticable constitution, which caused the strife; nor can I conceive any course of conduct which could so effectually have destroyed the previous system of mismanagement, and cleared the ground for future improvement, as that continued stoppage of supplies which the Assembly in its intemperance effected. It broke down at once the whole of that vicious appropriation of public funds, which was the great bane of provincial legislation, and has left the abuses of the Colony so long unfed, that a reforming Government may hereafter work upon an unencumbered soil.

The inevitable result of the animosities of race, and of the constant collision of the different powers of the State, which I have described, was a thorough disorganization of the institutions and administrative system of the country. I do not think that I necessarily cast any stigma on my predecessors in Lower Canada, or on the uniform good intentions which the Imperial Government has clearly evinced towards every class, and every race in the Colony, when I assert, that a country which has been agitated by these social and political dissensions, has suffered under great misgovernment. The blame rests not on individuals, but on the vicious system, which has generated the manifold and deep-rooted abuses that pervade every department of the public service, and constitute the real grievances of the Colony. These grievances are common to the whole people of Lower Canada; and it is not one race, or one party only, that suffers by their existence; they have hindered the prosperity, and endangered the security of all; though, unquestionably, the interests which have most materially been retarded by misgovernment, are the English. From the highest to the lowest officers of the executive Government, no important department is so organized as to act vigorously and completely, throughout the Province; and every duty which a Government owes to its subjects is imperfectly discharged.

The defective system of administration in Lower Canada, commences at the very source of power; and the efficiency of the public service is impaired throughout, by the entire want in the Colony of any vigorous administration of the prerogative of the Crown. The fact is, that, according to the present system, there is no real representative of the Crown in the Province; there is in it, literally, no power which originates and conducts the executive Government. The Governor, it is true, is said to represent the Sovereign, and the authority of the Crown is, to a certain extent, delegated to him; but he is, in fact, a mere subordinate officer, receiving his orders from the Secretary of State, responsible to him for his conduct, and guided by his instructions. Instead of selecting a Governor, with an entire confidence in his ability to use his local knowledge of the real state of affairs in the Colony in the manner which local observation and practical experience best prescribe to him, it has been the policy of the Colonial Department, not only at the outset, to instruct a Governor as to the general policy which he was to carry into effect, but to direct him, from time to time, by instructions, sometimes very precise, as to the course which he was to pursue, in every important particular of his administration. Theoretically irresponsible to the colonial legislature, the Governor was, in effect, the only officer in the Colony who was at all responsible;

inasmuch as the Assembly, by centring their attacks on him, and making him appear the sole cause of the difficulties of the Government, could occasion him so much vexation, and represent him in so unfavourable a light at home, that it frequently succeeded in imposing on him the necessity of resigning, or on the Colonial Minister, that of recalling him. In order to shelter himself from this responsibility, it has inevitably, and I must say very justifiably, been the policy of Governors to take care that the double responsibility shall be as light as possible; to endeavour to throw it, as much as possible, on the home Government, and to do as little as possible without previously consulting the Colonial Minister at home, and receiving his instructions. It has, therefore, been the tendency of the local Government to settle every thing by reference to the Colonial Department in Downing Street. Almost every question on which it was possible to avoid, even with great inconvenience, an immediate decision, has been habitually the subject of reference; and this applies not merely to those questions on which the local executive and legislative bodies happened to differ, wherein the reference might be taken as a kind of appeal, but to questions of a strictly local nature, on which it was next to impossible for the Colonial Office to have any sufficient information. It had become the habit of the Colonial Office to originate these questions, to entertain applications from individuals, to refer these applications to the Governor, and, on his answer, to make a decision. The Governor has been enabled by this system to shift responsibility on the Colonial Office, inasmuch as in every important case he was, in reality, carrying into effect the order of the authority to which he was responsible. But the real vigour of the executive has been essentially impaired; distance and delay have weakened the force of its decisions; and the Colony has, in every crisis of danger, and almost every detail of local management, felt the mischief of having its executive authority exercised on the other side of the Atlantic.

Nor has any thing been gained, either in effectual responsibility or sound information, by thus transferring the details of executive Government to the Colonial Department at home. The complete and unavoidable ignorance in which the British public, and even the great body of its legislators, are with respect to the real interests of distant communities, so entirely different from their own, produces a general indifference, which nothing but some great colonial crisis ever dispels; and responsibility to Parliament, or to the public opinion of Great Britain, would, except in these great and rare occasions, be positively mischievous, if it were not impossible. The repeated changes caused by political events at home having no connexion with colonial affairs, have left, to most of the various representatives of the Colonial Department in Parliament, too little time to acquire even an elementary knowledge of the condition of those numerous and heterogeneous communities for which they have had both to administer and legislate. The persons with whom the real management of these affairs has or ought to have rested, have been the permanent but utterly irresponsible members of the office. Thus the real government of the Colony has been entirely dissevered from the slight nominal responsibility which exists. Apart even from this great and primary evil of the system, the pressure of multifarious business thus thrown on the Colonial Office, and the repeated changes of its ostensible directors, have produced disorders in the management of public business which have occasioned serious mischief, and very great irritation. . . .

One of the greatest of all the evils arising from this system of irresponsible government, was the mystery in which the motives and actual purposes of their rulers were hid from the colonists themselves. The most important business of Government was carried on, not in open discussions or public acts, but in a secret correspondence between the Governor and the Secretary of State. Whenever this mystery was dispelled, it was long after the worst effects had been produced by doubt and misapprehension; and the Colonies have been frequently the last to learn the things that most concerned them, by the publication of papers on the order of the British Houses of Parliament.

The Governor, thus slightly responsible, and invested with functions so ill-defined, found himself at the head of a system, in which all his advisers and subordinates had still less responsibility, and duties still less defined. Disqualified at first by want of local information, and very often, subsequently, by an entire absence of all acquaintance with the business of civil government, the Governor, on his arrival in the Colony, found himself under the necessity of being, in many respects, guided by the persons whom he found in office. In no country, therefore, could there be a greater necessity for a proper demarcation of the business of each public officer, and of a greater responsibility resting on each. Now, I do not at all exaggerate the real state of the case when I assert, that there is no head of any of the most important departments of public business in the Colony. The limited powers of the local government in a Colony necessarily obviate the necessity of any provision for some of the most important departments which elsewhere require a superintending mind. But the mere ordinary administration of justice, police, education, public works and internal communications, of finance and of trade, would require the superintendence of persons competent to advise the Governor, on their own responsibility, as to the measures which should be adopted; and the additional labours which fall on the heads of such departments in other countries, in devising improvements of the system and the laws relating to each, would certainly afford additional occupation, growing out of the peculiarly defective legislation and administration of Lower Canada. Yet, of no one of these departments is there any responsible head, by whose advice the Governor may safely be guided. There are some subordinate and very capable officers in each department, from whom he is, in fact, compelled to get information from time to time. But there is no one to whom he, or the public, can look for the correct management and sound decision on the policy of each of these important departments.

The real advisers of the Governor have, in fact, been the Executive Council; and an institution more singularly calculated for preventing the responsibility of the acts of Government resting on any body, can hardly be imagined. It is a body, of which the constitution somewhat resembles that of the Privy Council; it is bound by a similar oath of secrecy; it discharges in the same manner certain anomalous judicial functions; and its 'consent and advice' are required in some cases in which the observance of that form has been thought a requisite check on the exercise of particular prerogatives of the Crown. But in other respects it bears a greater resemblance to a Cabinet, the Governor being in the habit of taking its advice on most of the important questions of his policy. But as there is no division into departments in the Council, there is no individual responsibility, and no individual superintendence. Each member of the Council takes an equal part in all the business brought before it. The power of removing members being very rarely exercised, the Council is, in fact, for the most part composed of persons placed in it long ago; and the Governor is obliged either to take the advice of persons in whom he has no confidence, or to consult only a portion of the Council. The secrecy of the proceedings adds to the irresponsibility of the body; and when the Governor takes an important step, it is not known, or not authentically known, whether he has taken the advice of this Council or not, what members he has consulted, or by the advice of which of the body he has been finally guided. The responsibility of the Executive Council has been constantly demanded by the reformers of Upper Canada, and occasionally by those of the Lower Province. But it is really difficult to conceive how a desirable responsibility could be attained, except by altering the working of this cumberous machine, and placing the business of the various departments of Government in the hands of competent public officers.

In the ordinary course of public business in the Colony, almost all matters come, in fact, before the Governor, or his immediate assistant, the Civil Secretary of the Province. The Civil Secretary's office is, in fact, the one general public office in which almost every species of business originates, or through which it passes in some stage or other. The applications which every day reach this office show the singular want of proper organization in the Province, and the great confusion of ideas respecting the functions of Government, generated in the minds of the people. A very considerable proportion consist of requests to the Governor to interfere with the course of civil justice. Every decision of subordinate officers is made matter of appeal; and no reference to the proper department satisfies the applicants, who imagine that they have a right to claim a personal investigation of every case by the Governor or the Civil Secretary. The appeals from the past are equally numerous; and it appears to be expected that every new Governor should sit in judgment on every decision of any or all of his predecessors, which happens to have dissatisfied the applicant. But if such is the bad organization and imperfection of the system at the seat of Government, it may be easily believed that the remainder of the Province enjoyed no very vigorous or complete administration. In fact, beyond the walls of Quebec, all regular administration of the country appeared to cease; and there literally was hardly a single public officer of the civil Government, except in Montreal and Three Rivers, to whom any order could be directed. The Solicitor General commonly resides at Montreal; and in each of the districts there is a Sheriff. In the rest of the Province there is no Sheriff, no Mayor, no constable, no superior administrative officer of any kind. There are no county, no municipal, no parochial officers, either named by the Crown, or elected by the people. There is a body of unpaid Justices of the Peace, whom I will describe more particularly hereafter. The officers of the militia used to be employed for purposes of police, as far as regarded the service of criminal warrants; but their services were voluntary, and not very assiduous; and the whole body is now completely disorganized. In every case in which any information was required by the Government, or any service was to be performed in a remote part of the Province, it was necessary either to send some one to the spot, or to find out, by inquiry at the seat of Government, the name of some resident there whom it was advisable and safe to consult on the subject, or direct to do the act required. In the state of parties in the country, such a step could hardly ever be taken, without trusting to very suspicious information, or delegating power to persons who would be, or be suspected of being, likely to abuse it.

This utter want of any machinery of executive Government in the Province is not, perhaps, more striking than might be observed in some of the most flourishing portions of the American continent. But in the greater part of the States to which I refer, the want of means at the disposal of the central executive is amply supplied by the efficiency of the municipal institutions; and even where these are wanting, or imperfect, the energy and self-governing habits of an Anglo-Saxon population enable it to combine whenever a necessity arises. But the French population of Lower Canada possesses neither such institutions, nor such a character. Accustomed to rely entirely on the Government, it has no power of doing any thing for itself, much less of aiding the central authority.

The utter want of municipal institutions giving the people any control over their local affairs, may indeed be considered as one of the main causes of the failure of representative government, and of the bad administration of the country. If the wise example of those countries in which a free representative government has alone worked well, had been in all respects followed in Lower Canada, care would have been taken that, at the same time that a Parliamentary system, based on a very extended suffrage, was introduced into the country, the people should have been entrusted with a complete control over their own local affairs, and been trained for taking their part in the concerns of the Province, by their experience in the management of that local business which was most interesting and most easily intelligible to them. But the inhabitants of Lower Canada were unhappily initiated into self-government at exactly the wrong end, and those who were not trusted with the management of a parish, were enabled, by their votes, to influence the destinies of a State. During my stay in the Province, I appointed a commission to inquire into its municipal institutions, and the practicability of introducing an effective and free system for the management of local affairs. The gentlemen entrusted with this inquiry had, when they were interrupted in their labours, made considerable progress towards preparing a report, which will, I hope, develop, in a full and satisfactory manner, the extent of the existing evil, and the nature of the practicable remedies.

There never has been, in fact, any institution in Lower Canada, in which any portion of the French population have been brought together for any administrative purpose, nor is there among the divisions of the country any one which has been constituted with a view to such an end. The larger divisions, called 'districts', are purely judicial divisions. The counties may be called merely Parliamentary divisions; for I know of no purpose for which they appear to have been constituted, except for the election of members for the House of Assembly; and during the present suspension of representative government, they are merely arbitrary and useless geographical divisions. There are no hundreds, or corresponding sub-divisions of counties. The parishes are purely ecclesiastical divisions, and may be altered by the Catholic Bishops. The only institution in the nature of local management, in which the people have any voice, is the *fabrique*, by which provision is made for the repairs of the Catholic churches.

The townships are inhabited entirely by a population of British and American origin; and may be said to be divisions established for surveying, rather than any other purposes. The eastern townships present a lamentable contrast in the management of all local matters to the bordering state of Vermont, in which the municipal institutions are the most complete, it is said, of any part even of New England. In any new settled district of New England, a small number of families settling within a certain distance of each other, are immediately empowered by law to assess themselves for local purposes, and to elect local officers. The settlers in the eastern townships, many of whom are natives of New England, and all of whom can contrast the state of things on their own with that which is to be seen on the other side of the line, have a serious and general cause of discontent in the very inferior management of all their own local concerns. The Government appears even to have discouraged the American settlers from introducing their own municipal institutions by common assent. . . .

But the want of municipal institutions has been and is most glaringly remarkable in Quebec and Montreal. These cities were incorporated a few years ago by a temporary provincial Act, of which the renewal was rejected in 1836. Since that time these cities have been without any municipal government; and the disgraceful state of the streets, and the utter absence of lighting, are consequences which arrest the attention of all, and seriously affect the comfort and security of the inhabitants.

The worst effects of this most faulty system of general administration will be developed in the view which I shall hereafter give of the practices adopted with respect to the public lands, and the settlement of the Province, but which I postpone for the present, because I purpose considering this subject with reference to all the North American Provinces. But I must here notice the mischievous results prominently exhibited in the provision which the government of Lower Canada makes for the first want of a people, the efficient administration of justice.

The law of the Province and the administration of justice are, in fact, a patch-work of the results of the interference at different times of different legislative powers, each proceeding on utterly different and generally incomplete views, and each utterly regardless of the other. The law itself is a mass of incoherent and conflicting laws, part French, part English, and with the line between each very confusedly drawn. Thus the criminal law is the criminal law of England as it was introduced in 1774, with such modifications as have since been made by the provincial legislature, it being now disputed whether the provincial legislature had any power to make any change whatever in that law, and it not being at all clear what is the extent of the phrase 'criminal law'. The civil law is the ancient civil law, also modified in some, but unfortunately very few, respects; and these modifications have been almost exclusively effected by Acts of the British Parliament and by ordinances of the Governor and Council constituted under the Quebec Act. The French law of evidence prevails in all civil matters, with a special exception of 'commercial' cases, in which it is provided that the English law is to be adopted; but no two lawyers agree in their definition of 'commercial'. . . .

It is . . . a lamentable fact, which must not be concealed, that there does not exist in the minds of the people of this Province the slightest confidence in the administration of criminal justice; nor were the complaints, or the apparent grounds for them, confined to one party. . . .

I cannot close this account of the system of criminal justice, without making some remarks with respect to the body by which it is administered in its primary stages and minor details to the great mass of the people of the Province. I mean the magistracy; and I cannot but express my regret, that among the few institutions for the administration of justice throughout the country, which have been adopted in Lower Canada from those of England, should be that of unpaid Justices of the Peace. I do not mean in any way to disparage the character, or depreciate the usefulness, of that most respectable body in this country. But the warmest admirer of that institution must admit that its benefits result entirely from the peculiar character of the class from which our magistracy is selected; and that without the general education, the moral responsibility imposed by their high station in the eyes of their countrymen, the check exercised by the opinion of their own class, and of an intelligent and vigilant public, and the habits of public business, which almost every Englishman, more or less, acquires, even the country gentlemen of England could not wield their legally irresponsible power as Justices of the Peace to the satisfaction of their country-men. What, then, must be conceived of the working of this institu-tion in a colony, by a class over whom none of these checks exist, and whose station in life and education would alone almost uni-versally exclude them from a similar office at home? When we transplant the institutions of England into our colonies, we ought at least to take care beforehand that the social state of the colony should possess those peculiar materials on which alone the excel-lence of those institutions depends in the mother country. The body of Justices of the Peace scattered over the whole of Lower Canada, are named by the Governor, on no very accurate local information, there being no lieutenants or similar officers of counties in this, as in the Upper Province. The real property qualification required for the magistracy is so low, that in the country parts almost everyone possesses it; and it only excludes some of the most respectable per-sons in the cities. In the rural districts the magistrates have no clerks. The institution has become unpopular among the Canadi-ans, owing to their general belief that the appointments have been made with a party and national bias. It cannot be denied that many most respectable Canadians were long left out of the commission of the peace, without any adequate cause, and it is still more undeni-able, that most disreputable persons of both races have found their way into it, and still continue to abuse the power thus vested in them. Instances of indiscretion, of ignorance, and of party feeling, and accusations of venality, have been often adduced by each party. Whether these representations be exaggerated or not, or whether they apply to a small or to a large portion of the magistracy, it is undeniable that the greatest want of confidence in the practical working of the institution exists; and I am therefore of opinion, that whilst this state of society continues, and, above all, in the present exasperation of parties, a small stipendiary magistracy would be much better suited to both Upper and Lower Canada. . . .

In the course of the preceding account, I have already inciden-tally given a good many of the most important details of the pro-vision for education made in Lower Canada. I have described the general ignorance of the people, and the abortive attempt which was made, or rather which was professed to be made, for the purpose of establishing a general system of public instruction; I have described the singular abundance of a somewhat defective education which exists for the higher classes, and which is solely in the hands of the Catholic priesthood. It only remains that I should add, that though the adults who have come from the Old Country are generally more or less educated, the English are hardly better off than the French for the means of education for their children, and indeed possess scarcely any, except in the cities.

There exists at present no means of college education for Protestants in the Province; and the desire of obtaining general, and still more, professional instruction, yearly draws a great many young men into the United States. . . .

The inhabitants of the North American Continent, possessing an amount of material comfort, unknown to the peasantry of any other part of the world, are generally very sensible to the importance of education. And the noble provision which every one of the northern States of the Union has gloried in establishing for the education of its youth, has excited a general spirit of emulation amongst the neighbouring Provinces, and a desire, which will probably produce some active efforts, to improve their own educational institutions.

It is therefore much to be regretted, that there appear to exist obstacles to the establishment of such a general system of instruction as would supply the wants, and, I believe, meet the wishes of the entire population. The Catholic clergy, to whose exertions the French and Irish population of Lower Canada are indebted for whatever means of education they have ever possessed, appear to be very unwilling that the State should in any way take the instruction of youth out of their hands. Nor do the clergy of some other denominations exhibit generally a less desire to give to education a sectarian character, which would be peculiarly mischievous in this Province, inasmuch as its inevitable effect would be to aggravate and perpetuate the existing distinctions of origin. But as the laity of every denomination appear to be opposed to these narrow views, I feel confident that the establishment of a strong popular government in this Province would very soon lead to the introduction of a liberal and general system of public education.

I am grieved to be obliged to remark, that the British Government has, since its possession of this Province, done, or even attempted, nothing for the promotion of general education. Indeed the only matter in which it has appeared in connexion with the subject, is one by no means creditable to it. For it has applied the Jesuits' estates, part of the property destined for purposes of education, to supply a species of fund for secret service; and for a number of years it has maintained an obstinate struggle with the Assembly in order to continue this misappropriation. . . .

It is a subject of very just congratulation, that religious differences have hardly operated as an additional cause of dissension in Lower Canada; and that a degree of practical toleration, known in very few communities, has existed in this Colony from the period of the conquest down to the present time.

The French Canadians are exclusively Catholics, and their church has been left in possession of the endowments which it had at the conquest. The right to tithe is enjoyed by their priests; but as it is limited by law to lands of which the proprietor is a Catholic, the priest loses his tithe the moment that an estate passes, by sale or otherwise, into the hands of a Protestant. This enactment, which is at variance with the true spirit of national endowments for religious purposes, has a natural tendency to render the clergy averse to the settlement of Protestants in the seigniories. But the Catholic priesthood of this Province have, to a very remarkable degree, conciliated the good-will of persons of all creeds; and I know of no parochial clergy in the world whose practice of all the Christian virtues, and zealous discharge of their clerical duties, is more universally admitted, and has been productive of more beneficial consequences. Possessed of incomes sufficient, and even large, according to the notions entertained in the country, and enjoying the advantage of education, they have lived on terms of equality and kindness with the humblest and least instructed inhabitants of the rural districts. Intimately acquainted with the wants and characters of their neighbours, they have been the promoters and dispensers of charity, and the effectual guardians of the morals of the people; and in the general absence of any permanent institutions of civil government, the Catholic Church has presented almost the only semblance of stability and organization, and furnished the only effectual support for civilization and order. The Catholic clergy of Lower Canada are entitled to this expression of my esteem, not only because it is founded on truth, but because a grateful recognition of their eminent services, in resisting the arts of the disaffected, is especially due to them from one who has administered the government of the Province in these troubled times.

The Constitutional Act, while limiting the application of the clergy reserves in the townships to a Protestant clergy, made no provision for the extension of the Catholic clerical institution, in the event of the French population settling beyond the limits of the seigniories. Though I believe that some power exists, and has been in a few cases used, for the creation of new Catholic parishes, I am convinced that this absence of the means of religious instruction has been the main cause of the indisposition of the French population to seek new settlements, as the increase of their numbers pressed upon their resources. It has been rightly observed, that the religious observances of the French Canadians are so intermingled with all their business, and all their amusements, that the priests and the church are with them, more than with any other people, the centres of their little communities. In order to encourage them to spread their population, and to seek for comfort and prosperity in new settlements, a wise government would have taken care to aid, in every possible way, the diffusion of their means of religious instruction.

The Protestant population of Lower Canada have been of late somewhat agitated by the question of the clergy reserves. The meaning of the ambiguous phrase 'Protestant clergy' has been discussed with great ardour in various quarters; and each disputant has displayed his ingenuity in finding reasons for a definition in accordance with his own inclination, either to the aggrandizement of his own sect, or the establishment of religious equality. Owing to the small numbers of the British population, to the endowment of the Catholic Church in most of the peopled and important districts of the Colony, and, above all, to the much more formidable and extensive causes of dissension existing in the Province, the dispute of the various Protestant denominations for the funds reserved for a 'Protestant clergy', has not assumed the importance which it has acquired in Upper Canada. In my account of that Province I shall give a more detailed explanation of the present position of this much-disputed question. I have reason to know, that the apprehension of measures tending to establish the predominance of a particular creed and clergy, has produced an irritation in this Province which has very nearly deprived the Crown of the support of some portions of the British population, in a period of very imminent danger. I must therefore most strongly recommend, that any plan by which the question of clergy reserves shall be set at rest in Upper Canada, should also be extended to the Lower Province. The endowments of the Catholic Church, and the services of its numerous and zealous parochial clergy, have been of the greatest benefit to the large body of Catholic emigrants from Ireland, who have relied much on the charitable as well as religious aid which they have received from the priesthood. The priests have an almost unlimited influence over the lower classes of Irish; and this influence is said to have been very vigorously exerted last winter, when it was much needed, to secure the loyalty of a portion of the Irish during the troubles. The general loyalty exhibited by the Irish settlers in the Canadas, during the last winter, and the importance of maintaining it unimpaired in future times of difficulty, render it of the utmost moment that the feelings and interests of the Catholic clergy and population should invariably meet with due consideration from the Government.

Setting on one side the management of the Crown Lands, and the revenue derived therefrom, which will be treated of fully in another part, it is not necessary that I should, on the present occasion, enter into any detailed account of the financial system of Lower Canada, my object being merely to point out the working of the general system of Government, as operating to produce the present condition of the Province. I need not inquire whether its fiscal, monetary or commercial arrangements have been in accordance with the best principles of public economy. But I have reason to believe that improvements may be made in the mode of raising and expending the Provincial revenue. During my stay in Canada, the evils of the banking and monetary systems of the

Province forced themselves on my attention. I am not inclined, however, to regard these evils as having been in anywise influential in causing the late disorders. I cannot regard them as indicative of any more mismanagement or error than are observable in the measures of the best governments with respect to questions of so much difficulty; and though the importance of finding some sufficient remedy for some of these disorders has, as I shall hereafter explain, very materially influenced my views of the general plan to be adopted for the government of this and the other North American Colonies, I regard the better regulation of the financial and monetary systems of the Province as a matter to be settled by the local Government, when established on a permanent basis.

With the exception of the small amount now derived from the casual and territorial funds, the public revenue of Lower Canada is derived from duties imposed, partly by imperial and partly by provincial statutes. These duties are, in great proportion, levied upon articles imported into the Colony from Great Britain and foreign countries; they are collected at the principal ports by officers of the Imperial Customs.

The amount of the revenue has within the last four years diminished from about £150,000, to little more than £100,000 per annum. This diminution is ascribed principally to the decreased consumption of spirituous liquors, and some other articles of foreign import, in consequence of the growth of native manufactures of such articles. Nevertheless, as the permanent expenditure of the civil Government only amounts to about £60,000 a year, there remains still a considerable surplus to be disposed of for local purposes, in the mischievous manner which I have described in the preceding pages. A vigorous and efficient government would find the whole revenue hardly adequate for its necessities; but in the present state of things, I consider the existence and application of this surplus revenue as so prejudicial, that I should, as the less of two evils, recommend a reduction of the duties levied, were it possible to do this without an equal diminution of the revenue of Upper Canada, which can by no means afford it.

The financial relations between these two Provinces are a source of great and increasing disputes. The greater part, almost the whole of the imports of Upper Canada entering at the ports of

Lower Canada, the Upper Province has urged and established its claim to a proportion of the duties levied on them. This proportion is settled, from time to time, by Commissioners appointed from each Province. Lower Canada now receives about three, and Upper Canada about two-fifths of the whole amount: nor is this the greatest cause of dissension and dissatisfaction. The present revenue of Upper Canada being utterly inadequate to its expenditure, the only means that the Province will have of paying the interest of its debt, will be by increasing its Customs' duties. But as these are almost all levied in Lower Canada, this cannot be done without raising the taxation also of the Lower Canadians, who have, as it is, a large surplus revenue. It was for the better settlement of these points of difference, that the union of the two Canadas was proposed in 1822; and the same feeling produces a great part of the anxiety now manifested for that measure by a portion of the people of Upper Canada.

A considerable revenue is raised from all these Provinces by the post-office establishment common to all of them, and subordinate to the General Post Office in England. The surplus revenue, which appears from a Report to the House of Assembly to amount to no less than £10,000 per annum, is transmitted to England. The Assembly made it a matter of great complaint that an important internal public institution of the Provinces should be entirely regulated and administered by the rulers and servants of an English public office, and that so large an amount of revenue, raised entirely without the consent of the Colonies, in a manner not at all free from objections, should be transmitted to the mother country. I cannot but say that there is great justice in these complaints, and I am decidedly of opinion that if any plan of a united Government of these Provinces should be adopted, the control and revenue of the Post Office should be given up to the Colony.

For the reasons I have before explained, there is hardly the semblance of direct taxation in Lower Canada for general and local purposes. This immunity from taxation has been sometimes spoken of as a great privilege of the people of Lower Canada, and a great proof of the justice and benevolence of their Government. The description which I have given of the singularly defective provision made for the discharge of the most important duties of both the general and the local government will, I think, make it appear that this apparent saving of the pockets of the people has been caused by their privation of many of the institutions which every civilized community ought to possess. A people can hardly be congratulated on having had at little cost a rude and imperfect administration of justice, hardly the semblance of police, no public provision for education, no lighting, and bad pavements in its cities, and means of communication so imperfect, that the loss of time, and wear and tear caused in taking any article to market, may probably be estimated at ten times the expense of good roads. If the Lower Canadians had been subjected, or rather had been taught to subject themselves to a much greater amount of taxation, they would probably at this time have been a much wealthier, a much better governed, a much more civilized, and a much more contented people.

UPPER CANADA

The information which I have to give respecting the state of Upper Canada, not having been acquired in the course of any actual administration of the government of that Province, will necessarily be much less ample and detailed than that which I have laid before Your Majesty respecting Lower Canada. My object will be to point out the principal causes to which a general observation of the Province induces me to attribute the late troubles; and even this task will be performed with comparative ease and brevity, inasmuch as I am spared the labour of much explanation and proof, by being able to refer to the details which I have given, and the principles which I have laid down, in describing the institutions of the Lower Province.

At first sight it appears much more difficult to form an accurate idea of the state of Upper than of Lower Canada. The visible and broad line of demarcation which separates parties by the distinctive character of race, happily has no existence in the Upper Province. The quarrel is one of an entirely English, if not British population. Like all such quarrels, it has, in fact, created, not two, but several parties; each of which has some objects in common with some one of those to which it is opposed. They differ on one point, and agree on another; the sections, which unite together one day, are strongly opposed the next; and the very party, which acts as one, against a common opponent, is in truth composed of divisions seeking utterly different or incompatible objects. It is very difficult to make out from the avowals of parties the real objects of their struggles, and still less easy is it to discover any cause of such importance as would account for its uniting any large mass of the people in an attempt to overthrow, by forcible means, the existing form of Government.

The peculiar geographical character of the Province greatly increases the difficulty of obtaining very accurate information. Its inhabitants scattered along an extensive frontier, with very imperfect means of communication, and a limited and partial commerce, have, apparently no unity of interest or opinion. The Province has no great centre with which all the separate parts are connected, and which they are accustomed to follow in sentiment and action; nor is there that habitual intercourse between the inhabitants of different parts of the country, which, by diffusing through all a knowledge of the opinions and interests of each, makes a people one and united, in spite of extent of territory and dispersion of population. Instead of this, there are many petty local centres, the sentiments and the interests (or at least what are fancied to be so) of which, are distinct, and perhaps opposed. It has been stated to me by intelligent persons from England, who had travelled through the Province for purposes of business, that this isolation of the different districts from each other was strikingly apparent in all attempts to acquire information in one district respecting the agricultural or commercial character of another; and that not only were very gross attempts made to deceive an inquirer on these points, but that even the information which had been given in a spirit of perfect good faith, generally turned out to be founded in great misapprehension. From these causes a stranger who visits any one of these local centres, or who does not visit the whole, is almost necessarily ignorant of matters, a true knowledge of which is essential to an accurate comprehension of the real position of parties, and of the political prospects of the country.

The political contest which has so long been carried on in the Assembly and the press appears to have been one, exhibiting throughout its whole course the characteristical features of the purely political part of the contest in Lower Canada; and, like that, originating in an unwise distribution of power in the constitutional system of the Province. The financial disputes which so long occupied the contending parties in Lower Canada, were much more easily and wisely arranged in the Upper Province; and the struggle, though extending itself over a variety of questions of more or less importance, avowedly and distinctly rested on the demand for responsibility in the executive Government.

In the preceding account of the working of the constitutional system in Lower Canada, I have described the effect which the irresponsibility of the real advisers of the Governor had in lodging permanent authority in the hands of a powerful party, linked together not only by common party interests, but by personal ties. But in none of the North American Provinces has this exhibited itself for so long a period or to such an extent, as in Upper Canada, which has long been entirely governed by a party commonly designated throughout the Province as the 'family compact', a name not much more appropriate than party designations usually are, inasmuch as there is, in truth, very little of family connexion among the persons thus united. For a long time this body of men, receiving at times accessions to its numbers, possessed almost all the highest public offices, by means of which, and of its influence in the Executive Council, it wielded all the powers of government; it maintained influence in the legislature by means of its predominance in the Legislative Council; and it disposed of the large number of petty posts which are in the patronage of the Government all over the Province. Successive Governors, as they came in their turn, are said to have either submitted quietly to its influence, or, after a short and unavailing struggle, to have yielded to this well-organized party the real conduct of affairs. The bench, the magistracy, the high offices of the Episcopal Church, and a great part of the legal profession, are filled by the adherents of this party: by grant or purchase, they have acquired nearly the whole of the waste lands of the Province; they are all-powerful in the chartered banks, and, till lately, shared among themselves almost exclusively all offices of trust and profit. The bulk of this party consists, for the most part, of native-born inhabitants of Colony, or of emigrants who settled in it before the last war with the United States; the principal members of it belong to the Church of England, and the maintenance of the claims of that church has always been one of its distinguishing characteristics.

A monopoly of power so extensive and so lasting could not fail, in process of time, to excite envy, create dissatisfaction, and ultimately provoke attack; and an opposition consequently grew up in the Assembly which assailed the ruling party, by appealing to popular principles of government, by denouncing the alleged jobbing and profusion of the official body, and by instituting inquiries into abuses, for the purpose of promoting reform, and especially economy. The question of the greatest importance, raised in the course of these disputes, was that of the disposal of the clergy reserves; and, though different modes of applying these lands, or rather the funds derived from them, were suggested, the reformers, or opposition, were generally very successful in their appeals to the people, against the project of the tory or official party, which was that of devoting them exclusively to the maintenance of the English Episcopal Church. The reformers, by successfully agitating this and various economical questions, obtained a majority. Like almost all popular colonial parties, it managed its power with very little discretion and skill, offended a large number of the constituencies, and, being baffled by the Legislative Council, and resolutely opposed by all the personal and official influences of the official body, a dissolution again placed it in a minority in the Assembly. This turn of fortune was not confined to a single instance; for neither party has for some time possessed the majority in two successive Parliaments. The present is the fifth of these alternating Houses of Assembly.

The reformers, however, at last discovered that success in the elections insured them very little practical benefit. For the official party not being removed when it failed to command a majority in the Assembly, still continued to wield all the powers of the executive Government, to strengthen itself by its patronage, and to influence the policy of the Colonial Governor and of the Colonial Department at home. By its secure majority in the Legislative Council, it could effectually control the legislative powers of the Assembly. It could choose its own moment for dissolving hostile

Assemblies; and could always insure, for those that were favourable to itself, the tenure of their seats for the full term of four years allowed by the law. Thus the reformers found that their triumph at elections could not in any way facilitate the progress of their views, while the executive Government remained constantly in the hands of their opponents. They rightly judged that, if the higher offices and the Executive Council were always held by those who could command a majority in the Assembly, the constitution of the Legislative Council was a matter of very little moment, inasmuch as the advisers of the Governor could always take care that its composition should be modified so as to suit their own purposes. They concentrated their powers, therefore, for the purpose of obtaining the responsibility of the Executive Council; and I cannot help contrasting the practical good sense of the English reformers of Upper Canada with the less prudent course of the French majority in the Assembly of Lower Canada, as exhibited in the different demands of constitutional change, most earnestly pressed by each. Both, in fact, desired the same object, namely, an extension of popular influence in the Government. The Assembly of Lower Canada attacked the Legislative Council; a body, of which the constitution was certainly the most open to obvious theoretical objections, on the part of all the advocates of popular institutions, but, for the same reason, most sure of finding powerful defenders at home. The reformers of Upper Canada paid little attention to the composition of the Legislative Council, and directed their exertions to obtaining such an alteration of the Executive Council as might have been obtained without any derangement of the constitutional balance of power; but they well knew, that if once they obtained possession of the Executive Council, and the higher offices of the Province, the Legislative Council would soon be unable to offer any effectual resistance to their meditated reforms.

It was upon this question of the responsibility of the Executive Council that the great struggle has for a long time been carried on between the official party and the reformers; for the official party, like all parties long in power, was naturally unwilling to submit itself to any such responsibility as would abridge its tenure, or cramp its exercise of authority. Reluctant to acknowledge any responsibility to the people of the Colony, this party appears to have paid a somewhat refractory and nominal submission to the Imperial Government, relying in fact on securing a virtual independence by this nominal submission to the distant authority of the Colonial Department, or to the powers of a Governor, over whose policy they were certain, by their facilities of access, to obtain a paramount influence.

The views of the great body of the reformers appear to have been limited, according to their favourite expression, to the making the Colonial Constitution 'an exact transcript' of that of Great Britain; and they only desired that the Crown should in Upper Canada, as at home, entrust the administration of affairs to men possessing the confidence of the Assembly. It cannot be doubted, however, that there were many of the party who wished to assimilate the institutions of the Province rather to those of the United States than to those of the mother country. A few persons, chiefly of American origin, appear to have entertained these designs from the outset; but the number had at last been very much increased by the despair which many of those who started with more limited views conceived of their being ever carried into effect under the existing form of Government.

Each party, while it possessed the ascendancy, has been accused by its opponents of having abused its power over the public funds in those modes of local jobbing which I have described as so common in the North American Colonies. This, perhaps, is to be attributed partly to the circumstances adverted to above, as increasing the difficulty of obtaining any accurate information as to the real circumstances of the Province. From these causes it too often happened that the members of the House of Assembly came to the meeting of the legislature ignorant of the real character of the general interests entrusted to their guardianship, intent only on promoting sectional objects, and anxious chiefly to secure for the county they happen to represent, or the district with which they are connected, as large a proportion as possible of any funds which the legislature may have at its disposal. In Upper Canada, however, the means of doing this were never so extensive as those possessed by the Lower Province; and the great works which the Province commenced on a very extended scale, and executed in a spirit of great carelessness and profusion, have left so little surplus revenue, that this Province alone, among the North American Colonies, has fortunately for itself been compelled to establish a system of local assessments, and to leave local works, in a great measure, to the energy and means of the localities themselves. It is asserted, however, that the nature of those great works, and the manner in which they were carried on, evinced merely a regard for local interests, and a disposition to strengthen party influence. The inhabitants of the less thickly peopled districts complained that the revenues of the Province were employed in works by which only the frontier population would benefit. The money absorbed by undertakings which they described as disproportioned to the resources and to the wants of the Province, would, they alleged, have sufficed to establish practicable means of communication over the whole country; and they stated, apparently not without foundation, that had this latter course been pursued, the population and the resources of the Province would have been so augmented as to make the works actually undertaken both useful and profitable. The carelessness and profusion which marked the execution of these works, the management of which, it was complained, was entrusted chiefly to members of the ruling party, were also assumed to be the result of a deliberate purpose, and to be permitted, if not encouraged, in order that a few individuals might be enriched at the expense of the community. Circumstances to which I shall hereafter advert, by which the further progress of these works has been checked, and the large expenses incurred in bringing them to their present state of forwardness, have been rendered unavailing, have given greater force to these complaints, and, in addition to the discontent produced by the objects of the expenditure, the governing party has been made responsible for a failure in the accomplishment of these objects, attributable to causes over which it had no control. But to whatever extent these practices may have been carried, the course of the Parliamentary contest in Upper Canada has not been marked by that singular neglect of the great duties of a legislative body, which I have remarked in the proceedings of the Parliament of Lower Canada. The statute book of the Upper Province abounds with useful and well constructed measures of reform, and presents an honourable contrast to that of the Lower Province.

While the parties were thus struggling, the operation of a cause, utterly unconnected with their disputes, suddenly raised up a very considerable third party, which began to make its appearance among the political disputants about the time that the quarrel was at its height. I have said that in Upper Canada there is no animosity of races; there is nevertheless a distinction of origin, which has exercised a very important influence on the composition of parties, and appears likely, sooner or later, to become the prominent and absorbing element of political division. The official and reforming parties which I have described, were both composed, for the most part, and were almost entirely led, by native-born Canadians, American settlers, or emigrants of a very ancient date; and as one section of this more ancient population possessed, so another was the only body of persons that claimed, the management of affairs, and the enjoyment of offices conferring emolument or power, until the extensive emigration from Great Britain, which followed the disastrous period of 1825 and 1826, changed the state of things, by suddenly doubling the population, and introducing among the ancient disputants for power, an entirely new class of persons. The new-comers, however, did not for a long time appear as a distinct party in the politics of Upper Canada. A large number of the higher class of emigrants, particularly the half-pay officers, who were induced to settle in this Province, had belonged to the Tory party in England, and, in conformity with their ancient predilections, naturally arrayed themselves on the side of the official party, contending with the representatives of the people. The mass of the humbler order of emigrants, accustomed in the mother country to complain of the corruption and profusion of the Government, and to seek for a reform of abuses, by increasing the popular influence in the representative body, arrayed themselves on the side of those who represented the people, and attacked oligarchical power and abuses; but there was still a great difference of opinion between each of the two Canadian parties and that section of the British which for a while acted with it. Each of the Canadian parties, while it differed with the other about the tenure of political powers in the Colony, desired almost the same degree of practical independence of the mother country; each felt and each betrayed in its political conduct a jealousy of the emigrants, and a wish to maintain the powers of office and the emoluments of the professions in the hands of persons born or long resident in the Colony. The British, on the contrary, to whichever party they belong, appear to agree in desiring that the connexion with the mother country should be drawn closer. They differ very little among themselves, I imagine, in desiring such a change as should assimilate the Government of Upper Canada, in spirit as well as in form, to the Government of England, retaining an executive sufficiently powerful to curb popular excesses, and giving to the majority of the people, or to such of them as the less liberal would trust with political rights, some substantial control over the administration of affairs. But the great common object was, and is, the removal of those disqualifications to which British emigrants are subject, so that they might feel as citizens, instead of aliens, in the land of their adoption.

Such was the state of parties, when Sir F. Head, on assuming the government of the Colony, dismissed from the Executive Council some of the members who were most obnoxious to the House of Assembly, and requested three individuals to succeed them. Two of these gentlemen, Dr. Rolph, and Mr. R. Baldwin, were connected with the reforming party, and the third, Mr. Dunn, was an Englishman, who had held the office of Receiver General for nearly fourteen years, and up to that time had abstained from any interference in politics. These gentlemen were, at first, reluctant to take office, because they feared that, as there were still three of the former Council left, they should be constantly maintaining a doubtful struggle for the measures which they considered necessary. They were, however, at length induced to forego their scruples, chiefly upon the representations of some of their friends, that when they had a Governor who appeared sincere in his professions of reform, and who promised them his entire confidence, it was neither generous nor prudent to persist in a refusal which might be taken to imply distrust of his sincerity; and they accordingly accepted office. Among the first acts of the Governor, after the appointment of this Council, was, however, the nomination to some vacant offices of individuals, who were taken from the old official party, and this without any communication with his Council. These appointments were attacked by the House of Assembly, and the new Council, finding that their opinion was never asked upon these, or other matters, and that they were seemingly to be kept in ignorance of all those public measures, which popular opinion nevertheless attributed to their advice, remonstrated privately on the subject with the Governor. Sir Francis desired them to make a formal representation to him on the subject; they did so, and this produced such a reply from him, as left them no choice but to resign. The occasion of the differences which had caused the resignation, was made the subject of communication between the Governor and the Assembly, so that the whole community were informed of the grounds of the dispute.

The contest which appeared to be thus commenced on the question of the responsibility of the Executive Council, was really decided on very different grounds. Sir F. Head, who appears to have thought that the maintenance of the connexion with Great Britain depended upon his triumph over the majority of the Assembly, embarked in the contest, with a determination to use every influence in his power, in order to bring it to a successful issue. He succeeded, in fact, in putting the issue in such a light before the Province, that a great portion of the people really imagined that they were called upon to decide the question of separation by their votes. The dissolution, on which he ventured, when he thought the public mind sufficiently ripe, completely answered his expectations. The British, in particular, were roused by the proclaimed danger to the connexion with the mother country; they were indignant at some portions of the conduct and speeches of certain members of the late majority, which seemed to mark a determined preference of American over British Institutions. They were irritated by indications of hostility to British emigration, which they saw, or fancied they saw, in some recent proceedings of the Assembly. Above all, not only they, but a great many others, had marked with envy the stupendous public works which were at that period producing their effect in the almost marvellous growth of the wealth and population of the neighbouring state of New York; and they reproached the Assembly with what they considered an unwise economy, in preventing the undertaking or even completion of similar works, that might, as they fancied, have produced a similar development of the resources of Upper Canada. The general support of the British determined the elections in favour of the Government; and though very large and close minorities, which in many cases supported the defeated candidates, marked the force which the reformers could bring into the field, even in spite of the disadvantages under which they laboured from the momentary prejudices against them, and the unusual manner in which the Crown, by its representative, appeared to make itself a party in an electioneering contest, the result was the return of a very large majority hostile in politics to that of the late Assembly.

It is rather singular, however, that the result which Sir F. Head appears really to have aimed at, was by no means secured by this apparent triumph. His object in all his previous measures, and in the nomination of the Executive Councillors, by whom he replaced the retiring members, was evidently to make the Council a means of administrative independence for the Governor. Sir F. Head would seem to have been, at the commencement of his administration, really desirous of effecting certain reforms which he believed to be needful, and of rescuing the substantial power of the Government from the hands of the party by which it had been so long monopolized. The dismissal of the old members of the Executive Council was the consequence of this intention; but though willing to take measures for the purpose of emancipating himself from the thraldom in which it was stated that other Governors had been held, he could not acquiesce in the claims of the House of Assembly to have a really responsible colonial executive. The result of the elections was to give him, as he conceived, a House of Assembly pledged to support him, as Governor, in the exercise of the independent authority he had claimed. On the very first occasion, however, on which he attempted to protect an officer of the Government, unconnected with the old official party, from charges which, whether well or ill founded, were obviously brought forward on personal grounds, he found that the new House was even more determined than its predecessor to assert its right to exercise a substantial control over the Government; and that, unless he was disposed to risk a collision with both branches of the legislature, then composed of similar materials, and virtually under one influence, he must succumb. Unwilling to incur this risk, when, as he justly imagined, there was no party upon whose support he could rely to bear him safely through the contest, he yielded the point. . . . From that time he never attempted to assert the independence which the new House of Assembly had been elected to secure. The Government consequently reverted in effect to the party which he had found in office when he assumed the Governorship, and which it had been his first act to dispossess. In their hands it still remains; and I must state that it is the general opinion, that never was the power of the 'family compact' so extensive or so absolute as it has been from the first meeting of the existing Parliament down to the present time.

It may, indeed, be fairly said, that the real result of Sir F. Head's policy was to establish that very administrative influence of the leaders of a majority in the legislature which he had so obstinately disputed. The Executive Councillors of his nomination, who seem to have taken office almost on the express condition of being mere ciphers, are not in fact, then, the real Government of the Province. It is said that the new officers of Government whom Sir F. Head appointed from without the pale of official eligibility, feel more apprehension of the present House than, so far as can be judged, was ever felt by their predecessors with regard to the most violent of the reforming Houses of Assembly. Their apprehension, however, is not confined to the present House; they feel that, under no conceivable contingency, can they expect an Assembly disposed to support them; and they accordingly appear to desire such a change in the colonial system as might make them dependent upon the Imperial Government alone, and secure them against all interference from the legislature of the Province, whatever party should obtain a preponderance in the Assembly.

While the nominal Government thus possesses no real power, the legislature, by whose leaders the substantial power is enjoyed, by no means possesses so much of the confidence of the people, as a legislature ought to command, even from those who differ from it on the questions of the day. I say this without meaning to cast any imputation on the Members of the House of Assembly, because, in fact, the circumstances under which they were elected, were such as to render them peculiarly objects of suspicion and reproach to a large number of their countrymen. They were accused of having violated their pledges at the election. It is said that many of them came forward, and were elected, as being really reformers, though opposed to any such claims to colonial independence as might involve a separation from the mother country. There seems to be no doubt that in several places, where the Tories succeeded, the electors were merely desirous of returning members who would not hazard any contest with England, by the assertion of claims which, from the proclamation of the Lieutenant-Governor, they believed to be practically needless; and who should support Sir F. Head in those economical reforms which the country desired, far more than political changes – reforms, for the sake of which alone political changes had been sought. In a number of other instances, too, the elections were carried by the unscrupulous exercise of the influence of the Government, and by a display of violence on the part of the Tories, who were emboldened by the countenance afforded to them by the authorities. It was stated, but I believe without any sufficient foundation, that the Government made grants of land to persons who had no title to them, in order to secure their votes. This report originated in the fact, that patents for persons who were entitled to grants, but had not taken them out, were sent down to the polling places, to be given to the individuals entitled to them, if they were disposed to vote for the Government candidate. The taking such measures, in order to secure their fair right of voting to the electors in a particular interest, must be considered rather as an act of official favouritism, than as an electoral fraud. But we cannot wonder that the defeated party put the very worst construction on acts which gave some ground for it; and they conceived, in consequence, a strong resentment against the means by which they believed that the representative of the Crown had carried the elections, his interference in which in any way was stigmatized by them as a gross violation of constitutional privilege and propriety.

It cannot be matter of surprise, that such facts and such impressions produced in the country an exasperation and a despair of good Government, which extended far beyond those who had actually been defeated at the poll. For there was nothing in the use which the leaders of the Assembly have made of their power, to soften the discontent excited by their alleged mode of obtaining it. Many even of those who had supported the successful candidates, were disappointed in every expectation which they had formed of

the policy to be pursued by their new representatives. No economical reforms were introduced. The Assembly, instead of supporting the Governor, compelled his obedience to itself, and produced no change in the administration of affairs, except that of
reinstating the 'family compact' in power. On some topics, on
which the feelings of the people were very deeply engaged, as, for
instance, the clergy reserves, the Assembly is accused of having
shown a disposition to act in direct defiance of the known sentiments of a vast majority of its constituents. The dissatisfaction
arising from these causes, was carried to its height, by an Act, that
appeared in defiance of all constitutional right, to prolong the
power of a majority which, it was supposed, counted on not being
able to retain its existence after another appeal to the people. This
was the passing an Act preventing the dissolution of the existing,
as well as any future Assembly, on the demise of the Crown. The
Act was passed in expectation of the approaching decease of his
late Majesty; and it has, in fact, prolonged the existence of the
present Assembly from the period of a single year to one of four. It
is said that this step is justified by the example of the other North
American Colonies. But it is certain that it nevertheless caused very
great dissatisfaction, and was regarded as an unbecoming usurpa-
tion of power.

It was the prevalence of the general dissatisfaction thus caused,
that emboldened the parties who instigated the insurrection to an
attempt, which may be characterized as having been as foolishly
contrived and as ill-conducted, as it was wicked and treasonable.
This outbreak, which common prudence and good management
would have prevented from coming to a head, was promptly
quelled by the alacrity with which the population, and especially
the British portion of it, rallied round the Government. The proximity of the American frontier, the nature of the border country,
and the wild and daring character, together with the periodical
want of employment of its population, have unfortunately
enabled a few desperate exiles to continue the troubles of their
country, by means of the predatory gangs which have from time
to time invaded and robbed, under the pretext of revolutionizing
the Province. But the general loyalty of the population has been
evinced by the little disposition that has been exhibited by any

portion of it to accept of the proffered aid of the refugees and foreign invaders, and by the unanimity with which all have turned
out to defend their country.

It has not, indeed, been exactly ascertained what proportion of
the inhabitants of Upper Canada were prepared to join Mackenzie
in his treasonable enterprise, or were so disposed that we may suppose they would have arrayed themselves on his side, had he
obtained any momentary success, as indeed was for some days
within his grasp. Even if I were convinced that a large proportion
of the population would, under any circumstances, have lent themselves to his projects, I should be inclined to attribute such a disposition merely to the irritation produced by those temporary
causes of dissatisfaction with the government of the Province
which I have specified, and not to any settled design on the part of
any great number, either to subvert existing institutions, or to
change their present connexion with Great Britain for a junction
with the United States. I am inclined to view the insurrectionary
movements which did take place as indicative of no deep-rooted
disaffection, and to believe that almost the entire body of the
reformers of this Province sought only by constitutional means to
obtain those objects for which they had so long peaceably strug-
gled before the unhappy troubles occasioned by the violence of a
few unprincipled adventurers and heated enthusiasts.

It cannot, however, be doubted, that the events of the past year
have greatly increased the difficulty of settling the disorders of
Upper Canada. A degree of discontent, approaching, if not
amounting, to disaffection, has gained considerable ground. The
cause of dissatisfaction continue to act on the minds of the reformers; and their hope of redress, under the present order of things,
has been seriously diminished. The exasperation caused by the
conflict itself, the suspicions and terrors of that trying period, and
the use made by the triumphant party of the power thrown into
their hands, have heightened the passions which existed before. It
certainly appeared too much as if the rebellion had been purposely
invited by the Government, and the unfortunate men who took
part in it deliberately drawn into a trap by those who subsequently
inflicted so severe a punishment on them for their error. It seemed,
too, as if the dominant party made use of the occasion afforded it

by the real guilt of a few desperate and imprudent men, in order to persecute or disable the whole body of their political opponents. A great number of perfectly innocent individuals were thrown into prison, and suffered in person, property and character. The whole body of reformers were subjected to suspicion, and to harassing proceedings, instituted by magistrates, whose political leanings were notoriously adverse to them. Severe laws were passed, under colour of which, individuals very generally esteemed were punished without any form of trial.

The two persons who suffered the extreme penalty of the law unfortunately engaged a great share of the public sympathy; their pardon had been solicited in petitions signed, it is generally asserted, by no less than 30,000 of their countrymen. The rest of the prisoners were detained in confinement a considerable time. A large number of the subordinate actors in the insurrection were severely punished, and public anxiety was raised to the highest pitch by the uncertainty respecting the fate of the others, who were from time to time partially released. It was not until the month of October last that the whole of the prisoners were disposed of, and a partial amnesty proclaimed, which enabled the large numbers who had fled the country, and so long, and at such imminent hazard, hung on its frontier, to return in security to their homes. I make no mention of the reasons which, in the opinion of the local government, rendered these different steps advisable, because my object is not to discuss the propriety of its conduct, but to point out the effect which it necessarily had in augmenting irritation.

The whole party of the reformers, a party which I am inclined to estimate as very considerable, and which has commanded large majorities in different Houses of Assembly, has certainly felt itself assailed by the policy pursued. It sees the whole powers of Government wielded by its enemies, and imagines that it can perceive also a determination to use these powers inflexibly against all the objects which it most values. The wounded private feelings of individuals, and the defeated public policy of a party, combine to spread a wide and serious irritation; but I do not believe that this has yet proceeded so far as to induce at all a general disposition to look to violent measures for redress. The reformers have been gradually recovering their hopes of regaining their ascendancy by constitutional means; the sudden pre-eminence which the question of the clergy reserves and rectories has again assumed during the last summer, appears to have increased their influence and confidence; and I have no reason to believe that any thing can make them generally and decidedly desirous of separation, except some such act of the Imperial Government as shall deprive them of all hopes of obtaining real administrative power, even in the event of their again obtaining a majority in the Assembly. With such a hope before them, I believe that they will remain in tranquil expectation of the result of the general election which cannot be delayed beyond the summer of 1840.

To describe the character and objects of the other parties in this Province would not be very easy; and their variety and complication is so great, that it would be of no great advantage were I to explain the various shades of opinion that mark each. In a very laboured essay, which was published in Toronto during my stay in Canada, there was an attempt to classify the various parties in the Province under six different heads. Some of these were classified according to strictly political opinions, some according to religion, and some according to birthplace; and each party, it was obvious, contained in its ranks a great many who would, according to the designations used, have as naturally belonged to some other. But it is obvious, from all accounts of the different parties, that the nominal Government, that is, the majority of the Executive Council, enjoy the confidence of no considerable party, and that the party called the 'family compact', which possesses the majority in both branches of the legislature, is, in fact, supported at present by no very large number of persons of any party. None are more hostile to them than the greater part of that large and spirited British-born population, to whose steadfast exertions the preservation of the Colony during the last winter is mainly attributable, and who see with indignation that a monopoly of power and profit is still retained by a small body of men, which seems bent on excluding from any participation in it the British emigrants. Zealously co-operating with the dominant party in resisting treason and foreign invasion, this portion of the population, nevertheless, entertains a general distrust and dislike of them; and though many of the most prominent of the British emigrants have always acted and still invariably act in opposition to the reformers, and dissent from their views of responsible government, I am very much inclined to think that they, and certainly the great mass of their countrymen, really desire such a responsibility of the Government, as would break up the present monopoly of office and influence.

Besides those causes of complaint which are common to the whole of the Colony, the British settlers have many peculiar to themselves. The emigrants who have settled in the country within the last ten years, are supposed to comprise half the population. They complain that while the Canadians are desirous of having British capital and labour brought into the Colony, by means of which their fields may be cultivated, and the value of their unsettled possessions increased, they refuse to make the Colony really attractive to British skill and British capitalists. They say that an Englishman emigrating to Upper Canada, is practically as much an alien in that British Colony as he would be if he were to emigrate to the United States. . . .

The great practical question, however, on which these various parties have for a long time been at issue, and which has within a very few months again become the prominent matter in debate, is that of the clergy reserves. The prompt and satisfactory decision of this question is essential to the pacification of Canada; and as it was one of the most important questions referred to me for investigation, it is necessary that I should state it fully, and not shrink from making known the light in which it has presented itself to my mind. The disputes on this subject are now of long standing. By the Constitutional Act a certain portion of the land in every township was set apart for the maintenance of a 'Protestant' clergy. In that portion of this Report which treats of the management of the waste lands, the economical mischiefs which have resulted from this appropriation of territory, are fully detailed; and the present disputes relate solely to the application, and not to the mode of raising, the funds, which are now derived from the sale of the clergy reserves. Under the term 'Protestant Clergy', the clergy of the Church of England have always claimed the sole enjoyment of these funds. The members of the Church of Scotland have claimed to be put entirely on a level with the Church of England, and have demanded that these funds should be equally divided between both. The various denominations of Protestant Dissenters have asserted that the term includes them, and that out of these funds an equal provision should be made for all Christians who do not belong to the Church of Rome. But a great body of all Protestant denominations, and the numerous Catholics who inhabit the Province, have maintained that any such favour towards anyone, or even all of the Protestant sects, would be most unadvisable, and have either demanded the equal application of those funds to the purposes of all religious creeds whatsoever, or have urged the propriety of leaving each body of religionists to maintain its own establishment, to repeal or disregard the law, and to apply the clergy funds to the general purposes of the Government, or to the support of a general system of education.

The supporters of these different schemes having long contended in this Province, and greatly inconvenienced the Imperial Government, by constant references to its decision, the Secretary of State for the Colonies proposed to leave the determination of the matter to the provincial legislatures, pledging the Imperial Government to do its utmost to get a Parliamentary sanction to whatever course they might adopt. Two Bills, in consequence, passed the last House of Assembly, in which the reformers had the ascendancy, applying these funds to the purposes of education; and both these Bills were rejected by the Legislative Council.

During all this time, however, though much irritation had been caused by the exclusive claims of the Church of England, and the favour shown by the Government to one, and that a small religious community, the clergy of that church, though an endowed, were not a dominant, priesthood. They had a far larger share of the public money than the clergy of any other denomination; but they had no exclusive privileges, and no authority, save such as might spring from their efficient discharge of their sacred duties, or from the energy, ability or influence of members of their body. But the last public act of Sir John Colborne, before quitting the Government of the Province in 1835, which was the establishment of the fifty-seven rectories, has completely changed the aspect of the question. It is understood that every rector possesses all the spiritual and other privileges enjoyed by an English rector; and that though he may have no right to levy tithes (for even this has been made a question), he is in all other respects in precisely the same position as a clergyman of the Established Church in England. This is regarded by all other teachers of religion in the country as having at once degraded them to a position of legal inferiority to the clergy of the Church of England; and it has been resented most warmly. In the opinion of many persons, this was the chief pre-disposing cause of the recent insurrection, and it is an abiding and unabated cause of discontent. Nor is this to be wondered at. The Church of England in Upper Canada, by numbering in its ranks all those who belong to no other sect, represents itself as being more numerous than any single denomination of Christians in the country. Even admitting, however, the justice of the principle upon which this enumeration proceeds, and giving that Church credit for all that it thus claims, its number could not amount to one-third, probably not a fourth, of the population. It is not, therefore, to be expected that the other sects, three at least of whom, the Methodists, the Presbyterians and the Catholics, claim to be individually more numerous than the Church of England, should acquiesce quietly in the supremacy thus given to it. And it is equally natural that the English Dissenters and Irish Catholics, remembering the position which they have occupied at home, and the long and painful struggle through which alone they have obtained the imperfect equality they now possess, should refuse to acquiesce for themselves in the creation of a similar establishment in their new country, and thus to bequeath to their children a strife as arduous and embittered as that from which they have so recently and imperfectly escaped.

But for this act, it would have been possible, though highly impolitic, to have allowed the clergy reserves to remain upon their former undetermined and unsatisfactory footing. But the question as to the application of this property, must now be settled, if it is intended that the Province is to be free from violent and perilous agitation. Indeed, the whole controversy, which had been in a great measure suspended by the insurrection, was, in the course of the last summer, revived with more heat than ever by the most inopportune arrival in the Colony of opinions given by the English Law Officers of the Crown in favour of the legality of the establishment of the rectories. Since that period, the question has again absorbed public attention; and it is quite clear that it is upon this practical point that issue must sooner or later be joined on all the constitutional questions to which I have previously adverted. I am well aware that there are not wanting some who represent the agitation of this question as merely the result of its present unsettled character, and who assert, that if the claims of the English Church to the exclusive enjoyment of this property were established by the Imperial Parliament, all parties, however loud their present pretensions, or however vehement their first complaints, would peacefully acquiesce in an arrangement which would then be inevitable. This might be the case if the establishment of some dominant church were inevitable. But it cannot be necessary to point out that, in the immediate vicinity of the United States, and with their example before the people of Canada, no injustice, real or fancied, occasioned and supported by a British rule, would be regarded in this light. The result of any determination on the part of the British Government or legislature to give one sect a predominance and superiority, would be, it might be feared, not to secure the favoured sect, but to endanger the loss of the Colony, and, in vindicating the exclusive pretensions of the English Church, to hazard one of the fairest possessions of the British Crown.

I am bound, indeed, to state, that there is a degree of feeling, and an unanimity of opinion, in the question of ecclesiastical establishments over the northern part of the continent of America, which it will be prudent not to overlook in the settlement of this question. The superiority of what is called 'the voluntary principle' is a question on which I may almost say that there is no difference of opinion in the United States; and it cannot be denied, that on this, as on other points, the tone of thought prevalent in the Union has exerted a very considerable influence over the neighbouring Provinces. Similar circumstances, too, have had the effect of accustoming the people of both countries to regard this question in a very different light from that in which it appears in the Old World; and the nature of the question is indeed entirely different in old and new countries. The apparent right which time and custom give to the maintenance of an ancient and respected institution cannot exist in a recently settled country, in which every thing is new; and the establishment of a dominant church there is a creation of exclusive privileges in favour of one out of many religious denominations, and that composing a small minority, at the expense not merely of the majority, but of many as large minorities. The church, too, for which alone it is proposed that the State should provide, is the church which, being that of the wealthy, can best provide for itself, and has the fewest poor to supply with gratuitous religious instruction. Another consideration, which distinguishes the grounds on which such a question must be decided in old and new countries, is, that the state of society in the latter is not susceptible of such an organization as is necessary for the efficiency of any Church Establishment of which I know, more especially of one so constituted as the Established Church of England; for the essence of the Establishment is its parochial clergy. The services of a parochial clergy are almost inapplicable to a colony, where a constantly varying population is widely scattered over the country. Any clergy there must be rather missionary than parochial.

A still stronger objection to the creation of a Church Establishment in this Colony is, that not merely are the members of the Church of England a small minority at present; but, inasmuch as the majority of emigrants are not members of the Church of England, the disproportion is likely to increase, instead of disappearing, in the course of time. The mass of British emigrants will be either from the middle classes of Great Britain, or the poorer classes of Ireland; the latter, almost exclusively Catholics, and the former in a great proportion either Scotch Presbyterians or English Dissenters.

It is most important that this question should be settled, and so settled as to give satisfaction to the majority of the people of the two Canadas, whom it equally concerns. And I know of no mode of doing this but by repealing all provisions in Imperial Acts that relate to the application of the clergy reserves, and the funds arising from them, leaving the disposal of the funds to the local legislature, and acquiescing in whatever decision it may adopt. The views which I have expressed on this subject sufficiently mark my conviction, that, without the adoption of such a course, the most mischievous practical cause of dissension will not be removed.

I feel it my duty also, in this as in the Lower Province, to call especial attention to the policy which has been, and which ought to be, pursued towards the large Catholic population of the Province. On this subject I have received complaints of a general spirit of intolerance and disfavour towards all persons of this creed, to which I am obliged to give considerable credit, from the great respectability and undoubted loyalty of those from whom the complaints were received. . . . The Catholics constitute at least a fifth of the whole population of Upper Canada. Their loyalty was most generally and unequivocally exhibited at the late outbreak. Nevertheless, it is said that they are wholly excluded from all share in the government of the country and the patronage at its disposal. . . .

The Irish Catholics complain very loudly and justly of the existence of Orangeism in this Colony. They are justly indignant that, in a Province which their loyalty and bravery have materially contributed to save, their feelings are outraged by the symbols and processions of this association. It is somewhat difficult to understand the nature and objects of the rather anomalous Orangeism of Upper Canada. Its members profess to desire to uphold the Protestant religion, but to be free from those intolerant feelings towards their Catholic countrymen, which are the distinctive marks of the Irish Orangemen. They assert, that their main object, to which the support of the English Church is subsidiary, is to maintain the connexion with Great Britain. They have sworn, it is said, many ignorant Catholics into their body; and at their public dinners, after drinking the 'pious, glorious and immortal memory', with all the usual formality of abuse of the Catholics, they toast the health of the Catholic Bishop, M'Donnell. It would seem that their great purpose has been to introduce the machinery, rather than the tenets of Orangeism; and the leaders probably hope to make use of this kind of permanent conspiracy and illegal organization to gain political power for themselves. In fact, the Catholics scarcely appear to view this institution with more jealousy than the reformers of the Province. It is an Irish Tory institution, having not so much a religious as a political bearing. The Irish Catholics who have been initiated have entered it chiefly from its supposed national character, and probably with as little regard to the political as to the religious objects with which it is connected. Still the organization of this body enables its leaders to exert a powerful influence over the populace; and it is stated that, at the last general election, the Tories succeeded in carrying more than one seat by means of the violence of the organized mob thus placed at their disposal. It is not, indeed, at the last election only that the success of the Government candidate has been attributed to the existence of this association. At former elections, especially those for the county of Leeds, it is asserted that the return of the Canadian Deputy Grand Master, and of the then Attorney General, his colleague, was procured by means of a violent and riotous mob of Orangemen, who prevented the voters in the opposition interest from coming up to the poll. In consequence of this and other similar outrages, the Assembly presented an address to Sir Francis Head, begging 'that his Excellency would be pleased to inform the House whether the Government of the Province had taken, or determined to take, any steps to prevent or discourage public processions of Orange societies, or to discourage the formation and continuance of such societies'. To this Address the Governor made the following reply: – 'The Government of this Province has neither taken, nor has it determined to take, any steps to prevent or discourage the formation or continuance of such societies.' It is to be presumed that this answer proceeded from a disbelief of the truth of those charges of outrage and riot which were made the foundation of the Address. But it can excite no surprise that the existence of such an institution, offending one class by its contemptuous hostility to their religion, and another by its violent opposition to their politics, and which had been sanctioned by the Governor, as was conceived, on account of its political tendencies, should excite among both classes a deep feeling of indignation, and add seriously to the distrust with which the Government was regarded.

In addition to the irritation engendered by the position of parties, by the specific causes of dispute to which I have adverted, and by those features in the Government of the Colony which deprive the people of all power to effect a settlement of the questions by which the country is most deeply agitated, or to redress abuses in the institutions, or in the administration of the Province, there are permanent causes of discontent, resulting from the existence of deep-seated impediments in the way of its industrial progress. The

Province is without any of those means by which the resources of a country are developed, and the civilization of a people is advanced or upheld. The general administration of justice, it is true, appears to be much better in Upper than in Lower Canada. Courts of Justice, at least, are brought into every man's neighbourhood by a system of circuits; and there is still some integrity in juries. But there are general complaints of the union of political and judicial functions in the Chief Justice; not because any suspicion attaches to that Judge's discharge of his duties, but on account of the party grounds upon which his subordinates are supposed to be appointed, and the party bias attributed to them. Complaints, too, similar to those which I have adverted to in the Lower Province, are made against the system by which the Sheriffs are appointed. It is stated, that they are selected exclusively from the friends or dependents of the ruling party; that very insufficient securities are taken from them; and that the money arising from executions and sales, which are represented as unhappily very numerous in this Province, generally remains in their hands for at least a year. For reasons also which I have specified in my account of the Lower Province, the composition of the magistracy appears to be a serious cause of mischief and dissatisfaction.

But, independently of these sources of complaint, are the impediments which I have mentioned. A very considerable portion of the Province has neither roads, post offices, mills, schools, nor churches. The people may raise enough for their own subsistence, and may even have a rude and comfortless plenty, but they can seldom acquire wealth; nor can even wealthy land-owners prevent their children from growing up ignorant and boorish, and from occupying a far lower mental, moral and social position that they themselves fill. Their means of communication with each other, or the chief towns of the Province, are limited and uncertain. With the exception of the labouring class, most of the emigrants who have arrived within the last ten years, are poorer now than at the time of their arrival in the Province. There is no adequate system of local assessment to improve the means of communication; and the funds occasionally voted for this purpose are, under the present system, disposed of by a House of Assembly which represents principally the interests of the more settled districts, and which, it is alleged, has been chiefly intent in making their disposal a means of strengthening the influence of its members in the constituencies which they represent. These funds have consequently almost always been applied in that part of the country where they were least needed; and they have been too frequently expended so as to produce scarcely any perceptible advantages. Of the lands which were originally appropriated for the support of schools throughout the country, by far the most valuable portion has been diverted to the endowment of the University, from which those only derive any benefit who reside in Toronto, or those who, having a large assured income, are enabled to maintain their children in that town at an expense which has been estimated at £50 per annum for each child. Even in the most thickly peopled districts there are but few schools, and those of a very inferior character; while the more remote settlements are almost entirely without any.

Under such circumstances there is little stimulus to industry or enterprise, and their effect is aggravated by the striking contrast presented by such of the United States as border upon this Province, and where all is activity and progress. I shall hereafter, in connexion with the disposal of the public lands, advert to circumstances affecting not Upper Canada merely, but the whole of our North American Colonies in an almost equal degree, which will illustrate in detail the causes and results of the more prominent of these evils. I have referred to the topic in this place in order to notice the inevitable tendency of these inconveniences to aggravate whatever discontent may be produced by purely political causes, and to draw attention to the fact, that those who are most satisfied with the present political state of the Province, and least disposed to attribute economical injuries or social derangement to the form or the working of the Government, feel and admit that there must have been something wrong to have caused so striking a difference in progress and wealth between Upper Canada and the neighbouring states of the Union. I may also observe, that these evils affect chiefly that portion of the people which is composed of British emigrants, and who have had no part in the causes to which they are attributable. The native-born Canadians, as they generally inhabit the more settled districts of the Province, are the owners of nearly all the waste lands, and have almost exclusively had the application of all public funds, might be expected to have escaped from the evils alluded to, and even to have profited by the causes out of which they have sprung. The number of those who have thus profited is, however, comparatively small; the majority of this class, in common with the emigrant population, have suffered from the general depression, and share in the discontent and restlessness which this depression has produced.

The trade of the country is, however, a matter which appears to demand a notice here, because so long as any such marked and striking advantages in this respect are enjoyed by Americans, as at present arise from causes which Government has the power to remove, it is impossible but that many will look forward with desire to political changes. There are laws which regulate, or rather prohibit, the importation of particular articles, except from England, especially of tea, which were framed originally to protect the privileges of monopolies here; but which have been continued in the Province after the English monopoly has been removed. It is not that these laws have any appreciable effect in raising the price of the commodities in question: almost all used in the Province is smuggled across the frontier, but their operation is at once injurious to the fair dealer, who is undersold by persons who have obtained their articles in the cheaper market of the United States, and to the Province which can neither regulate the traffic, nor make it a source of revenue. It is probable, indeed, that the present law has been allowed to continue through inadvertence; but, if so, it is no very satisfactory evidence of the care or information of the Imperial Government that it knows or feels so little the oppressive influence of the laws to which it subjects its dependencies.

Another and more difficult topic connected with this subject, is the wish of this Province that it should be allowed to make use of New York as a port of entry. At present the rate of duty upon all goods coming from the United States, whatever may be their nature, or the port in Europe from which they have been shipped, is such as to compel all importers to receive the articles of their trade through the Saint Lawrence, the navigation of which river opens generally several weeks later than the time at which goods may be obtained in all the parts of Upper Canada bordering upon

Lake Ontario, by way of Oswego. The dealer, therefore, must submit to an injurious delay in his business, or must obtain his goods in the autumn, and have his capital lying dead for six months. Either of these courses must lessen the amount of traffic, by diminishing the quantity, or increasing the price, of all commodities; and the mischief is seriously enhanced by the monopoly which the present system places in the hands of what are called the 'forwarders' on the Saint Lawrence and the Rideau Canal. If goods might be shipped from England to be landed at New York in bond, and to be admitted into Upper Canada free of duty, upon the production of a certificate from the officer of customs at the English port from which they are shipped, this inconvenience would be removed, and the people of the Province would in reality benefit by their connexion with England, in the superior cheapness of their articles, without paying for it as highly as they do at present in the limitation of their commerce.

I have already stated, in my account of Lower Canada, the difficulties and disputes which are occasioned by the financial relations of the two Provinces. The state of affairs, however, which causes these disputes is of far greater practical mischief to Upper Canada. That Province some years ago conceived the very noble project of removing or obviating all the natural impediments to the navigation of the Saint Lawrence; and the design was to make these works on a scale so commensurate with the capabilities of that broad and deep river, as to enable sea-going vessels to navigate its whole course to the head of Lake Huron. The design was, perhaps, too vast, at least for the first effort of a State at that time comparatively so small and poor; but the boldness with which the people undertook it, and the immense sacrifices which they made in order to achieve it, are gratifying indications of a spirit which bids fair hereafter to render Upper Canada as thriving a country as any State of the American Union. The House of Assembly, with this object in view, took a large portion of the shares of the Welland Canal, which had been previously commenced by a few enterprising individuals. It then commenced the great ship canal, called the Cornwall Canal, with a view of enabling ships of considerable draught to avoid the Long Sault Rapids; and this work was, at an immense outlay, brought very far towards a completion.

It is said that there was great mismanagement, and perhaps no little jobbing, in the application of the funds, and the execution of the work. But the greatest error committed was the undertaking the works in Upper, without ensuring their continuation in Lower Canada. For the whole of the works in the Upper Province, when completed, would be comparatively, if not utterly, useless, without the execution of similar works on that part of the St. Lawrence which lies between the Province line and Montreal. But this co-operation the Lower Canadian Assembly refused or neglected to give; and the works of the Cornwall Canal are now almost suspended, from the apparent inutility of completing them.

The necessary expense of these great undertakings was very large; and the prodigality superadded thereto, has increased it to such an extent, that this Province is burthened with a debt of more than a million of pounds; the whole revenue, which is about £60,000, being hardly adequate to pay the interest. The Province has already been fortunately obliged to throw the whole support of the few and imperfect local works which are carried on in different parts of the Province on local assessments; but it is obvious that it will soon be obliged to have recourse to direct taxation to meet its ordinary civil expenditure. For the custom duties cannot be increased without the consent of Lower Canada; and that consent it is useless to expect from any House of Assembly chosen under the suspended constitution. The canals, of which the tolls would, if the whole series of necessary works were completed, in all probability render the past outlay a source of profit, instead of loss, remain in a state of almost hopeless suspension: the Cornwall Canal being unfinished, and the works already completed daily falling into decay, and the Welland Canal, which has been a source of great commercial benefit, being now in danger of becoming useless, from want of money to make the necessary repairs. After all its great hopes, and all the great sacrifices which it has made to realize them, Upper Canada now finds itself loaded with an enormous debt, which it is denied the means of raising its indirect taxation to meet, and mocked by the aspect of those unfinished works, which some small combined efforts might render a source of vast wealth and prosperity, but which now are a source of useless expense and bitter disappointment.

It may well be believed that such a state of things is not borne without repining by some of the most enterprising and loyal people of the Province. It is well known that the desire of getting over these difficulties has led many persons in this Province to urge the singular claim to have a convenient portion of Lower Canada taken from that Province, and annexed to Upper Canada; and that it induces many to desire an union of the Provinces as the only efficient means of settling all these disputes on a just and permanent footing. But it cannot be matter of surprise, that in despair of any sufficient remedies being provided by the Imperial Government, many of the most enterprising colonists of Upper Canada look to that bordering country, in which no great industrial enterprise ever feels neglect, or experiences a check, and that men the most attached to the existing form of government would find some compensation in a change, whereby experience might bid them hope that every existing obstacle would be speedily removed, and each man's fortune share in the progressive prosperity of a flourishing State.

A dissatisfaction with the existing order of things, produced by causes such as I have described, necessarily extends to many who desire no change in the political institutions of the Province. Those who most admire the form of the existing system, wish to see it administered in a very different mode. Men of all parties feel that the actual circumstances of the Colony are such as to demand the adoption of widely different measures from any that have yet been pursued in reference to them. They ask for greater firmness of purpose in their rulers, and a more defined and consistent policy on the part of the Government; something, in short, that will make all parties feel that an order of things has been established to which it is necessary that they should conform themselves, and which is not to be subject to any unlooked for and sudden interruption consequent upon some unforeseen move in the game of politics in England. Hitherto the course of policy adopted by the English Government towards this Colony, has had reference to the state of parties in England, instead of the wants and circumstances of the Province; neither party could calculate upon a successful result to their struggles for any particular object, because though they might be able to estimate accurately enough their strength in the Colony, they could not tell how soon some hidden spring might be put in motion in the Colonial Office in England which would defeat their best laid plans, and render utterly unavailing whole years of patient effort.

THE EASTERN PROVINCES AND NEWFOUNDLAND

Though I have stated my opinion that my inquiries would have been very incomplete, had they been confined to the two Canadas, the information which I am enabled to communicate with respect to the other North American Colonies is necessarily very limited. As, however, in these Provinces, with the exception of Newfoundland, there are no such discontents as threaten the disturbance of the public tranquillity, I did not think it necessary to institute any minute inquiries into the details of the various departments of Government. . . .

It is not necessary. . . that I should enter into any lengthened account of the nature or working of the form of government established in these Provinces, because in my account of Lower Canada I have described the general characteristics of the system common to all, and adduced the example of these Provinces in illustration of the defects of their common system. In all these Provinces we find representative government coupled with an irresponsible executive; we find the same constant collision between the branches of the Government; the same abuse of the powers of the representative bodies, owing to the anomaly of their position, aided by the want of good municipal institutions, and the same constant interference of the Imperial administration in matters which should be left wholly to the Provincial Governments. And if in these Provinces there is less formidable discontent and less obstruction to the regular course of Government, it is because in them there has been recently a considerable departure from the ordinary course of the colonial system, and a nearer approach to sound constitutional practice.

This is remarkably the case in New Brunswick, a province which was till a short time ago one of the most constantly harassed by collisions between the executive and legislative powers; the collision has now been in part terminated by the concession of all the revenues of the Province to the Assembly. The policy of this concession, with reference to the extent and mode in which it was made, will be discussed in the separate Report on the disposal and management of public lands; but the policy of the Government in this matter has at any rate put an end to disputes about the revenue, which were on the point of producing a constant Parliamentary conflict between the Crown and the Assembly in many respects like that which has subsisted in Lower Canada; but a more important advance has been made towards the practice of the British Constitution in a recent change which has been made in the Executive and Legislative Councils of the Colony, whereby, as I found from the representatives of the present official body in the delegation from New Brunswick, the administrative power of the Province had been taken out of the hands of the old official party, and placed in those of members of the former liberal opposition. The constitutional practice had been, in fact, fully carried into effect in this Province; the Government had been taken out of the hands of those who could not obtain the assent of the majority of the Assembly, and placed in the hands of those who possessed its confidence; the result is, that the Government of New Brunswick, till lately one of the most difficult in the North American Colonies, is now the most harmonious and easy.

In Nova Scotia some, but not a complete approximation has been made to the same judicious course. The Government is in a minority in the House of Assembly, and the Assembly and the Legislative Council do not perfectly harmonize. But the questions which divide parties at present happen really to be of no very great magnitude; and all are united and zealous in the great point of maintaining the connexion with Great Britain. . . .

The political history of Prince Edward's Island is contained in the system pursued with regard to its settlement, and the appropriation of its lands, which is fully detailed in the subsequent view of that department of government in the North American Colonies; and its past and present disorders are but the sad result of that fatal error which stifled its prosperity in the very cradle of its existence, by giving up the whole island to a handful of distant proprietors. Against this system, this small and powerless community has in vain been struggling for some years: a few active and influential proprietors in London have been able to drown the remonstrances, and defeat the efforts of a distant and petty Province: for the ordinary evils of distance are, in the instance of Prince Edward's Island, aggravated by the scantiness of its population, and the confined extent of its territory. This island, most advantageously situated for the supply of the surrounding Colonies, and of all the fisheries, possesses a soil peculiarly adapted to the production of grain; and, from its insular position, is blessed with a climate far more genial than a great part of the continent which lies to the southward. Had its natural advantages been turned to proper account, it might at this time have been the granary of the British Colonies, and, instead of barely supporting a poor and unenterprising population of 40,000, its mere agricultural resources would, according to Major Head, have maintained in abundance a population of at least ten times that number. Of nearly 1,400,000 acres contained in the island, only 10,000 are said to be unfit for the plough. Only 100,000 are now under cultivation. No one can mistake the cause of this lamentable waste of the means of national wealth. It is the possession of almost the whole soil of the island by absentee proprietors, who would neither promote nor permit its cultivation, combined with the defective Government which first caused and has since perpetuated the evil. The simple legislative remedy for all this mischief having been suggested by three successive Secretaries of State, has been embodied in an Act of the local legislature, which was reserved for the Royal Assent; and the influence of the proprietors in London was such, that that assent was for a long time withheld. The question was referred to me during my stay in Canada; and I believe I may have the satisfaction of attributing to the recommendation which I gave, in accordance with the earnest representations of the Lieutenant-Governor, Sir Charles Fitzroy, the adoption at last of a measure intended to remove the abuse that has so long retarded the prosperity of this Colony.

The present condition of these Colonies presents none of those alarming features which mark the state of the two Canadas. The loyalty and attachment to the mother country which animate their inhabitants, is warm and general. But their varied and ample resources are turned to little account. Their scanty population exhibits, in most portions of them, an aspect of poverty, backwardness and stagnation; and wherever a better state of things is visible, the improvement is generally to be ascribed to the influx of American settlers or capitalists. Major Head describes his journey through a great part of Nova Scotia as exhibiting the melancholy spectacle of 'half the tenements abandoned, and lands every where falling into decay'; 'and the lands,' he tells us, 'that were purchased 30 and 40 years ago, at 5s. an acre, are now offered for sale at 3s.' 'The people of Prince Edward's Island are,' he says, 'permitting Americans to take out of their hands all their valuable fisheries, from sheer want of capital to employ their own population in them.' 'The country on the noble river, St. John's,' he states, 'possesses all that is requisite, except "that animation of business which constitutes the value of a new settlement."' But the most striking indication of the backward state of these Provinces, is afforded by the amount of the population. These Provinces, among the longest settled on the North American Continent, contain nearly 30,000,000 of acres, and a population, estimated at the highest, at no more, than 365,000 souls, giving only one inhabitant for every 80 acres. In New Brunswick, out of 16,500,000 acres, it is estimated that at least 15,000,000 are fit for cultivation; and the population being estimated at no more than 140,000, there is not one inhabitant for 100 acres of cultivable land.

It is a singular and melancholy feature in the condition of these Provinces, that the resources rendered of so little avail to the population of Great Britain, are turned to better account by the enterprising inhabitants of the United States. While the emigration from the Province is large and constant, the adventurous farmers of New England cross the frontier, and occupy the best farming lands. Their fishermen enter our bays and rivers, and in some cases monopolize the occupations of our own unemployed countrymen; and a great portion of the trade of the St. John's is in their hands. Not only do the citizens of a foreign nation do this, but they do it with British capital. Major Head states, 'that an American merchant acknowledged to him that the capital with which his countrymen carried on their enterprises in the neighbourhood of St. John's, was chiefly supplied by Great Britain; and,' he adds, as a fact within his own knowledge, 'that wealthy capitalists at Halifax, desirous of an investment for their money, preferred lending it in the United States to applying it to speculation in New Brunswick, or to lending it to their own countrymen in that Province.'

I regret to say, that Major Head also gives the same account respecting the difference between the aspect of things in these Provinces, and the bordering State of Maine. On the other side of the line, good roads, good schools, and thriving farms afford a mortifying contrast to the condition in which a British subject finds the neighbouring possessions of the British Crown.

With respect to the Colony of Newfoundland, I have been able to obtain no information whatever, except from sources open to the public at large. The Assembly of that island signified their intention of making an appeal to me respecting some differences with the Governor, which had their immediate origin in a dispute with a Judge. Owing, probably, to the uncertain and tardy means of communication between Quebec and that island, I received no further communication on this or any other subject, until after my arrival in England, when I received an Address expressive of regret at my departure.

I know nothing, therefore, of the state of things in Newfoundland, except that there is, and long has been, the ordinary colonial collision between the representative body on one side, and the executive on the other; that the representatives have no influence on the composition or the proceedings of the executive Government; and that the dispute is now carried on, as in Canada, by impeachments of various public officers on one hand, and prorogations on the other. I am inclined to think that the cause of these disorders is to be found in the same constitutional defects as those which I have signalized in the rest of the North American Colonies. If it be true, that there exists in this island a state of society which renders it unadvisable that the whole of the local government should be entirely left to the inhabitants, I believe that it would be much better to incorporate this Colony with a larger community, than to attempt to continue the present experiment of governing it by a constant collision of constitutional powers.

DISPOSAL OF PUBLIC LANDS

I have mentioned the peculiar importance which, in newly-settled societies, is attached to works for creating and improving the means of communication. But in such communities, and especially when only a small proportion of the land has been occupied by settlers, there is a still more momentous subject of public concern. I allude to an operation of Government, which has a paramount influence over the happiness of individuals, and the progress of society towards wealth and greatness. I am speaking of the disposal, by the Government, of the lands of the new country. In old countries no such matter ever occupies public attention; in new colonies, planted on a fertile and extensive territory, this is the object of the deepest moment to all, and the first business of the Government. Upon the manner in which this business is conducted, it may almost be said that every thing else depends. If lands are not bestowed on the inhabitants and new-comers with a generous hand, the society endures the evils of an old and over-peopled state, with the superadded inconveniences that belong to a wild country. They are pinched for room even in the wilderness, are prevented from choosing the most fertile soils and favourable situations, and are debarred from cultivating that large extent of soil, in proportion to the hands at work, which can alone compensate, in quantity of produce, for the rude nature of husbandry in the wilderness. If, on the other hand, the land is bestowed with careless profusion, great evils of another kind are produced. Large tracts become the property of individuals, who leave their lands unsettled and untouched. Deserts are thus interposed between the industrious settlers; the natural difficulties of communication are greatly enhanced; the inhabitants are not merely scattered over a wide space of country, but are separated from each other by impassable wastes; the cultivator is cut off or far remove from a market in which to dispose of his surplus produce, and procure other commodities; and the greatest obstacles exist to co-operation in labour, to exchange, to the division of employments, to combination for municipal or other public purposes, to the growth of towns, to public worship, to regular education, to the spread of news, to the acquisition of common knowledge, and even to the civilizing influences of mere intercourse for amusement. Monotonous and stagnant indeed must ever be the state of a people who are permanently condemned to such separation from each other. If, moreover, the land of a new country is so carelessly surveyed that the boundaries of property are incorrectly or inadequately defined, the Government lays up a store of mischievous litigation for the people. Whatever delay takes place in perfecting the titles of individuals to lands alienated by the Government, occasions equal uncertainty and insecurity of property. If the acquisition of land, in whatever quantities, is made difficult or troublesome, or is subjected to any needless uncertainty or delay, applicants are irritated, settlement is hindered, and immigration to the colony is discouraged, as emigration from it is promoted. If very different methods of proceeding have effect in the same colony, or in different parts of the same group of colonies, the operation of some can scarcely fail to interfere with or counteract the operation of others; so that the object of the Government must somewhere, or at some time, be defeated. And frequent changes of system are sure to be very injurious, not only by probably displeasing those who either obtain land just before, or desire to obtain some just after, each change, but also by giving a character of irregularity, uncertainty, and even mystery, to the most important proceeding of Government. In this way settlement and emigration are discouraged; inasmuch as the people, both of the Colony and of the mother country, are deprived of all confidence in the permanency of any system, and of any familiar acquaintance with any of the temporary methods. It would be easy to cite many other examples of the influence of Government in this matter. I will mention but one more here. If the disposal of public lands is administered partially – with favour to particular persons or classes – a sure result is, the anger of all who do not benefit by such favouritism (the far greater number, of course), and consequently, the general unpopularity of the Government.

Under suppositions the reverse of these, the best, instead of the worst, effects would be produced; a constant and regular supply of new land in due proportion to the wants of a population increasing by births and immigration; all the advantages to which facilities of transport and communication are essential; certainty of limits and security of title to property in land; the greatest facilities in acquiring the due quantity; the greatest encouragements to immigration and settlement; the most rapid progress of the people in material comfort and social improvement, and a general sense of obligation to the Government. What a contrast do the two pictures present! Neither of them is over coloured; and a mere glance at both suffices to show that in the North American Colonies of England, as in the United States, the function of authority most full of good or evil consequences has been the disposal of public land. . . .

In the United States, ever since the year 1796, the disposal of public land not already appropriated to particular states, has been strictly regulated by a law of Congress; not by different laws for the various parts of the country, but by one law for the whole of the public lands, and a law which we may judge to have been conducive to the prosperity of the people, both from its obvious good effects, and from its almost unquestioned continuance for so many years. In the British North American Colonies, with one partial exception, there never has been, until quite recently, any law upon the subject. The whole of the public lands have been deemed the property of the Crown, and the whole of the administration for disposing of them to individuals, with a view to settlement, has been conducted by officers of the Crown; under instructions from the Treasury or the Colonial Department in England. The Provincial Assemblies, except quite recently in New Brunswick and Upper Canada, have never had any voice in this matter; nor is the popular control in those two cases much more than nominal. The Imperial Parliament has never interfered but once, when, leaving all other things untouched, it enacted the unhappy system of 'Clergy Reserves'. With these very slight exceptions, the Lords of the Treasury and Colonial Secretary of State for the time being have been the only legislators; and the provincial agents of the Colonial Secretary, responsible to him alone, have been the sole executors.

The system of the United States appears to combine all the chief requisites of the greatest efficiency. It is uniform throughout the vast federation; it is unchangeable save by Congress, and has never been materially altered; it renders the acquisition of new land easy, and yet, by means of a price, restricts appropriation to the actual wants of the settler; it is so simple as to be readily understood; it provides for accurate surveys and against needless delays; it gives an instant and secure title; and it admits of no favouritism, but distributes the public property amongst all classes and persons upon precisely equal terms. That system has promoted an amount of immigration and settlement, of which the history of the world affords no other example; and it has produced to the United States a revenue which has averaged about half a million sterling per annum, and has amounted in one twelvemonth to above four millions sterling, or more than the whole expenditure of the Federal Government.

In the North American Colonies there never has been any system. Many different methods have been practised, and this not only in the different colonies, but in every Colony at different times, and within the same Colony at the same time. The greatest diversity and most frequent alteration would almost seem to have been the objects in view. In only one respect has there been uniformity. Every where the greatest profusion has taken place, so that in all the Colonies, and nearly in every part of each Colony, more, and very much more land has been alienated by the Government, than the grantees had at the time, or now have the means of reclaiming from a state of wilderness; and yet in all the Colonies until lately, and in some of them still, it is either very difficult or next to impossible for a person of no influence to obtain any of the public land. More or less in all the Colonies, and in some of them to an extent which would not be credited, if the fact were not established by unquestionable testimony, the surveys have been inaccurate, and the boundaries, or even the situation of estates, are proportionably uncertain. Every where needless delays have harassed and exasperated applicants; and every where, more or less, I am sorry but compelled to add, gross favouritism has prevailed in the disposal of public lands. . . .

The results of long misgovernment in this department are such as might have been anticipated by any person understanding the subject. The administration of the public lands, instead of always yielding a revenue, cost for a long while more than it produced. But this is, I venture to think, a trifling consideration when compared with others. There is one in particular which has occurred to every observant traveller in these regions, which is a constant theme of boast in the States bordering upon our Colonies, and a subject of loud complaint within the Colonies. I allude to the striking contrast which is presented between the American and the British sides of the frontier line in respect to every sign of productive industry, increasing wealth, and progressive civilization.

By describing one side, and reversing the picture, the other would be also described. On the American side, all is activity and bustle. The forest has been widely cleared; every year numerous settlements are formed, and thousands of farms are created out of the waste; the country is intersected by common roads; canals and railroads are finished, or in the course of formation; the ways of communication and transport are crowded with people, and enlivened by numerous carriages and large steam-boats. The observer is surprised at the number of harbours on the lakes, and the number of vessels they contain; while bridges, artificial landing-places, and commodious wharves are formed in all directions as soon as required. Good houses, warehouses, mills, inns, villages, towns, and even great cities, are almost seen to spring up out of the desert. Every village has its schoolhouse and place of public worship. Every town has many of both, with its township buildings, its book stores, and probably one or two banks and newspapers; and the cities, with their fine churches, their great hotels, their exchanges, courthouses and municipal halls, of stone or marble, so new and fresh as to mark the recent existence of the forest where they now stand, would be admired in any part of the Old World. On the British side of the line, with the exception of a few favoured spots, where some approach to American prosperity is apparent, all seems waste and desolate. There is but one railroad in all British America, and that, running between the St. Lawrence and Lake Champlain, is only fifteen miles long. The ancient city of Montreal, which is naturally the commercial capital of the Canadas, will not bear the least comparison, in any respect, with Buffalo, which is a creation of yesterday. But it is not in the difference between the larger towns on the two sides that we shall find the best evidence of our own inferiority. That painful but undeniable truth is most manifest in the country districts through which the line of national separation passes for 1,000 miles. There, on the side of both the Canadas, and also of New Brunswick and Nova Scotia, a widely scattered population, poor, and apparently unenterprising, though hardy and industrious, separated from each other by tracts of intervening forest, without towns and markets, almost without roads, living in mean houses, drawing little more than a rude subsistence from ill-cultivated land, and seemingly incapable of improving their condition, present the most instructive contrast to their enterprising and thriving neighbours on the American side. . . . This view is confirmed by another fact equally indisputable. Throughout the frontier, from Amherstburg to the ocean, the market value of land is much greater on the American than on the British side. In not a few parts of the frontier this difference amounts to as much as a thousand per cent., and in some cases even more. . . . It might be supposed by persons unacquainted with the frontier country, that the soil on the American side is of very superior natural fertility. I am positively assured that this is by no means the case; but that, on the whole, superior natural fertility belongs to the British territory. In Upper Canada, the whole of the great peninsula between Lakes Erie and Huron, comprising nearly half the available land of the Province, consists of gently-undulating alluvial soil, and, with a smaller proportion of inferior land than probably any other tract of similar extent in that part of North America, is generally considered the best grain country on that continent. The soil of the border townships of Lower Canada is allowed, on all hands, to be superior to that of the border townships of New York, Vermont, and New Hampshire; while the lands of New Brunswick, equal in natural fertility to those of Maine, enjoy superior natural means of communication. I do not believe that the universal difference in the value of land can any where be fairly attributed to natural causes.

Still less can we attribute to such causes another circumstance, which in some measure accounts for the different values of property, and which has a close relation to the subject of the public lands. I mean the great amount of re-emigration from the British Colonies to the border States. This is a notorious fact. Nobody denies it; almost every colonist speaks of it with regret. . . .[*Calculations indicate*] that the number of people who have emigrated from Upper Canada to the United States, since 1829, must be equal to more than half the number who have entered the Province during the eight years. Mr. Baillie, the present Commissioner of Crown Lands in New Brunswick, says, 'a great many emigrants arrive in the Province, but they generally proceed to the United States, as there is not sufficient encouragement for them in this Province.' Mr. Morris, the present Commissioner of Crown Lands, and Surveyor General of Nova Scotia, speaks in almost similar terms of the emigrants who reach that Province by way of Halifax.

I am far from asserting that the very inferior value of land in the British Colonies, and the re-emigration of immigrants, are altogether occasioned by mismanagement in the disposal of public lands. Other defects and errors of government must have had a share in producing these lamentable results; but I only speak the opinion of all the more intelligent, and, let me add, some of the most loyal of Your Majesty's subjects in North America when I say that this has been the principal cause of these great evils. . . .

Of the lands granted in Upper and Lower Canada, upwards of 3,000,000 acres consist of 'Clergy Reserves', being for the most part lots of 200 acres each, scattered at regular intervals over the whole face of the townships, and remaining, with few exceptions, entirely wild to this day. The evils produced by the system of reserving land for the clergy have become notorious, even in this country; and a common opinion I believe prevails here, not only that the system has been abandoned, but that measures of remedy have been adopted. This opinion is incorrect in both points. In respect of every new township in both Provinces, reserves are still made for the clergy, just as before; and the Act of the Imperial Parliament, which permits the sale of clergy reserves, applies to only one-fourth of the quantity. The Select Committee of the House of Commons on the Civil Government of Canada reported, in 1828, that 'these reserved lands, as they are at present distributed over the country, retard more than any other circumstance the improvement of the Colony, lying as they do in detached portions in each township, and intervening between the occupations of actual settlers, who have no means of cutting roads through the woods and morasses, which thus separate them from their neighbours.' This description is perfectly applicable to the present state of things. In no perceptible degree has the evil been remedied.

The system of clergy reserves was established by the Act of 1791, commonly called the Constitutional Act, which directed that, in respect of all grants made by the Crown, a quantity equal to one-seventh of the land so granted should be reserved for the clergy. A quantity equal to one-seventh of all grants would be one-eighth of each township, or of all the public land. Instead of this proportion, the practice has been, ever since the Act passed, and in the clearest violation of its provisions, to set apart for the clergy in Upper Canada a seventh of all the land, which is a quantity equal to a sixth of the land granted. There have been appropriated for this purpose 300,000 acres, which, legally, it is manifest, belong to the public. And of the amount for which clergy reserves have been sold in that Province, namely £ 317,000 (of which about £ 100,000 have been already received and invested in the English funds), the sum of about £ 45,000 should belong to the public.

In Lower Canada, the same violation of the law has taken place, with this difference – that upon every sale of Crown and clergy reserves, a fresh reserve for the clergy has been made, equal to a fifth of such reserves. The result has been the appropriation for the clergy of 673,567 acres, instead of 446,000, being an excess of 227,559 acres, or half as much again as they ought to have received. The Lower Canada fund already produced by sales amounts to £ 50,000, of which, therefore, a third, or about £ 16,000, belong to the public. If, without any reform of this abuse, the whole of the unsold clergy reserves in both Provinces should fetch the average price at which such lands have hitherto sold, the public would be wronged to the amount of about £ 280,000; and the reform of this abuse will produce a certain and almost immediate gain to the public of £ 60,000. . . . I am desirous of stating my own conviction that the clergy have had no part in this great misappropriation of the public property, but that it has arisen entirely from heedless misconception, or some other error, of the civil government of both Provinces.

The great objection to reserves for the clergy is, that those for whom the land is set apart never have attempted, and never could successfully attempt, to cultivate or settle the property, and that, by that special appropriation, so much land is withheld from settlers, and kept in a state of waste, to the serious injury of all settlers in its neighbourhood. But it would be a great mistake to suppose that this is the only practice by which such injury has been, and still is, inflicted on actual settlers. In the two Canadas, especially, the practice of rewarding, or attempting to reward, public services by grants of public land, has produced, and is still producing, a degree of injury to actual settlers which it is difficult to conceive without having witnessed it. The very principle of such grants is bad, inasmuch as, under any circumstances, they must lead to an amount of appropriation beyond the wants of the community, and greatly beyond the proprietor's means of cultivation and settlement. In both the Canadas, not only has this principle been pursued with reckless profusion, but the local executive Governments have managed, by violating or evading the instructions which they received from the Secretary of State, to add incalculably to the mischiefs that would have arisen at all events.

In Upper Canada, 3,200,000 acres have been granted to 'U. E. Loyalists', being refugees from the United States who settled in the Province before 1787, and their children; 730,000 acres to militiamen, 450,000 acres to discharged soldiers and sailors, 255,000 acres to magistrates and barristers, 136,000 acres to Executive Councillors and their families, 50,000 acres to five Legislative Councillors and their families, 36,900 acres to clergymen as private property, 264,000 acres to persons contracting to make surveys, 92,526 acres to officers of the army and navy, 500,000 acres for the endowment of schools, 48,520 acres to Colonel Talbot, 12,000 acres to the heirs of General Brock, and 12,000 acres to Doctor Mountain, a former Bishop of Quebec; making altogether, with the clergy reserves, nearly half of all the surveyed land in the Province. In Lower Canada, exclusively of grants to refugee loyalists, as to the amount of which the Crown Lands' Department could furnish me with no information, 450,000 acres have been granted to militiamen, to Executive Councillors 72,000 acres, to Governor Milnes about 48,000 acres, to Mr. Cushing and another upwards of 100,000 acres (as a reward for giving information in a case of high treason), to officers and soldiers 200,000 acres, and to 'leaders of townships' 1,457,209 acres, making altogether, with the clergy reserves, rather more than half of the surveyed lands originally at the disposal of the Crown.

In Upper Canada, a very small proportion (perhaps less than a tenth) of the land thus granted has been even occupied by settlers, much less reclaimed and cultivated. In Lower Canada, with the exception of a few townships bordering on the American frontier, which have been comparatively well settled, in despite of the proprietors, by American squatters, it may be said that nineteen-twentieths of these grants are still unsettled, and in a perfectly wild state.

No other result could have been expected in the case of those classes of grantees whose station would preclude them from settling in the wilderness, and whose means would enable them to avoid exertion for giving immediate value to their grants; and, unfortunately, the land which was intended for persons of a poorer order, who might be expected to improve it by their labour, has, for the most part, fallen into the hands of land-jobbers of the class just mentioned, who have never thought of settling in person, and who retain the land in its present wild state, speculating upon its acquiring a value at some distant day, when the demand for land shall have increased through the increase of population. . . .

[*In spite of the British Government's attempt to introduce a sale system, immense quantities of land have continued to be disposed of by free grants. Surveys have been inaccurate.*]

In the United States, the title to land purchased of the Government is obtained immediately and securely on payment of the purchase-money. In all the British Colonies, there is more or less of useless formality and consequent delay in procuring a complete title to land which has been paid for. . . . A recent Act of the Legislature of Upper Canada has greatly mitigated this evil, which however remains in full force in Lower Canada. . . . The results of this general mismanagement are thus illustrated by the chief agent for emigrants in Upper Canada.

'The principal evils to which settlers in a new township are subject result from the scantiness of population. A township contains 80,000 acres of land; one-seventh is reserved for the clergy and one-seventh for the Crown; consequently five-sevenths remain for the disposal of Government, a large proportion of which is taken up by grants to U. E. loyalists, militiamen, officers and others: the far greater part of these grants remain in an unimproved state.

These blocks of wild land place the actual settler in an almost hopeless condition; he can hardly expect, during his lifetime, to see his neighbourhood contain a population sufficiently dense to support mills, schools, post-offices, places of worship, markets or shops; and without these, civilization retrogrades. Roads under such circumstances can neither be opened by the settlers, nor kept in proper repair, even if made by the Government. The inconvenience arising from want of roads is very great, and is best illustrated by an instance which came under my own observation in 1834. I met a settler from the township of Warwick on the Caradoc Plains, returning from the grist mill at Westminster, with the flour and bran of thirteen bushels of wheat; he had a yoke of oxen and a horse attached to his waggon, and had been absent nine days, and did not expect to reach home until the following evening. Light as his load was, he assured me that he had to unload wholly or in part several times, and, after driving his waggon through the swamps, to pick out a road through the woods where the swamps or gullies were fordable, and to carry the bags on his back and replace them in the waggon. Supposing the services of the man and his team to be worth two dollars per day, the expense of transport would be twenty dollars. As the freight of wheat from Toronto to Liverpool [England] is rather less the 2s. 6d. per bushel, it follows that a person living in this city could get the same wheat ground on the banks of the Mersey, and the flour and bran returned to him at a much less expense than he could transport it from the rear of Warwick to Westminster and back – a distance less than 90 miles. Since 1834 a grist-mill has been built in Adelaide, the adjoining township, which is a great advantage to the Warwick settlers; but the people in many parts of the Province still suffer great inconvenience from the same cause.' . . .

One of the most remarkable instances of evils resulting from profuse grants of land is to be found in Prince Edward's Island. Nearly the whole of this island (about 1,400,000 acres) was alienated in one day, in very large grants, chiefly to absentees, and upon conditions which have been wholly disregarded. The extreme improvidence which dictated these grants is obvious: the neglect of the Government as to enforcing the conditions of the grants, in spite of the constant efforts of the people and the legislature to force upon its attention the evils under which they laboured, is not less so. The great bulk of the island is still possessed by absentees, who hold it as a sort of reversionary interest, which requires no present attention, but may become valuable some day or other through the growing wants of the inhabitants. But in the mean time, the inhabitants are subjected to the greatest inconvenience, nay, to the most serious injury, from the state of property in land. The absent proprietors neither improve the land, nor will let others improve it. They retain the land, and keep it in a state of wilderness. . . .

In the above enumeration of facts, I do not profess to have exhausted the long catalogue of evils and abuses which were brought to my notice. But I have stated enough, I trust, to establish the position with which I set out, – that the disposal of public lands in a new country has more influence on the prosperity of the people than any other branch of Government; and further to make it evident, that the still existing evils which have been occasioned by mismanagement in this department, are so great and general as to require a comprehensive and effectual remedy, applied to all the Colonies, before any merely political reform can be expected to work well.

EMIGRATION

I now proceed to another subject, which, though ultimately connected with the colonization and improvement of the Provinces, must yet be considered separately; for it is one in which not the colonial population only, but the people of the United Kingdom have a deep and immediate interest. I allude to the manner in which the emigration of the poorer classes from Great Britain and Ireland to the North American Colonies has hitherto been conducted.

About nine years ago, measures were for the first time taken to ascertain the number of immigrants arriving at Quebec by sea. The number during these nine years have been 263,089; and there have been as many in one year (1832) as 51,746. In the year before, the number was 50,254; in 1833, 21,752; in 1834, 30,935; in 1835, 12,527; in 1836, 27,728; in 1837, 22,500; and in 1838, only

4,992. The great diminution in 1838 was occasioned solely, I
believe, by the vague fears entertained in this country of dangers
presented by the distracted state of the Colonies. I am truly surprised, however, that emigration of the poorer classes to the
Canadas did not almost entirely cease some years ago; and that
this would have been the case, if the facts which I am about to state
had been generally known in the United Kingdom, there can, I
think, be no rational doubt.

Dr. Morrin, a gentleman of high professional and personal character, Inspecting Physician of the Port of Quebec, and Commissioner of the Marine and Emigrant Hospital, says: 'I am almost at
a loss for words to describe the state in which the emigrants frequently arrived; with a few exceptions, the state of the ships was
quite abominable; so much so, that the harbour-master's boatmen
had no difficulty, at the distance of gun-shot, either when the wind
was favourable or in a dead calm, in distinguishing by the odour
alone a crowded emigrant ship. I have known as many as from 30
to 40 deaths to have taken place, in the course of a voyage, from
typhus fever, on board a ship containing from 500 to 600 passengers; and within six weeks after the arrival of some vessels, and the
landing of the passengers at Quebec, the hospital has received
upwards of 100 patients at different times from among them. On
one occasion, I have known nearly 400 patients at one time in the
Emigrant Hospital of Quebec, for whom there was no sufficient
accommodation; and in order to provide them with some shelter,
Dr. Painchaud, the then attending physician, with the aid of other
physicians, incurred a personal debt to the Quebec Bank to a considerable amount, which, however, was afterwards paid by the
Provincial Legislature.' . . . 'The mortality was considerable among
the emigrants at that time, and was attended with most disastrous
consequences; children being left without protection, and wholly
dependent on the casual charity of the inhabitants of the city. As
to those who were not sick on arriving, I have to say that they were
generally forcibly landed by the masters of vessels, without a
shilling in their pockets to procure them a night's lodging, and very
few of them with the means of subsistence for more than a very
short period. They commonly established themselves along the
wharfs and at the different landing-places, crowding into any place

of shelter they could obtain, where they subsisted principally upon the charity of the inhabitants. For six weeks at a time from the commencement of the emigrant-ship season, I have known the shores of the river along Quebec, for about a mile and a half, crowded with these unfortunate people, the places of those who might have moved off being constantly supplied by fresh arrivals, and there being daily drafts of from 10 to 30 taken to the hospital with infectious disease. The consequence was it spread among the inhabitants of the city, especially in the districts in which these unfortunate creatures had established themselves. Those who were not absolutely without money, got into low taverns and boarding-houses and cellars, where they congregated in immense numbers, and where their state was not any better than it had been on board ship. This state of things existed within my knowledge from 1826 to 1832, and probably for some years previously.'

Dr. Morrin's testimony is confirmed by that of Dr. Skey, Deputy Inspector General of Hospitals, and President of the Quebec Emigrants Society. He says, 'Upon the arrival of emigrants in the river, a great number of sick have landed. A regular importation of contagious disease into this country has annually taken place; that disease originated on board ship, and was occasioned, I should say, by bad management in consequence of the ships being ill-found, ill-provisioned, overcrowded, and ill-ventilated. I should say that the mortality during the voyage has been dreadful; to such an extent that, in 1834, the inhabitants of Quebec, taking alarm at the number of shipwrecks, at the mortality of the passengers, and the fatal diseases which accumulated at the Quarantine Establishment at Grosse Isle and the Emigrant Hospital of this city, involving the inhabitants of Quebec in the calamity, called upon the Emigrants Society to take the subject into consideration, and make representations to the Government thereon.'

The circumstances described took place under the operation of the Act 9th Geo. 4, commonly called the Passengers Act, which was passed in 1825, repealed in 1827, and re-enacted in 1828. In 1835, an amended Passengers Act was passed, the main features of which, so far as they differed from the former Act, are stated to have been suggested by the Quebec Emigrants Society. Mr. Jessopp, Collector of Customs at the Port of Quebec, speaking of emigration under the last Act, says, 'It very often happens that poorer emigrants have not a sufficiency of provisions for the voyage; that they should have a sufficiency of provisions, might be enforced under the Act, which authorizes the inspection of provisions by the outport agent for emigrants. Many instances have come to my knowledge in which, from insufficiency of provisions, emigrants have been thrown upon the humanity of the captain, or the charity of their fellow-passengers. It will appear, also, from the fact that many vessels have more emigrant passengers than the number allowed by law, that sufficient attention is not paid at the outport to enforce the provisions of the Act, as to the proportions between the numbers and the tonnage. Such instances have not occurred this season [1838], emigration having almost ceased, in consequence, I presume, of the political state of the Province; but, last year, there were several instances in which prosecution took place. Vessels are chartered for emigration by persons whose sole object is to make money, and who make a trade of evading the provisions of the Act. This applies particularly to vessels coming from Ireland. We have found, in very many instances, that, in vessels chartered in this way, the number was greater than allowed by law; and the captains have declared, that the extra numbers smuggled themselves, or were smuggled, on board, and were only discovered after the vessel had been several days at sea. This might be prevented by a stricter examination of the vessel. The Imperial Act requires that the names, ages, sex and occupation of each passenger should be entered in a list, certified by the customs officer at the outport, and delivered by the captain with the ship's papers to the officers of the customs here. Lists, purporting to be correct, are always delivered to the tide-surveyor, whose duty it is to muster the passengers, and compare them with the list; and this list, in many instances, is wholly incorrect as to names and ages.' . . . 'The object of the falsification of the ages is to defraud the revenue by evading the tax upon emigrants.' . . . 'The falsification of names produces no inconvenience; and I have only referred to it for the purpose of showing the careless manner in which the system is worked by the agents in the United Kingdom.' But Dr. Poole, Inspecting Physician of the Quarantine Station at Grosse Isle, further explains the fraud, saying, 'These falsifications are, first, for the purpose of evading the emigrant tax, which is levied in proportion to age, and the common fraud is to understate the age; and, secondly, for the purpose of carrying more passengers than the law allows, by counting grown persons as children, of which last, the law allows a larger proportion to tonnage than of grown persons. This fraud is very common, of frequent occurrence, and it arises manifestly from want of inspection at home.'

From this and other evidence, it will appear that the Amended Passengers Act alone, as it has been hitherto administered, would have afforded no efficient remedy of the dreadful evils described by Dr. Morrin and Dr. Skey. Those evils have, however, been greatly mitigated by two measures of the provincial Government: first, the application of a tax upon passengers from the United Kingdom, to providing shelter, medical attendance, and the means of further transport to destitute emigrants; secondly, the establishment of the Quarantine Station at Grosse Isle, a desert island some miles below Quebec, where all vessels arriving with cases of contagious disease are detained; the diseased persons are removed to a hospital, and emigrants not affected with disease are landed, and subjected to some discipline for the purpose of cleanliness, the ship also being cleaned while they remain on shore. By these arrangements, the accumulation of wretched paupers at Quebec, and the spread of contagious disease, are prevented. An arrangement, made only in 1837, whereby the Quarantine physician at Grosse Isle decides whether or not an emigrant ship shall be detained there or proceed on its voyage, has, to use the words of Dr. Poole, 'operated as a premium to care and attention on the part of the captain, and has had a salutary effect on the comfort of the emigrants.'

I cordially rejoice in these improvements, but would observe that the chief means by which the good has been accomplished indicates the greatness of the evil that remains. The necessity of a Quarantine Establishment for preventing the importation of contagious disease from Britain to her Colonies, as if the emigrants had departed from one of those Eastern countries which are the home of the plague, shows beyond a doubt either that our very system of emigration is most defective, or that it is most carelessly administered. . . .

The Agent General's Report, which was laid before Parliament last year, does not even allude to another feature of our system of emigration, on which I have yet to offer some remarks. However defective the present arrangements for the passage of emigrants, they are not more so than the means employed to provide for the comfort and prosperity of this class after their arrival in the Colonies. Indeed, it may be said that no such means are in existence. It will be seen, from the very meagre evidence of the Agent for Emigrants at Quebec, that the office which he holds is next to useless. I cast no blame on the officer, but would only explain, that he has no powers, nor scarcely any duties to perform. Nearly all that is done for the advantage of poor emigrants, after they have passed the Lazaretto, is performed by the Quebec and Montreal Emigrants Societies – benevolent associations of which I am bound to speak in the highest terms of commendation; to which, indeed, we owe whatever improvement has taken place in the yet unhealthy mid-passage, but which, as they were instituted for the main purpose of relieving the inhabitants of the two cities from the miserable spectacle of crowds of unemployed and starving emigrants, so have their efforts produced little other good than that of facilitating the progress of poor emigrants to the United States, where the industrious of every class are always sure of employment at good wages. In the Report on Emigration, to which I have alluded before, I find favourable mention of the principle of entrusting some parts of the conduct of emigration rather to 'charitable committees' than to 'an ordinary department of Government'. From this doctrine I feel bound to express my entire dissent. I can scarcely imagine any obligation which it is more incumbent on Government to fulfill, than that of guarding against an improper selection of emigrants, and securing to poor persons disposed to emigrate every possible facility and assistance, from the moment of their intending to leave this country to that of their comfortable establishment in the Colony. No less an obligation is incurred by the Government, when, as is now the case, they invite poor persons to emigrate by tens of thousands every year. It would, indeed, be very mischievous if the Government were to deprive emigrants of self-reliance, by doing every thing for them: but when the State leads great numbers of people into a situation in which it is impossible that they should do well without assistance, then the obligation to assist them begins; and it never ends, in my humble opinion, until those who have relied on the truth and paternal care of the Government, are placed in a situation to take care of themselves. . . .

It is far from my purpose, in laying these facts before Your Majesty, to discourage emigration to Your North American colonies. On the contrary, I am satisfied that the chief value of those colonies to the mother country consists in their presenting a field where millions even, of those who are distressed at home, might be established in plenty and happiness. All the gentlemen whose evidence I have last quoted, are warm advocates of systematic emigration. I object, along with them, only to such emigration as now takes place – without forethought, preparation, method or system of any kind.

GENERAL REVIEW AND RECOMMENDATIONS

I have now brought under review the most prominent features of the condition and institutions of the British Colonies in North America. It has been my painful task to exhibit a state of things which cannot be contemplated without grief by all who value the well-being of our colonial fellow-countrymen, and the integrity of the British Empire. I have described the operation of those causes of division which unhappily exist in the very composition of society; the disorder produced by the working of an ill-contrived constitutional system, and the practical mismanagement which these fundamental defects have generated in every department of Government.

It is not necessary that I should take any pains to prove that this is a state of things which should not, which cannot continue. Neither the political nor the social existence of any community can bear much longer the operation of those causes, which have in Lower Canada already produced a long practical cessation of the regular course of constitutional government, which have occasioned the violation and necessitated the absolute suspension of the provincial constitution, and which have resulted in two insurrections, two substitutions of martial for civil law, and two periods of a general abeyance of every guarantee that is considered essential for the protection of a British subject's rights. I have already described the state of feeling which prevails among each of the contending parties, or rather races; their all-pervading and irreconcileable enmity to each other; the entire and irremediable disaffection of the whole French population, as well as the suspicion with which the English regard the Imperial Government; and the determination of the French, together with the tendency of the English to seek for a redress of their intolerable present evils in the chances of a separation from Great Britain. The disorders of Lower Canada admit of no delay; the existing form of government is but a temporary and forcible subjugation. The recent constitution is one of which neither party would tolerate the re-establishment, and of which the bad working has been such, that no friend to liberty or to order could desire to see the Province again subjected to its mischievous influence. Whatever may be the difficulty of discovering a remedy, its urgency is certain and obvious.

Nor do I believe that the necessity for adopting some extensive and decisive measure for the pacification of Upper Canada, is at all less imperative. From the account which I have given of the causes of disorder in that Province, it will be seen that I do not consider them by any means of such a nature as to be irremediable, or even to be susceptible of no remedy, that shall not effect an organic change in the existing constitution. It cannot be denied indeed that the continuance of the many practical grievances, which I have described as subjects of complaint, and, above all, the determined resistance to such a system of responsible government as would give the people a real control over its own destinies, have, together with the irritation caused by the late insurrection, induced a large portion of the population to look with envy at the material prosperity of their neighbours in the United States, under a perfectly free and eminently responsible government; and, in despair of obtaining such benefits under their present institutions, to desire the adoption of a Republican constitution, or even an incorporation with the American Union. But I am inclined to think that such feelings have made no formidable or irreparable progress; on the contrary, I believe that all the discontented parties, and especially the reformers of Upper Canada, look with considerable confidence to the result of my mission. The different parties believe that when the case is once fairly put before the mother country, the desired changes in the policy of their government will be readily granted: they are now tranquil, and I believe loyal; determined to abide the decision of the Home Government, and to defend their property and their country against rebellion and invasion. But I cannot but express my belief, that this is the last effort of their almost exhausted patience, and that the disappointment of their hopes on the present occasion, will destroy for ever their expectation of good resulting from British connexion. I do not mean to say that they will renew the rebellion, much less do I imagine that they will array themselves in such force as will be able to tear the government of their country from the hands of the great military power which Great Britain can bring against them. If now frustrated in their expectations, and kept in hopeless subjection to rulers irresponsible to the people, they will, at best, only await in sullen prudence the contingencies which may render the preservation of the Province dependent on the devoted loyalty of the great mass of its population.

With respect to the other North American Provinces, I will not speak of such evils as imminent, because I firmly believe that whatever discontent there may be, no irritation subsists which in any way weakens the strong feeling of attachment to the British Crown and Empire. Indeed, throughout the whole of the North American Provinces there prevails among the British population an affection for the mother country, and a preference for its institutions, which a wise and firm policy, on the part of the Imperial Government, may make the foundation of a safe, honourable and enduring connexion. But even this feeling may be impaired, and I must warn those in whose hands the disposal of their destinies rests, that a blind reliance on the all-enduring loyalty of our countrymen may be carried too far. It is not politic to waste and cramp their resources, and to allow the backwardness of the British Provinces every where to present a melancholy contrast to the progress and prosperity of the United States. Throughout the course of the preceding pages, I have constantly had occasion to refer to this contrast. I have not hesitated to do so, though no man's just pride in his country, and firm attachments to its institutions, can be more deeply shocked by the mortifying admission of inferiority. But I should ill discharge my duty to Your Majesty, I should give but an imperfect view of the real condition of these Provinces, were I to detail mere statistical facts without describing the feelings which they generate in those who observe them daily, and daily experience their influence on their own fortunes. The contrast which I have described, is the theme of every traveller who visits these countries, and who observes on one side of the line the abundance, and on the other the scarcity of every sign of material prosperity which thriving agriculture and flourishing cities indicate, and of that civilization which schools and churches testify even to the outward senses. While it excites the exultation of the enemies of British institutions, its reality is more strongly evinced by the reluctant admission of Your Majesty's most attached subjects. It is no true loyalty to hide from Your Majesty's knowledge the existence of an evil which it is in Your Majesty's power, as it is Your Majesty's benevolent pleasure, to remove. For the possibility of reform is yet afforded by the patient and fervent attachment which Your Majesty's English subjects in all these Provinces still feel to their allegiance and their mother country. Calm reflection and loyal confidence have retained these feelings unimpaired, even by the fearful drawback of the general belief that every man's property is of less value on the British than on the opposite side of the boundary. It is time to reward this noble confidence, by showing that men have not indulged in vain the hope that there is a power in British institutions to rectify existing evils, and to produce in their place a well-being which no other dominion could give. It is not in the terrors of the law, or in the might of our armies, that the secure and honourable bond of connexion is to be found. It exists in the beneficial operation of those British institutions which link the utmost development of freedom and civilization with the stable authority of an hereditary monarchy, and which, if rightly organized and fairly administered in the Colonies, as in Great Britain, would render a change of institutions only an additional evil to the loss of the protection and commerce of the British Empire.

But while I count thus confidently on the possibility of a permanent and advantageous retention of our connexion with these important Colonies, I must not disguise the mischief and danger of holding them in their present state of disorder. I rate the chances of successful rebellion as the least danger in prospect. I do not doubt that the British Government can, if it choose to retain these dependencies at any cost, accomplish its purpose. I believe that it has the means of enlisting one part of the population against the other, and of garrisoning the Canadas with regular troops sufficient to awe all internal enemies. But even this will not be done without great expense and hazard. The experience of the last two years furnishes only a foretaste of the cost to which such a system of government will subject us. On the lowest calculation, the addition of a million a year to our annual colonial expenditure will barely enable us to attain this end. Without a change in our system of government, the discontent which now prevails, will spread and advance. As the cost of retaining these Colonies increases, their value will rapidly diminish. And if by such means the British Nation shall be content to retain a barren and injurious sovereignty, it will but tempt the chances of foreign aggression, by keeping continually exposed to a powerful and ambitious neighbour a distant dependency, in which an invader would find no resistance, but might rather reckon on active co-operation from a portion of the resident population.

I am far from presenting this risk in a manner calculated to irritate the just pride which would shrink from the thoughts of yielding to the menaces of a rival nation. Because, important as I consider the foreign relations of this question, I do not believe that there is now any very proximate danger of a collision with the United States, in consequence of that power desiring to take advantage of the disturbed state of the Canadas. In the Dispatch of the 9th of August I have described my impression of the state of feeling with respect to the Lower Canadian insurrection, which had existed, and was then in existence, in the United States. Besides the causes of hostile feeling which originate in the mere juxta-position of that power to our North American Provinces, I described the influence which had undoubtedly been exercised by that mistaken political sympathy with the insurgents of Lower Canada, which the inhabitants of the United States were induced to entertain. There is no people in the world so little likely as that of the United States to sympathize with the real feelings and policy of the French Canadians; no people so little likely to share in their anxiety to preserve ancient and barbarous laws, and to check the industry and improvement of their country, in order to gratify some idle and narrow notion of a petty and visionary nationality. The Americans who have visited Lower Canada, perfectly understand the real truth of the case; they see that the quarrel is a quarrel of races; and they certainly show very little inclination to take part with the French Canadians and their institutions. Of the great number of American travellers, coming from all parts of the Union, who visited Quebec during my residence there, and whose society I, together with the gentlemen attached to my mission, had the advantage of enjoying, not one ever expressed to any of us any approbation of, what may be termed, the national objects of the French Canadians, while many did not conceal a strong aversion to them. There is no people in the world to whom the French Canadian institutions are more intolerable, when circumstances compel submission to them. But the mass of the American people had judged of the quarrel from a distance: they had been obliged to form their judgment on the apparent grounds of the controversy; and were thus deceived, as all those are apt to be who judge under such circumstances, and on such grounds. The contest bore some resemblance to that great struggle of their own forefathers, which they regard with the highest pride. Like that, they believed it to be a contest of a Colony against the Empire, whose misconduct alienated their own country: they considered it to be a contest undertaken by a people professing to seek independence of distant control, and extension of popular privileges; and, finally, a contest of which the first blow was struck in consequence of a violation of a colonial constitution, and the appropriation of the colonial revenues without the consent of the colonists. It need not surprise us, that such apparently probable and sufficient causes were generally taken, by the people of the United States, as completely accounting for the whole dispute; that the analogy between the Canadian insurrection and the War of Independence was considered to be satisfactorily made out; and that a free and high-spirited people eagerly demonstrated its sympathy with those whom it regarded as gallantly attempting, with unequal means, to assert that glorious cause which its own fathers had triumphantly upheld.

In the case of Upper Canada, I believe the sympathy to have been much more strong and durable; and though the occasion of the contest was apparently less marked, I have no doubt that this was more than compensated by the similarity of language and manners, which enabled the rebels of the Upper Province to present their case much more easily and forcibly to those whose sympathy and aid they sought. The incidents of any struggle of a large portion of a people with its Government, are sure, at some time or another, to elicit some sympathy with those who appear, to the careless view of a foreign nation, only as martyrs to the popular cause, and as victims of a Government conducted on principles differing from its own. And I have no doubt that if the internal struggle be renewed, the sympathy from without will, at some time or another, reassume its former strength.

For it must be recollected that the natural ties of sympathy between the English population of the Canadas and the inhabitants of the frontier States of the Union are peculiarly strong. Not only do they speak the same language, live under laws having the same origin, and preserve the same customs and habits, but there is a positive alternation, if I may so express it, of the populations of the two countries. While large tracts of the British territory are peopled by American citizens, who still keep up a constant connexion with their kindred and friends, the neighbouring States are filled with emigrants from Great Britain, some of whom have quitted Canada after unavailing efforts to find there a profitable return for their capital and labour; and many of whom have settled in the United States, while other members of their families, and the companions of their youth, have taken up their abode on the other side of the frontier. I had no means of ascertaining the exact degree of truth in some statements which I have heard respecting the number of Irish settled in the State of New York; but it is commonly asserted that there are no less than 40,000 Irish in the militia of that State. The intercourse between these two divisions of what is, in fact, an identical population, is constant and universal. The border townships of Lower Canada are separated from the United States by an imaginary line; a great part of the frontier of Upper Canada by rivers, which are crossed in ten minutes; and the rest by lakes, which interpose hardly a six hours' passage between the inhabitants of each side. Every man's daily occupations bring him in contact with his neighbours on the other side of the line; the daily wants of one country are supplied by the produce of the other; and the population of each is in some degree dependent on the state of trade and the demands of the other. Such common wants beget an interest in the politics of each country among the citizens of the other. The newspapers circulate in some places almost equally on the different sides of the line; and men discover that their welfare is frequently as much involved in the political condition of their neighbours as of their own countrymen.

The danger of any serious mischief from this cause appears to me to be less at the present moment than for some time past. The events of the last year, and the circulation of more correct information respecting the real causes of contention, have apparently operated very successfully against the progress or continuance of this species of sympathy; and I have the satisfaction of believing that the policy which was pursued during my administration of the government, was very efficient in removing it. The almost complete unanimity of the press of the United States, as well as the assurances of individuals well conversant with the state of public opinion in that country, convince me, that the measures which I adopted met with a concurrence that completely turned the tide of feeling in favour of the British Government. Nor can I doubt, from the unvarying evidence that I have received from all persons who have recently travelled through the frontier states of the Union that there hardly exists, at the present moment, the slightest feeling which can properly be called sympathy. Whatever aid the insurgents have recently received from citizens of the United States, may either be attributed to those national animosities which are the too sure result of past wars, or to those undisguised projects of conquest and rapine which, since the invasion of Texas, find but too much favour among the daring population of the frontiers. Judging from the character and behaviour of the Americans most prominent in the recent aggressions on Upper Canada, they seem to have been produced mainly by the latter cause: nor does any cause appear to have secured to the insurgents of Lower Canada any very extensive aid, except that in money and munitions of war, of which the source cannot very clearly be traced. Hardly any Americans took part in the recent disturbances in Lower Canada. Last year, the outbreak was the signal for numerous public meetings in all the great cities of the frontier States, from Buffalo to New York. At these the most entire sympathy with the insurgents was openly avowed; large subscriptions were raised, and volunteers invited to join. Since the last outbreak no such manifestations have taken place: the meetings which the Nelsons and others have attempted in New York, Philadelphia, Washington, and elsewhere, have ended in complete failure; and, at the present moment, there does not exist the slightest indication of any sympathy with the objects of the Lower Canadian insurgents, or of any desire to co-operate with them for political purposes. The danger, however, which may be apprehended from the mere desire to repeat the scenes of Texas in the Canadas, is a danger from which we cannot be secure while the disaffection of any considerable portion of the population continues to give an appearance of weakness to our Government. It is in vain to expect that such attempts can wholly be repressed by the federal Government; or that they could even be effectually counteracted by the utmost exertion of its authority, if any sudden turn of affairs should again revive a strong and general sympathy with insurrection in Canada. Without dwelling on the necessary weakness of a merely federal Government – without adverting to the difficulty which authorities, dependent for their very existence on the popular will, find in successfully resisting a general manifestation of public feeling, the impossibility which any Government would find in restraining a population like that which dwells along the thousand miles of this frontier, must be obvious to all who reflect on the difficulty of maintaining the police of a dispersed community.

Nor is this danger itself unproductive of feelings which are in their turn calculated to produce yet further mischief. The loyal people of Canada, indignant at the constant damage and terror occasioned by incursions from the opposite shore, naturally turn their hostility against the nation and the government which permit, and which they accuse even of conniving at the violation of international law and justice. Mutual recriminations are bandied about from one side to the other; and the very facilities of intercourse which keep alive the sympathy between portions of the two populations, afford at the same time occasions for the collision of angry passions and national antipathies. The violent party papers on each side, and the various bodies whose pecuniary interests a war would promote, foment the strife. A large portion of each population endeavours to incite its own government to war, and at the same time labours to produce the same result by irritating the national feelings of the rival community. Rumours are diligently circulated by the Canadian press; and every friendly act of the American people or government appears to be systematically subjected to the most unfavourable construction. It is not only to be apprehended that this state of mutual suspicion and dislike may be brought to a head by acts of mutual reprisals, but that the officers of the respective governments, in despair of preserving peace, may take little care to prevent the actual commencement of war.

Though I do not believe that there ever was a time in which the specific relations of the two countries rendered it less likely that the United States would imagine that a war with England could promote their own interests, yet it cannot be doubted that the disturbed state of the Canadas is a serious drawback on the prosperity of a great part of the Union. Instead of presenting an additional field for their commercial enterprise, these Provinces, in their present state of disorder, are rather a barrier to their industrial energies. The present state of things also occasions great expense to the federal Government, which has been under the necessity of largely augmenting its small army, on account chiefly of the troubles of Canada.

Nor must we forget, that whatever assurances and proofs of amicable feeling we may receive from the Government of the United States, however strong may be the ties of mutual pacific interests that bind the two nations together, there are subjects of dispute which may produce less friendly feelings. National interests are now in question between us, of which the immediate adjustment is demanded by every motive of policy. These interests cannot be supported with the necessary vigour, while disaffection in a most important part of our North American possessions appears to give an enemy a certain means of inflicting injury and humiliation on the Empire.

But the chances of rebellion or foreign invasion are not those which I regard as either the most probable or the most injurious.

The experience of the last two years suggests the occurrence of a much more speedy and disastrous result. I dread, in fact, the completion of the sad work of depopulation and impoverishment which is now rapidly going on. The present evil is not merely, that improvement is stayed, and that the wealth and population of these Colonies do not increase according to the rapid scale of American progress. No accession of population takes place by immigration, and no capital is brought into the country. On the contrary, both the people and the capital seem to be quitting these distracted Provinces. From the French portion of Lower Canada there has, for a long time, been a large annual emigration of young men to the northern states of the American Union, in which they are highly valued as labourers, and gain good wages, with their savings, from which they generally return to their homes in a few months or years. I do not believe that the usual amount of this emigration has been increased during the last year, except by a few persons, prominently compromised in the insurrection, who have sold their property, and made up their minds to a perpetual exile; but I think there is some reason to believe that, among the class of habitual emigrants whom I have described, a great many now take up their permanent residence in the United States. But the stationary habits and local attachments of the French Canadians render it little likely that they will quit their country in great numbers. I am not aware that there is any diminution of the British population from such a cause. The employment of British capital in the Province is not materially checked in the principal branch of trade; and the main evils are the withdrawal of enterprising British capitalists from the French portion of the country, the diminished employment of the capital now in the Province, and the entire stoppage of all increase of the population by means of immigration. But from Upper Canada the withdrawal both of capital and of population has been very considerable. I have received accounts from most respectable sources of a very numerous emigration from the whole of the Western and London districts. It was said by persons who professed to have witnessed it, that considerable numbers had, for a long time, daily passed over from Amherstburg and Sandwich to Detroit; and a most respectable informant stated, that he had seen, in one of the districts which I have mentioned, no less than 15 vacant farms together on the road-side. A body of the reforming party have avowed, in the most open manner, their intention of emigrating, from political motives, and publicly invited all who might be influenced by similar feelings to join in their enterprise. For this the Mississippi Emigration Society has been formed with the purpose of facilitating emigration from Upper Canada to the new territory of the Union, called Iowa, on the west bank of the Upper Mississippi. The prospectus of the undertaking, and the report of the deputies who were sent to examine the country in question, were given in the public press, and the advantages of the new colony strongly enforced by the reformers, and depreciatingly discussed by the friends of the Government. The number of persons who have thus emigrated is not, however, I have reason to believe, as great as it has often been represented. Many who might be disposed to take such a step, cannot sell their farms on fair terms; and though some, relying on the ease with which land is obtained in the United States, have been content to remove merely their stock and their chattels, yet there are others again who cannot at the last make the sacrifices which a forced sale would necessitate, and who continue, even under their present state of alarm, to remain in hopes of better times. In the districts which border on the St. Lawrence, little has in fact come of the determination to emigrate, which was loudly expressed at one time. And some even of those who actually left the country are said to have returned. But the instances which have come to my knowledge induce me to attach even more importance to the class than to the alleged number of the emigrants; and I can by no means agree with some of the dominant party, that the persons who thus leave the country, are disaffected subjects, whose removal is a great advantage to loyal and peaceable men. In a country like Upper Canada, where the introduction of population and capital is above all things needful for its prosperity, and almost for its continued existence, it would be more prudent as well as just, more the interest as well as the duty of Government to remove the causes of disaffection, than to drive out the disaffected. But there is no ground for asserting that all the reformers who have thus quitted the country, are disloyal and turbulent men; nor indeed is it very clear that all of them are reformers, and that the

increasing insecurity of person and property have not, without distinction of politics, driven out some of the most valuable settlers of
the Province. A great impression has been lately made by the
removal of one of the largest proprietors of the Province, a gentleman who arrived there not many years ago from Trinidad; who
has taken no prominent, and certainly no violent part in politics;
and who has now transferred himself and his property to the
United States, simply because in Upper Canada he can find no
secure investment for the latter, and no tranquil enjoyment of life.
I heard of another English gentleman, who, having resided in the
country for six or seven years, and invested large sums in bringing
over a superior breed of cattle and sheep, was, while I was there,
selling off his stock and implements, with a view of settling in Illi-
nois. I was informed of an individual who, 30 years ago, had gone
into the forest with his axe on his shoulder, and, with no capital at
starting, had, by dint of patient labour, acquired a farm and stock,
which he had sold for £2,000, with which he went into the United
States. This man, I was assured, was only a specimen of a numerous class, to whose unwearied industry the growth and prosperity
of the Colony are mainly to be ascribed. They are now driven from
it, on account of the present insecurity of all who, having in former times been identified in politics with some of those that subsequently appeared as prominent actors in the revolt, are regarded
and treated as rebels, though they had held themselves completely
aloof from all participation in schemes or acts of rebellion. Considerable alarm also exists as to the general disposition to quit the
country which was said to have been produced by some late measures of the authorities among that mild and industrious, but peculiar race of descendants of the Dutch, who inhabit the back part of
the Niagara district.

Such are the lamentable results of the political and social evils
which have so long agitated the Canadas; and such is their condition, that, at the present moment, we are called on to take immediate precautions against dangers so alarming as those of rebellion,
foreign invasion, and utter exhaustion and depopulation. When I
look on the various and deep-rooted causes of mischief which the
past inquiry has pointed out as existing in every institution, in the
constitutions, and in the very composition of society throughout a

great part of these Provinces, I almost shrink from the apparent presumption of grappling with these gigantic difficulties. Nor shall I attempt to do so in detail. I rely on the efficacy of reform in the constitutional system by which these Colonies are governed, for the removal of every abuse in their administration which defective institutions have engendered. If a system can be devised which shall lay in these countries the foundation of an efficient and popular government, ensure harmony, in place of collision, between the various powers of the State, and bring the influence of a vigorous public opinion to bear on every detail of public affairs, we may rely on sufficient remedies being found for the present vices of the administrative system.

The preceding pages have sufficiently pointed out the nature of those evils, to the extensive operation of which, I attribute the various practical grievances, and the present unsatisfactory condition of the North American Colonies. It is not by weakening, but strengthening the influence of the people on its Government; by confining within much narrower bounds than those hitherto allotted to it, and not by extending the interference of the imperial authorities in the details of colonial affairs, that I believe that harmony is to be restored, where dissension has so long prevailed; and a regularity and vigour hitherto unknown, introduced into the administration of these Provinces. It needs no change in the principles of government, no invention of a new constitutional theory, to supply the remedy which would, in my opinion, completely remove the existing political disorders. It needs but to follow out consistently the principles of the British Constitution, and introduce into the Government of these great Colonies those wise provisions, by which alone the working of the representative system can in any country be rendered harmonious and efficient. We are not now to consider the policy of establishing representative government in the North American Colonies. That has been irrevocably done; and the experiment of depriving the people of their present constitutional power, is not to be thought of. To conduct their Government harmoniously, in accordance with its established principles, is now the business of its rulers; and I know not how it is possible to secure that harmony in any other way, than by administering the Government on those principles which have been found perfectly efficacious in Great Britain. I would not impair a single prerogative of the Crown; on the contrary, I believe that the interests of the people of these Colonies require the protection of prerogatives, which have not hitherto been exercised. But the Crown must, on the other hand, submit to the necessary consequences of representative institutions; and if it has to carry on the Government in unison with a representative body, it must consent to carry it on by means of those in whom that representative body has confidence.

In England, this principle has been so long considered an indisputable and essential part of our constitution, that it has really hardly ever been found necessary to inquire into the means by which its observance is enforced. When a ministry ceases to command a majority in Parliament on great questions of policy, its doom is immediately sealed; and it would appear to us as strange to attempt, for any time, to carry on a Government by means of ministers perpetually in a minority, as it would be to pass laws with a majority of votes against them. The ancient constitutional remedies, by impeachment and a stoppage of the supplies, have never, since the reign of William III, been brought into operation for the purpose of removing a ministry. They have never been called for, because, in fact, it has been the habit of ministers rather to anticipate the occurrence of an absolutely hostile vote, and to retire, when supported only by a bare and uncertain majority. If colonial legislatures have frequently stopped the supplies, if they have harassed public servants by unjust or harsh impeachments, it was because the removal of an unpopular administration could not be effected in the Colonies by those milder indications of a want of confidence, which have always sufficed to attain the end in the mother country.

The means which have occasionally been proposed in the Colonies themselves appear to me by no means calculated to attain the desired end in the best way. These proposals indicate such a want of reliance on the willingness of the Imperial Government to acquiesce in the adoption of a better system, as, if warranted, would render an harmonious adjustment of the different powers of the State utterly hopeless. An elective Executive Council would not only be utterly inconsistent with monarchial government, but would really, under the nominal authority of the Crown, deprive the community of one of the great advantages of an hereditary monarchy. Every purpose of popular control might be combined with every advantage of vesting the immediate choice of advisers in the Crown, were the Colonial Governor to be instructed to secure the co-operation of the Assembly in his policy, by entrusting its administration to such men as could command a majority; and if he were given to understand that he need count on no aid from home in any difference with the Assembly, that should not directly involve the relations between the mother country and the Colony. This change might be effected by a single dispatch containing such instructions; or if any legal enactment were requisite, it would only be one that would render it necessary that the official acts of the Governor should be countersigned by some public functionary. This would induce responsibility for every act of the Government, and, as a natural consequence, it would necessitate the substitution of a system of administration, by means of competent heads of departments, for the present rude machinery of an Executive Council. The Governor, if he wished to retain advisers not possessing the confidence of the existing Assembly, might rely on the effect of an appeal to the people, and, if unsuccessful, he might be coerced by a refusal of supplies, or his advisers might be terrified by the prospect of impeachment. But there can be no reason for apprehending that either party would enter on a contest, when each would find its interest in the maintenance of harmony; and the abuse of the powers which each would constitutionally possess, would cease when the struggle for larger powers became unneccessary. Nor can I conceive that it would be found impossible or difficult to conduct a Colonial Government with precisely that limitation of the respective powers which has been so long and so easily maintained in Great Britain.

I know that it has been urged, that the principles which are productive of harmony and good government in the mother country, are by no means applicable to a colonial dependency. It is said that it is necessary that the administration of a colony should be carried on by persons nominated without any reference to the wishes of its people; that they have to carry into effect the policy, not of that people, but of the authorities at home; and that a colony which should name all its own administrative functionaries, would, in fact, cease to be dependent. I admit that the system which I propose would, in fact, place the internal government of the Colony in the hands of the colonists themselves; and that we should thus leave to them the execution of the laws, of which we have long entrusted the making solely to them. Perfectly aware of the value of our colonial possessions, and strongly impressed with the necessity of maintaining our connexion with them, I know not in what respect it can be desirable that we should interfere with their internal legislation in matters which do not affect their relations with the mother country. The matters, which so concern us, are very few. The constitution of the form of government, – the regulation of foreign relations, and of trade with the mother country, the other British Colonies, and foreign nations, – and the disposal of the public lands, are the only points of which the mother country requires a control. This control is now sufficiently secured by the authority of the Imperial legislature; by the protection which the Colony derives from us against foreign enemies; by the beneficial terms which our laws secure to its trade; and by its share of the reciprocal benefits which would be conferred by a wise system of colonization. A perfect subordination, on the part of the Colony, on these points, is secured by the advantages which it finds in the continuance of its connexion with the Empire. It certainly is not strengthened, but greatly weakened, by a vexatious interference on the part of the Home Government, with the enactment of laws for regulating the internal concerns of the Colony, or in the selection of the persons entrusted with their execution. The colonists may not always know what laws are best for them, or which of their countrymen are the fittest for conducting their affairs; but, at least, they have a greater interest in coming to a right judgment on these points, and will take greater pains to do so than those whose welfare is very remotely and slightly affected by the good or bad legislation of these portions of the Empire. If the colonists make bad laws, and select improper persons to conduct their affairs, they will generally be the only, always the greatest, sufferers; and, like the people of other countries, they must bear the ills which they bring on themselves, until they choose to apply the remedy. But it surely cannot be the duty or the interest of Great Britain to keep a most expensive military possession of these Colonies, in order that a Governor or Secretary of State may be able to confer colonial appointments on one rather than another set of persons in the Colonies. For this is really the only question at issue. The slightest acquaintance with these Colonies proves the fallacy of the common notion, that any considerable amount of patronage in them is distributed among strangers from the mother country. Whatever inconvenience a consequent frequency of changes among the holders of office may produce, is a necessary disadvantage of free government, which will be amply compensated by the perpetual harmony which the system must produce between the people and its rulers. Nor do I fear that the character of the public servants will, in any respect, suffer from a more popular tenure of office. For I can conceive no system so calculated to fill important posts with inefficient persons as the present, in which public opinion is too little consulted in the original appointment, and in which it is almost impossible to remove those who disappoint the expectations of their usefulness, without inflicting a kind of brand on their capacity or integrity.

I am well aware that many persons, both in the Colonies and at home, view the system which I recommend with considerable alarm, because they distrust the ulterior views of those by whom it was originally proposed, and whom they suspect of urging its adoption, with the intent only of enabling them more easily to subvert monarchial institutions, or assert the independence of the Colony. I believe, however, that the extent to which these ulterior views exist, has been greatly overrated. We must not take every rash expression of disappointment as an indication of a settled aversion to the existing constitution; and my own observation convinces me, that the predominant feeling of all the English population of the North American Colonies is that of devoted attachment to the mother country. I believe that neither the interests nor the feelings of the people are incompatible with a Colonial Government, wisely and popularly administered. The proofs, which many who are much dissatisfied with the existing administration of the Government, have given of their loyalty, are not to be denied or overlooked. The attachment constantly exhibited by the people of these Provinces towards the British Crown and Empire, has all the characteristics of a strong national feeling. They value the institutions of their country, not merely from a sense of the practical advantages which they confer, but from sentiments of national pride; and they uphold them the more, because they are accustomed to view them as marks of nationality, which distinguish them from their Republican neighbours. I do not mean to affirm that this is a feeling which no impolicy on the part of the mother country will be unable to impair; but I do most confidently regard it as one which may, if rightly appreciated, be made the link of an enduring and advantageous connexion. The British people of the North American Colonies are a people on whom we may safely rely, and to whom we must not grudge power. For it is not to the individuals who have been loudest in demanding the change, that I propose to concede the responsibility of the Colonial administration, but to the people themselves. Nor can I conceive that any people, or any considerable portion of a people, will view with dissatisfaction a change which would amount simply to this, that the Crown would henceforth consult the wishes of the people in the choice of its servants.

The important alteration in the policy of the Colonial Government which I recommend, might be wholly or in great part effected for the present by the unaided authority of the Crown; and I believe that the great mass of discontent in Upper Canada, which is not directly connected with personal irritation, arising out of the incidents of the late troubles, might be dispelled by an assurance that the government of the Colony should henceforth be carried on in conformity with the views of the majority in the Assembly. But I think that for the well-being of the Colonies, and the security of the mother country, it is necessary that such a change should be rendered more permanent than a momentary sense of the existing difficulties can ensure its being. I cannot believe that persons in power in this country will be restrained from the injudicious interference with the internal management of these Colonies, which I deprecate, while they remain the petty and divided communities which they now are. The public attention at home is distracted by the various and sometimes contrary complaints of these different contiguous Provinces. Each now urges its demands at different times, and in somewhat different forms, and the interests which each individual complainant represents as in peril, are too petty to attract the due attention of the Empire. But if these important and extensive Colonies should speak with one voice, if it were felt that every error of our colonial policy must cause a common suffering and a common discontent throughout the whole wide extent of British America, those complaints would never be provoked; because no authority would venture to run counter to the wishes of such a community, except on points absolutely involving the few Imperial interests, which it is necessary to remove from the jurisdiction of Colonial legislation.

It is necessary that I should also recommend what appears to me an essential limitation on the present powers of the representative bodies in these Colonies. I consider good government not to be attainable while the present unrestricted powers of voting public money, and of managing the local expenditure of the community, are lodged in the hands of an Assembly. As long as a revenue is raised, which leaves a large surplus after the payment of the necessary expenses of the civil Government, and as long as any member of the Assembly may, without restriction, propose a vote of public money, so long will the Assembly retain in its hands the powers which it every where abuses, of misapplying that money. The prerogative of the Crown which is constantly exercised in Great Britain for the real protection of the people, ought never to have been waived in the Colonies; and if the rule of the Imperial Parliament, that no money vote should be proposed without the previous consent of the Crown, were introduced into these Colonies, it might be wisely employed in protecting the public interests, now frequently sacrificed in that scramble for local appropriations, which chiefly serves to give an undue influence to particular individuals or parties.

The establishment of a good system of municipal institutions throughout these Provinces is a matter of vital importance. A general legislature, which manages the private business of every parish, in addition to the common business of the country, wields a power which no single body, however popular in its constitution, ought to have; a power which must be destructive of any constitutional balance. The true principle of limiting popular power is that apportionment of it in many different depositories which has been

adopted in all the most free and stable States of the Union. Instead
of confiding the whole collection and distribution of all the revenues raised in any country for all general and local purposes to a
single representative body, the power of local assessment, and the
application of the funds arising from it, should be entrusted to
local management. It is in vain to expect that this sacrifice of
power will be voluntarily made by any representative body. The
establishment of municipal institutions for the whole country
should be made a part of every colonial constitution; and the prerogative of the Crown should be constantly interposed to check
any encroachment on the functions of the local bodies, until the
people should become alive, as most assuredly they almost immediately would be, to the necessity of protecting their local privileges.

The establishment of a sound and general system for the management of the lands and the settlement of the Colonies, is a necessary part of any good and durable system of government. In a
report contained in the Appendix to the present, the plan which I
recommend for this purpose, will be fully developed.

These general principles apply, however, only to those changes
in the system of government which are required in order to rectify
disorders common to all the North American Colonies; but they
do not in any degree go to remove those evils in the present state
of Lower Canada which require the most immediate remedy. The
fatal feud of origin, which is the cause of the most extensive mischief, would be aggravated at the present moment by any change,
which should give the majority more power than they have hitherto possessed. A plan by which it is proposed to ensure the tranquil government of Lower Canada, must include in itself the means
of putting an end to the agitation of national disputes in the legislature, by settling, at once and for ever, the national character of
the Province. I entertain no doubts as to the national character
which must be given to Lower Canada; it must be that of the
British Empire; that of the majority of the population of British
America; that of the great race which must, in the lapse of no long
period of time, be predominant over the whole North American
Continent. Without effecting the change so rapidly or so roughly
as to shock the feelings and trample on the welfare of the existing

generation, it must henceforth be the first and steady purpose of the British Government to establish an English population, with English laws and language, in this Province, and to trust its government to none but a decidedly English legislature.

It may be said that this is a hard measure to a conquered people; that the French were originally the whole, and still are the bulk of the population of Lower Canada; that the English are new-comers, who have no right to demand the extinction of the nationality of a people, among whom commercial enterprise has drawn them. It may be said, that, if the French are not so civilized, so energetic, or so money-making a race as that by which they are surrounded, they are an amiable, a virtuous, and a contented people, possessing all the essentials of material comfort, and not to be despised or ill-used, because they seek to enjoy what they have, without emulating the spirit of accumulation, which influences their neighbours. Their nationality is, after all, an inheritance; and they must be not too severely punished, because they have dreamed of maintaining on the distant banks of the St. Lawrence, and transmitting to their posterity, the language, the manners, and the institutions of that great nation, that for two centuries gave the tone of thought to the European Continent. If the disputes of the two races are irreconcileable, it may be urged that justice demands that the minority should be compelled to acquiesce in the supremacy of the ancient and most numerous occupants of the Province, and not pretend to force their own institutions and customs on the majority.

But before deciding which of the two races is now to be placed in the ascendant, it is but prudent to inquire which of them must ultimately prevail; for it is not wise to establish to-day that which must, after a hard struggle, be reversed to-morrow. The pretensions of the French Canadians to the exclusive possession of Lower Canada, would debar the yet larger English population of Upper Canada and the Townships from access to the great natural channel of that trade which they alone have created, and now carry on. The possession of the mouth of the St. Lawrence concerns not only those who happen to have made their settlements along the narrow line which borders it, but all who now dwell, or will hereafter dwell, in the great basin of that river. For we must not look to the present alone. The question is, by what race is it likely that the wilderness which now covers the rich and ample regions surrounding the comparatively small and contracted districts in which the French Canadians are located, is eventually to be converted into a settled and flourishing country? If this is to be done in the British dominions, as in the rest of North America, by some speedier process than the ordinary growth of population, it must be by immigration from the English Isles, or from the United States, – the countries which supply the only settlers that have entered, or will enter, the Canadas in any large numbers. This immigration can neither be debarred from a passage through Lower Canada, nor even be prevented from settling in that Province. The whole interior of the British dominions must ere long, be filled with an English population, every year rapidly increasing its numerical superiority over the French. Is it just that the prosperity of this great majority, and of this vast tract of country, should be for ever, or even for a while, impeded by the artificial bar which the backward laws and civilization of a part, and part only, of Lower Canada, would place between them and the ocean? Is it to be supposed that such an English population will ever submit to such a sacrifice of its interests?

I must not, however, assume it to be possible that the English Government shall adopt the course of placing or allowing any check to the influx of English immigration into Lower Canada, or any impediment to the profitable employment of that English capital which is already vested therein. The English have already in their hands the majority of the larger masses of property in the country; they have the decided superiority of intelligence on their side; they have the certainty that colonization must swell their numbers to a majority; and they belong to the race which wields the Imperial Government, and predominates on the American Continent. If we now leave them in a minority, they will never abandon the assurance of being a majority hereafter, and never cease to continue the present contest with all the fierceness with which it now rages. In such a contest they will rely on the sympathy of their countrymen at home; and if that is denied them, they feel very confident of being able to awaken the sympathy of their neighbours of kindred origin. They feel that if the British Government intends to maintain its hold of the Canadas, it can rely on the English population alone; that if it abandons its colonial possessions, they must become a portion of that great Union which will speedily send forth its swarms of settlers, and, by force of numbers and activity, quickly master every race. The French Canadians, on the other hand, are but the remains of an ancient colonization, and are and ever must be isolated in the midst of an Anglo-Saxon world. Whatever may happen, whatever government shall be established over them, British or American, they can see no hope for their nationality. They can only sever themselves from the British Empire by waiting till some general cause of dissatisfaction alienates them, together with the surrounding colonies, and leaves them part of an English confederacy; or, if they are able, by effecting a separation singly, and so either merging in the American Union, or keeping up for a few years a wretched semblance of feeble independence, which would expose them more than ever to the intrusion of the surrounding population. I am far from wishing to encourage indiscriminately these pretensions to superiority on the part of any particular race; but while the greater part of every portion of the American Continent is still uncleared and unoccupied, and while the English exhibit such constant and marked activity in colonization, so long will it be idle to imagine that there is any portion of that Continent into which that race will not penetrate, or in which, when it has penetrated, it will not predominate. It is but a question of time and mode; it is but to determine whether the small number of French who now inhabit Lower Canada shall be made English, under a Government which can protect them, or whether the process shall be delayed until a much larger number shall have to undergo, at the rude hands of its uncontrolled rivals, the extinction of a nationality strengthened and embittered by continuance.

And is this French Canadian nationality one which, for the good merely of that people, we ought to strive to perpetuate, even if it were possible? I know of no national distinctions marking and continuing a more hopeless inferiority. The language, the laws, the character of the North American Continent are English; and every race but the English (I apply this to all who speak the English language) appears there in a condition of inferiority. It is to elevate them from that inferiority that I desire to give to the Canadians our English character. I desire it for the sake of the educated classes, whom the distinction of language and manners keeps apart from the great Empire to which they belong. At the best, the fate of the educated and aspiring colonist is, at present, one of little hope, and little activity; but the French Canadian is cast still further into the shade, by a language and habits foreign to those of the Imperial Government. A spirit of exclusion has closed the higher professions on the educated classes of the French Canadians, more, perhaps, than was absolutely necessary; but it is impossible for the utmost liberality on the part of the British Government to give an equal position in the general competition of its vast population to those who speak a foreign language. I desire the amalgamation still more for the sake of the humbler classes. Their present state of rude and equal plenty is fast deteriorating under the pressure of population in the narrow limits to which they are confined. If they attempt to better their condition, by extending themselves over the neighbouring country, they will necessarily get more and more mingled with an English population: if they prefer remaining stationary, the greater part of them must be labourers in the employ of English capitalists. In either case it would appear, that the great mass of the French Canadians are doomed, in some measure, to occupy an inferior position, and to be dependent on the English for employment. The evils of poverty and dependence would merely be aggravated in a ten-fold degree, by a spirit of jealous and resentful nationality, which should separate the working class of the community from the possessors of wealth and employers of labour.

I will not here enter into the question of the effect of the mode of life and division of property among the French Canadians on the happiness of the people. I will admit, for the moment, that it is as productive of well-being as its admirers assert. But, be it good or bad, the period in which it is practicable, is past; for there is not enough unoccupied land left in that portion of the country in which English are not already settled, to admit of the present French population possessing farms sufficient to supply them with their present means of comfort, under their system of husbandry. No population has increased by mere births so rapidly as that of the French Canadians has since the conquest. At that period their number was estimated at 60,000; it is now supposed to amount to more than seven times as many. There has been no proportional increase in cultivation, or of produce from the land already under cultivation; and the increased population has been in a great measure provided for by mere continued subdivision of estates. In a Report from a Committee of the Assembly in 1826, of which Mr. Andrew Steuart was chairman, it is stated, that since 1784 population of the seigniories had quadrupled, while the number of cattle had only doubled, and the quantity of land in cultivation had only increased one-third. Complaints of distress are constant, and the deterioration of the condition of a great part of the population admitted on all hands. A people so circumstanced must alter their mode of life. If they wish to maintain the same kind of rude, but well-provided agricultural existence, it must be by removing into those parts of the country in which the English are settled; or if they cling to their present residence, they can only obtain a livelihood by deserting their present employment, and working for wages on farms, or in commercial occupations under English capitalists. But their present proprietary and inactive condition is one which no political arrangements can perpetuate. Were the French Canadians to be guarded from the influx of any other population, their condition in a few years would be similar to that of the poorest of the Irish peasantry.

There can hardly be conceived a nationality more destitute of all that can invigorate and elevate a people, than that which is exhibited by the descendants of the French in Lower Canada, owing to their retaining their peculiar language and manners. They are a people with no history, and no literature. The literature of England is written in a language which is not theirs; and the only literature which their language renders familiar to them, is that of a nation from which they have been separated by eighty years of a foreign rule, and still more by those changes which the Revolution and its consequences have wrought in the whole political, moral and social state of France. Yet it is on a people whom recent history, manners and modes of thought, so entirely separate from them, that the French Canadians are wholly dependent for almost all the instruction and amusement derived from books: it is on this essentially foreign literature, which is conversant about events, opinions and habits of life, perfectly strange and unintelligible to them, that they are compelled to be dependent. Their newspapers are mostly written by natives of France, who have either come to try their fortunes in the Province, or been brought into it by the party leaders, in order to supply the dearth of literary talent available for the political press. In the same way their nationality operates to deprive them of the enjoyments and civilizing influence of the arts. Though descended from the people in the world that most generally love, and have most successfully cultivated the drama – though living on a continent, in which almost every town, great or small, has an English theatre, the French population of Lower Canada, cut off from every people that speaks its own language, can support no national stage.

In these circumstances. I should be indeed surprised if the more reflecting part of the French Canadians entertained at present any hope of continuing to preserve their nationality. Much as they struggle against it, it is obvious that the process of assimilation to English habits is already commencing. The English language is gaining ground, as the language of the rich and of the employers of labour naturally will. It appeared by some of the few returns, which had been received by the Commissioner of the Inquiry into the state of Education, that there are about ten times the number of French children in Quebec learning English, as compared with the English children who learn French. A considerable time must, of course, elapse before the change of a language can spread over a whole people; and justice and policy alike require, that while the people continue to use the French language, their Government should take no such means to force the English language upon them as would, in fact, deprive the great mass of the community of the protection of the laws. But, I repeat that the alteration of the character of the Province ought to be immediately entered on, and firmly, though cautiously, followed up; that in any plan, which may be adopted for the future management of Lower Canada, the first object ought to be that of making it an English Province; and that, with this end in view, the ascendancy should never again be placed in any hands but those of an English population. Indeed, at the present moment this is obviously necessary: in the state of mind in which I have described the French Canadian population, as not only now being, but as likely for a long while to remain, the trusting them with an entire control over this Province, would be, in fact, only facilitating a rebellion. Lower Canada must be governed now, as it must be hereafter, by an English population: and thus the policy, which the necessities of the moment force on us, is in accordance with that suggested by a comprehensive view of the future and permanent improvement of the Province.

The greater part of the plans which have been proposed for the future Government of Lower Canada, suggest either as a lasting or as a temporary and intermediate scheme, that the Government of that Province should be constituted on an entirely despotic footing, or on one that would vest it entirely in the hands of the British minority. It is proposed either to place the legislative authority in a Governor, with a Council formed of the heads of the British party, or to contrive some scheme of representation by which a minority, with the forms of representation, is to deprive a majority of all voice in the management of its own affairs.

The maintenance of an absolute form of government on any part of the North American Continent, can never continue for any long time, without exciting a general feeling in the United States against a power of which the existence is secured by means so odious to the people; and as I rate the preservation of the present general sympathy of the United States with the policy of our Government in Lower Canada, as a matter of the greatest importance, I should be sorry that the feeling should be changed for one which, if prevalent among the people, must extend over the surrounding Provinces. The influence of such an opinion would not only act very strongly on the entire French population, and keep up among them a sense of injury, and a determination of resistance to the Government, but would lead to just as great discontent among the English. In their present angry state of feeling, they might tolerate, for a while, any arrangement that would give them a triumph over the French; but I have greatly misunderstood their character, if they would long bear a Government in which they had no direct voice. Nor would their jealousy be obviated by the selection of a Council from the persons supposed to have their confidence. It is not easy to know who really possess that confidence; and I suspect that there would be no surer way of depriving a man of influence over them, than by treating him as their representative, without their consent.

The experience which we have had of a Government irresponsible to the people in these Colonies, does not justify us in believing that it would be very well administered. And the great reforms in the institutions of the Province which must be made, ere Lower Canada can ever be a well-ordered and flourishing community, can be effected by no legislature which does not represent a great mass of public opinion.

But the great objection to any government of an absolute kind is, that it is palpably of a temporary nature; that there is no reason to believe that its influence during the few years that it would be permitted to last, would leave the people at all more fit to manage themselves; that, on the contrary, being a mere temporary institution, it would be deficient in that stability which is the great requisite of government in times of disorder. There is every reason to believe that a professedly irresponsible government would be the weakest that could be devised. Every one of its acts would be discussed, not in the Colony, but in England, on utterly incomplete and incorrect information, and run the chance of being disallowed without being understood. The most violent outcry that could be raised by persons looking at them through the medium of English and constitutional notions, or by those who might hope thereby to promote the sinister purposes of faction at home, would be constantly directed against them. Such consequences as these are inevitable. The people of England are not accustomed to rely on the honest and discreet exercise of absolute power; and if they permit a despotism to be established in their Colonies, they feel bound, when their attention happens to be directed towards them, to watch its acts with vigilance. The Governor and Council would feel this responsibility in all their acts; unless they happened to be men of much more than ordinary nerve and earnestness, they would shape their policy so as merely to avoid giving a handle to attacks; and their measures would exhibit all that uncertainty and weakness which such a motive is sure to produce.

With respect to every one of those plans which propose to make the English minority an electoral majority by means of new and strange modes of voting or unfair divisions of the country, I shall only say, that if the Canadians are to be deprived of representative government, it would be better to do it in a straightforward way than to attempt to establish a permanent system of government on the basis of what all mankind would regard as mere electoral frauds. It is not in North America that men can be cheated by an unreal semblance of representative government, or persuaded that they are out-voted, when, in fact, they are disfranchised.

The only power that can be effectual at once in coercing the present disaffection, and hereafter obliterating the nationality of the French Canadians, is that of a numerical majority of a loyal and English population; and the only stable government will be one more popular than any that has hitherto existed in the North American Colonies. The influence of perfectly equal and popular institutions in effacing distinctions of race without disorder or oppression, and with little more than ordinary animosities of party in a free country, is memorably exemplified in the history of the state of Louisiana, the laws and population of which were French at the time of its cession to the American Union. And the eminent success of the policy adopted with regard to that State, points out to us the means by which a similar result can be effected in Lower Canada.

The English of Lower Canada, who seem to infer the means from the result, entertain and circulate the most extraordinary conceptions of the course really pursued in this instance. On the single fact, that in the constitution of Louisiana it is specified that the public acts of the State shall be 'in the language in which the constitution of the United States is written', it has been inferred that the federal Government in the most violent manner swept away the use of the French language and laws, and subjected the French population to some peculiar disabilities which deprived them, in fact, of an equal voice in the government of their State. Nothing can be more contrary to the fact. Louisiana, on its first cession was governed as a 'district'; its public officers were appointed by the federal Government; and, as was natural under the circumstances of the case, they were natives of the old States of the Union. In 1812, the district, having the requisite population, was admitted into the Union as a State, and admitted on precisely the same terms that any other population would have or has been. The constitution was framed so as to give precisely the same power to the majority as is enjoyed in the other States of the Union. No alteration was then made in the laws. The proof of this is afforded by a fact familiar to every person moderately acquainted with the jurisprudence of the age. The code, which is the glory of Louisiana and Mr. Livingstone, was subsequently undertaken under the auspices of the legislature, in consequence of the confusion daily arising in the administration of the English and French system of law in the same courts. This change of laws, effected in the manner most consonant to the largest views of legislation, was not forced on the legislature and people of the State by an external authority, but was the suggestion of their own political wisdom. Louisiana is not the only State in the Union which has been troubled by the existence of conflicting systems of law. The State of New York, till within a few years, suffered under the same evil, which it remedied in the same way, by employing a commission of its ablest lawyers to digest both systems of law into a common code. The contending populations of Lower Canada may well imitate these examples; and if, instead of endeavouring to force their respective laws upon each other, they would attempt an amalgamation of the two systems into one, adopting what is really best in both, the result would be creditable to the Province.

Every provision was made in Louisiana for securing to both races a perfectly equal participation in all the benefits of the Government. It is true that the intention of the federal Government to encourage the use of the English language was evinced by the provision of the constitution with respect to the language of the records; but those who will reflect how very few people ever read such documents, and how very recently it is that the English language has become the language of the law in this country, will see that such a provision could have little practical effect. In all cases in which convenience requires it, the different parties use their respective languages in the courts of justice, and in both branches of the legislature. In every judicial proceeding, all documents which pass between the parties are required to be in both languages, and the laws are published in both languages. Indeed the equality of the two languages is preserved in the legislature by a very singular contrivance; the French and English members speak their respective languages, and an interpreter, as I was informed, after every speech, explains its purport in the other language.

For a long time the distinction between the two races was the cause of great jealousy. The Americans crowded into the State in order to avail themselves of its great natural resources, and its unequalled commercial advantages; there, as every where else on that continent, their energy and habits of business gradually drew the greater part of the commercial business of the country into their hands; and though, I believe, a few of the richest merchants, and most of the owners of plantations, are French, the English form the bulk of the wealthier classes. Year after year their numbers have become greater, and it is now generally supposed that they constitute the numerical majority. It may be imagined that the French have borne this with a good deal of dissatisfaction; but as the advantages gained by the English are entirely the result, not of favour, but of their superiority in a perfectly free competition, this jealousy could excite no murmurs against the Government. The competition made the two races enemies at first, but it has gradually stirred the emulation of the less active race, and made them rivals. The jealousies in the city of New Orleans were so great at one time, that the legislature of the State, at the desire of the English, who complained of the inertness of the French, formed separate municipalities for the French and English parts of the city. These two municipalities are now actuated by a spirit of rivalry, and each undertakes great public works for the ornament and convenience of their respective quarters.

The distinction still lasts, and still causes a good deal of division; the society of each race is said to be in some measure distinct, but not by any means hostile; and some accounts represent the social mixture to be very great. All accounts represent the division of the races as becoming gradually less and less marked; their newspapers are printed in the two languages on opposite pages; their local politics are entirely merged in those of the Union; and instead of discovering in their papers any vestiges of a quarrel of races, they are found to contain a repetition of the same party recriminations and party arguments, which abound in all other parts of the federation.

The explanation of this amalgamation is obvious. The French of Louisiana, when they were formed into a state, in which they were a majority, were incorporated into a great nation, of which they constituted an extremely small part. The eye of every ambitious man turned naturally to the great centre of federal affairs, and the high prizes of federal ambition. The tone of politics was taken from those by whose hand its highest powers were wielded; the legislation and government of Louisiana were from the first insignificant, compared with the interests involved in the discussions at Washington. It became the object of every aspiring man to merge his French, and adopt completely an American nationality. What was the interest of individuals, was also the interest of the State. It was its policy to be represented by those who would acquire weight in the councils of the federation. To speak only a language foreign to that of the United States, was consequently a disqualification for a candidate for the posts of either senator or representative; the French qualified themselves by learning English, or submitted to the superior advantages of their English competitors. The representation of Louisiana in Congress is now entirely English, while each of the federal parties in the State conciliates the French feeling, by putting up a candidate of that race. But the result is, that the Union is never disturbed by the quarrels of these races; and the French language and manners bid fair, in no long time, to follow their laws, and pass away like the Dutch peculiarities of New York.

It is only by the same means – by a popular government, in which an English majority shall permanently predominate – that Lower Canada, if a remedy for its disorders be not too long delayed, can be tranquilly ruled.

On these grounds, I believe that no permanent or efficient remedy can be devised for the disorders of Lower Canada, except a fusion of the Government in that of one or more of the surrounding Provinces; and as I am of opinion that the full establishment of responsible government can only be permanently secured by giving these Colonies an increased importance in the politics of the Empire, I find in union the only means of remedying at once and completely the two prominent causes of their present unsatisfactory condition.

Two kinds of union have been proposed, – federal and legislative. By the first, the separate legislature of each Province would be preserved in its present form, and retain almost all its present attributes of internal legislation; the federal legislature exercising no power, save in those matters of general concern, which may have been expressly ceded to it by the constituent Provinces. A legislative union would imply a complete incorporation of the Provinces included in it under one legislature, exercising universal and sole legislative authority over all of them, in exactly the same manner as the Parliament legislates alone for the whole of the British Isles.

On my first arrival in Canada, I was strongly inclined to the project of a federal union, and it was with such a plan in view, that I discussed a general measure for the government of the Colonies, with the deputations from the Lower Provinces, and with various leading individuals and public bodies in both the Canadas. I was fully aware that it might be objected that a federal union would, in many cases, produce a weak and rather cumbrous Government; that a Colonial federation must have, in fact, little legitimate authority or business, the greater part of the ordinary functions of a federation falling within the scope of the Imperial Legislature and executive; and that the main inducement to federation, which is the necessity of conciliating the pretensions of independent states to the maintenance of their own sovereignty, could not exist in the case of colonial dependencies, liable to be moulded according to the pleasure of the supreme authority at home. In the course of the discussions which I have mentioned, I became aware also of great practical difficulties in any plan of federal government, particularly those that must arise in the management of the general revenues, which would in such a plan have to be again distributed among the Provinces. But I had still more strongly impressed on me the great advantages of a united Government; and I was gratified by finding the leading minds of the various Colonies strongly and generally inclined to a scheme that would elevate their countries into something like a national existence. I thought that it would be the tendency of a federation sanctioned and consolidated by a monarchial Government gradually to become a complete legislative union; and that thus, while conciliating the French of

Lower Canada, by leaving them the government of their own Province and their own internal legislation, I might provide for the protection of British interests by the general government, and for the gradual transition of the Provinces into a united and homogeneous community.

But the period of gradual transition is past in Lower Canada. In the present state of feeling among the French population, I cannot doubt that any power which they might possess would be used against the policy and the very existence of any form of British government. I cannot doubt that any French Assembly that shall again meet in Lower Canada will use whatever power, be it more or less limited, it may have, to obstruct the Government, and undo whatever has been done by it. Time, and the honest co-operation of the various parties, would be required to aid the action of a federal constitution; and time is not allowed, in the present state of Lower Canada, nor co-operation to be expected from a legislature, of which the majority shall represent its French inhabitants. I believe that tranquillity can only be restored by subjecting the Province to the vigorous rule of an English majority; and that the only efficacious government would be that formed by a legislative union.

If the population of Upper Canada is rightly estimated at 400,000, the English inhabitants of Lower Canada at 150,000, and the French at 450,000, the union of the two Provinces would not only give a clear English majority, but one which would be increased every year by the influence of English emigration; and I have little doubt that the French, when once placed, by the legitimate course of events and the working of natural causes, in a minority, would abandon their vain hopes of nationality. I do not mean that they would immediately give up their present animosities, or instantly renounce the hope of attaining their end by violent means. But the experience of the two Unions in the British Isles may teach us how effectually the strong arm of a popular legislature would compel the obedience of the refractory population; and the hopelessness of success, would gradually subdue the existing animosities, and incline the French Canadian population to acquiesce in their new state of political existence. I certainly should not like to subject the French Canadians to the rule of the identical English minority with which they have so long been contending; but from a majority, emanating from so much more extended a source, I do not think they would have any oppression or injustice to fear; and in this case, the far greater part of the majority never having been brought in to previous collision, would regard them with no animosity that could warp their natural sense of equity. The endowments of the Catholic Church in Lower Canada, and the existence of all its present laws, until altered by the united legislature, might be secured by stipulations similar to those adopted in the Union between England and Scotland. I do not think that the subsequent history of British legislation need incline us to believe, that the nation which has a majority in a popular legislature, is likely to use its power to tamper very hastily with the laws of the people to which it is united.

The union of the two Provinces would secure to Upper Canada the present great objects of its desire. All disputes as to the division or amount of the revenue would cease. The surplus revenue of Lower Canada would supply the deficiency of that part of the upper Province; and the Province thus placed beyond the possibility of locally jobbing the surplus revenue, which it cannot reduce, would, I think, gain as much by the arrangement as the Province, which would thus find a means of paying the interest of its debt. Indeed it would be by no means unjust to place this burthen on Lower Canada, inasmuch as the great public works for which the debt was contracted, are as much the concern of one Province as of the other. Nor is it to be supposed that, whatever may have been the mismanagement, in which a great part of the debt originated, the canals of Upper Canada will always be a source of loss, instead of profit. The completion of the projected and necessary line of public works would be promoted by such a union. The access to the sea would be secured to Upper Canada. The saving of public money, which would be ensured by the union of various establishments in the two Provinces, would supply the means of conducting the general Government on a more efficient scale than it has yet been carried on. And the responsibility of the executive would be secured by the increased weight which the representative body of the United Province would bring to bear on the Imperial Government and legislature.

But while I convince myself that such desirable ends would be secured by the legislative union of the two Provinces, I am inclined to go further, and inquire whether all these objects would not more surely be attained, by extending this legislative union over all the British Provinces in North America; and whether the advantages which I anticipate for two of them, might not, and should not in justice be extended over all. Such a union would at once decisively settle the question of races; it would enable all the Provinces to co-operate for all common purposes; and, above all, it would form a great and powerful people, possessing the means of securing good and responsible government for itself, and which, under the protection of the British Empire, might in some measure counterbalance the preponderant and increasing influence of the United States on the American Continent. I do not anticipate that a colonial legislature thus strong and thus self-governing, would desire to abandon the connexion with Great Britain. On the contrary, I believe that the practical relief from undue interference, which would be the result of such a change, would strengthen the present bond of feelings and interests; and that the connexion would only become more durable and advantageous, by having more of equality, of freedom, and of local independence. But at any rate, our first duty is to secure the well-being of our colonial countrymen; and if in the hidden decrees of that wisdom by which this world is ruled, it is written, that these countries are not for ever to remain portions of the Empire, we owe it to our honour to take good care that, when they separate from us, they should not be the only countries on the American Continent in which the Anglo-Saxon race shall be found unfit to govern itself.

I am, in truth, so far from believing that the increased power and weight that would be given to these Colonies by union would endanger their connexion with the Empire, that I look to it as the only means of fostering such a national feeling throughout them as would effectually counterbalance whatever tendencies may now exist towards separation. No large community of free and intelligent men will long feel contented with a political system which places them, because it places their country, in a position of inferiority to their neighbours. The colonist of Great Britain is linked, it is true, to a mighty Empire; and the glories of its history, the visible signs of its present power, and the civilization of its people, are calculated to raise and gratify his national pride. But he feels, also, that his link to that Empire is one of remote dependence; he catches but passing and inadequate glimpses of its power and prosperity; he knows that in its government he and his own countrymen have no voice. While his neighbour on the other side of the frontier assumes importance, from the notion that his vote exercises some influence on the councils, and that he himself has some share in the onward progress of a mighty nation, the colonist feels the deadening influence of the narrow and subordinate community to which he belongs. In his own, and in the surrounding Colonies, he finds petty objects occupying petty, stationary and divided societies; and it is only when the chances of an uncertain and tardy communication bring intelligence of what has passed a month before on the other side of the Atlantic, that he is reminded of the Empire with which he is connected. But the influence of the United States surrounds him on every side, and is for ever present. It extends itself as population augments and intercourse increases; it penetrates every portion of the continent into which the restless spirit of American speculation impels the settler or the trader; it is felt in all the transactions of commerce, from the important operations of the monetary system down to the minor details of ordinary traffic; it stamps, on all the habits and opinions of the surrounding countries, the common characteristics of the thoughts, feelings and customs of the American people. Such is necessarily the influence which a great nation exercises on the small communities which surround it. Its thoughts and manners subjugate them, even when nominally independent of its authority. If we wish to prevent the extension of this influence, it can only be done by raising up for the North American colonist some nationality of his own; by elevating these small and unimportant communities into a society having some objects of a national importance; and by thus giving their inhabitants a country which they will be unwilling to see absorbed even into one more powerful.

While I believe that the establishment of a comprehensive system of government, and of an effectual union between the different Provinces, would produce this important effect on the general feelings of their inhabitants, I am inclined to attach very great importance to the influence which it would have in giving greater scope and satisfaction to the legitimate ambition of the most active and prominent persons to be found in them. As long as personal ambition is inherent in human nature, and as long as the morality of every free and civilized community encourages its aspirations, it is one great business of a wise Government to provide for its legitimate development. If, as it is commonly asserted, the disorders of these Colonies have, in great measure, been fomented by the influence of designing and ambitious individuals, this evil will best be remedied by allowing such a scope for the desires of such men as shall direct their ambition into the legitimate chance of furthering, and not of thwarting, their Government. By creating high prizes in a general and responsible Government, we shall immediately afford the means of pacifying the turbulent ambitions, and of employing in worthy and noble occupations the talents which now are only exerted to foment disorder. We must remove from these Colonies the cause to which the sagacity of Adam Smith traced the alienation of the Provinces which now form the United States: we must provide some scope for what he calls 'the importance' of the leading men in the Colony, beyond what he forcibly terms the present 'petty prizes of the paltry raffle of colonial faction'. A general legislative union would elevate and gratify the hopes of able and aspiring men. They would no longer look with envy and wonder at the great arena of the bordering federation, but see the means of satisfying every legitimate ambition in the high offices of the Judicature and executive Government of their own Union.

Nor would a union of the various Provinces be less advantageous in facilitating a co-operation for various common purposes, of which the want is now very seriously felt. There is hardly a department of the business of government which does not require, or would not be better performed, by being carried on under the superintendence of a general Government; and when we consider the political and commercial interests that are common to these Provinces, it appears difficult to account for their having ever been divided into separate Governments, since they have all been portions of the same Empire, subject to the same Crown, governed by nearly the same laws and constitutional customs, inhabited, with one exception, by the same race, contiguous and immediately adjacent to each other, and bounded along their whole frontier by the territories of the same powerful and rival State. It would appear that every motive that has induced the union of various Provinces into a single State, exists for the consolidation of these Colonies under a common legislature and executive. They have the same common relation to the mother country; the same relation to foreign nations. When one is at war, the others are at war; and the hostilities that are caused by an attack on one, must seriously compromise the welfare of the rest. Thus the dispute between Great Britain and the State of Maine, appears immediately to involve the interests of none of these Colonies, except New Brunswick or Lower Canada, to one of which the territory claimed by us must belong. But if a war were to commence on this ground, it is most probable that the American Government would select Upper Canada as the most vulnerable, or, at any rate, as the easiest point of attack. A dispute respecting the fisheries of Nova Scotia would involve precisely the same consequences. A union for common defence against foreign enemies is the natural bond of connexion that holds together the great communities of the world; and between no parts of any Kingdom or State is the necessity for such an union more obvious than between the whole of these Colonies.

Their internal relations furnish quite as strong motives for union. The Post Office is at the present moment under the management of the same Imperial establishment. If, in compliance with the reasonable demands of the Colonies, the regulation of a matter so entirely of internal concern, and the revenue derived from it, were placed under the control of the provincial legislatures, it would still be advisable that the management of the Post Office throughout the whole of British North America should be conducted by one general establishment. In the same way, so great is the influence on the other Provinces of the arrangements adopted with respect to the disposal of public lands and colonization in anyone, that it is absolutely essential that this department of government should be conducted on one system, and by one authority. The necessity of common fiscal regulations is strongly felt by all the Colonies; and a common custom-house establishment would relieve them from the hindrances to their trade, caused by the duties now levied on all commercial intercourse between them. The monetary and banking system of all is subject to the same influences, and ought to be regulated by the same laws. The establishment of a common colonial currency is very generally desired. Indeed, I know of no department of government that would not greatly gain, both in economy and efficiency, by being placed under a common management. I should not propose, at first, to alter the existing public establishments of the different Provinces, because the necessary changes had better be left to be made by the united Government; and the judicial establishments should certainly not be disturbed until the future legislature shall provide for their re-construction, on an uniform and permanent footing. But even in the administration of justice, an union would immediately supply a remedy for one of the most serious wants under which all the Provinces labour, by facilitating the formation of a general appellate tribunal for all the North American Colonies.

But the interests which are already in common between all these Provinces are small in comparison with those which the consequences of such an union might, and I think I may say assuredly would, call into existence; and the great discoveries of modern art, which have throughout the world, and no where more than in America, entirely altered the character and the channels of communication between distant countries, will bring all the North American Colonies into constant and speedy intercourse with each other. The success of the great experiment of steam navigation across the Atlantic, opens a prospect of a speedy communication with Europe, which will materially affect the future state of all these Provinces. In a Dispatch which arrived in Canada after my departure, the Secretary of State informed me of the determination of Your Majesty's Government to establish a steam communication between Great Britain and Halifax; and instructed me to turn my attention to the formation of a road between that port and Quebec. It would, indeed, have given me sincere satisfaction, had I remained in the Province, to promote, by any means in my power, so highly desirable an object; and the removal of the usual restrictions on my authority as Governor-General, having given me the means of effectually acting in concert with the various provincial Governments, I might have been able to make some progress in the work. But I cannot point out more strikingly the evils of the present want of a general Government for these Provinces, than by adverting to the difficulty which would practically occur, under the previous and present arrangements of both executive and legislative authorities in the various Provinces, in attempting to carry such a plan into effect. For the various Colonies have no more means of concerting such common works with each other, than with the neighbouring States of the Union. They stand to one another in the position of foreign States, and of foreign States without diplomatic relations. The Governors may correspond with each other: the legislatures may enact laws, carrying the common purposes into effect in their respective jurisdictions; but there is no means by which the various details may speedily and satisfactorily be settled with the concurrence of the different parties. And, in this instance, it must be recollected that the communication and the final settlement would have to be made between, not two, but several of the Provinces. The road would run through three of them; and Upper Canada, into which it would not enter, would, in fact, be more interested in the completion of such a work than any even of the Provinces through which it would pass. The Colonies, indeed, have no common centre in which the arrangement could be made, except in the Colonial Office at home; and the details of such a plan would have to be discussed just where the interests of all parties would have the least means of being fairly and fully represented, and where the minute local knowledge necessary for such a matter would be least likely to be found.

The completion of any satisfactory communication between Halifax and Quebec, would, in fact, produce relations between these Provinces, that would render a general union absolutely necessary. Several surveys have proved that a railroad would be perfectly practicable the whole way. Indeed, in North America, the expense and difficulty of making a railroad, bears by no means the excessive proportion to those of a common road that it does in Europe. It appears to be a general opinion in the United States, that the severe snows and frosts of that continent very slightly impede, and do not prevent, the travelling on railroads; and if I am rightly informed, the Utica railroad, in the northern part of the State of New York, is used throughout the winter. If this opinion be correct, the formation of a railroad from Halifax to Quebec would entirely alter some of the distinguishing characteristics of the Canadas. Instead of being shut out from all direct intercourse with England during half the year, they would possess a far more certain and speedy communication throughout the winter than they now possess in summer. The passage from Ireland to Quebec would be a matter of 10 to 12 days, and Halifax would be the great port by which a large portion of the trade, and all the conveyance of passengers to the whole of British North America, would be carried on. But even supposing these brilliant prospects to be such as we could not reckon on seeing realized, I may assume that it is not intended to make this road without a well-founded belief that it will become an important channel of communication between the upper and lower Provinces. In either case, would not the maintenance of such a road, and the mode in which the Government is administered in the different Provinces, be matters of common interest to all? If the great natural channel of the St. Lawrence gives all the people who dwell in any part of its basin such an interest in the Government of the whole as renders it wise to incorporate the two Canadas, the artificial work which would, in fact, supersede the lower part of the St. Lawrence, as the outlet of a great part of the Canadian trade, and would make Halifax, in a great measure, an outport to Quebec, would surely in the same way render it advisable that the incorporation should be extended to Provinces through which such a road would pass.

With respect to the two smaller Colonies of Prince Edward's Island and Newfoundland, I am of opinion, that not only would most of the reasons which I have given for an union of the others apply to them, but that their smallness makes it absolutely necessary, as the only means of securing any proper attention to their interests, and investing them with that consideration, the deficiency of which they have so much reason to lament in all the disputes which yearly occur between them and the citizens of the United States, with regard to the encroachments made by the latter on their coasts and fisheries. . . .

I know of but one difficulty in the way of such an union; and that arises from the disinclination which some of the lower Provinces might feel to the transference of powers from their present legislatures to that of the Union. The objection to this would arise principally, I imagine, from their not liking to give up the immediate control which they now have over the funds by which their local expenditure is defrayed. I have given such a view of the evils of this system, that I cannot be expected to admit that an interference with it would be an objection to my plan. I think, however, that the Provinces would have a right to complain, if these powers of local management, and of distributing funds for local purposes, were taken from provincial Assemblies only to be placed in the yet more objectionable hands of a general legislature. Every precaution should, in my opinion, be taken to prevent such a power, by any possibility, falling into the hands of the legislature of the Union. In order to prevent that, I would prefer that the Provincial Assemblies should be retained, with merely municipal powers. But it would be far better, in point both of efficiency and of economy, that this power should be entrusted to the municipal bodies of much smaller districts; and the formation of such bodies would, in my opinion, be an essential part of any durable and complete umon.

With such views, I should without hesitation recommend the immediate adoption of a general legislative union of all the British Provinces in North America, if the regular course of government were suspended or perilled in the lower Provinces, and the neces- sity of the immediate adoption of a plan for their government, without reference to them, a matter of urgency; or if it were possi- ble to delay the adoption of a measure with respect to the Canadas until the project of a union could have been referred to the legisla- tures of the lower Provinces. But the state of the lower Provinces, though it justifies the proposal of an union, would not, I think, render it gracious, or even just, on the part of Parliament to carry it into effect without referring it for the ample deliberation and consent of the people of those Colonies. Moreover, the state of the two Canadas is such, that neither the feelings of the parties con- cerned, nor the interests of the Crown or the Colonies themselves will admit of a single Session, or even of a large portion of a Ses- sion of Parliament, being allowed to pass without a definite deci- sion by the Imperial legislature as to the basis on which it purposes to found the future Government of those Colonies.

In existing circumstances, the conclusion to which the foregoing considerations lead me, is that no time should be lost in proposing to Parliament a Bill for repealing the 31 Geo. 3;[2] restoring the union of the Canadas under one legislature; and re-constituting them as one Province.

The Bill should contain provisions by which any or all of the other North American Colonies may, on the application of the legislature, be, with the consent of the two Canadas, or their united legislature, admitted into the Union on such terms as may be agreed on between them.

As the mere amalgamation of the Houses of Assembly of the two Provinces would not be advisable, or give at all a due share of representation to each, a Parliamentary Commission should be appointed, for the purpose of forming the electoral divisions, and determining the number of members to be returned on the principle of giving representation, as near as may be, in proportion to population. I am averse to every plan that has been proposed for giving an equal number of members to the two Provinces, in order to attain the temporary end of out-numbering the French, because I think the same object will be obtained without any violation of the principle of representation, and without any such appearance of injustice in the scheme as would set public opinion, both in England and America, strongly against it; and because, when emigration shall have increased the English population in the Upper Province, the adoption of such a principle would operate to defeat the very purpose it is intended to serve. It appears to me that any such electoral arrangement, founded on the present provincial divisions, would tend to defeat the purposes of union, and perpetuate the idea of disunion.

At the same time, in order to prevent the confusion and danger likely to ensue from attempting to have popular elections in districts recently the seats of open rebellion, it will be advisable to give the Governor a temporary power of suspending by proclamation, stating specifically the grounds of his determination, the writs of electoral districts, in which he may be of opinion that elections could not safely take place.

2 The Constitutional Act of 1791.

The same commission should form a plan of local government by elective bodies subordinate to the general legislature, and exercising a complete control over such local affairs as do not come within the province of general legislation. The plan so framed should be made an Act of the Imperial Parliament, so as to prevent the general legislature from encroaching on the powers of the local bodies.

A general executive on an improved principle should be established, together with a Supreme Court of Appeal, for all the North American Colonies. The other establishments and laws of the two Colonies should be left unaltered, until the legislature of the Union should think fit to change them; and the security of the existing endowments of the Catholic Church in Lower Canada should be guaranteed by the Act.

The constitution of a second legislative body for the united legislature, involves questions of very great difficulty. The present constitution of the Legislative Councils of these Provinces has always appeared to me inconsistent with sound principles, and little calculated to answer the purpose of placing the effective check which I consider necessary on the popular branch of the legislature. The analogy which some persons have attempted to draw between the House of Lords and the Legislative Councils seems to me erroneous. The constitution of the House of Lords is consonant with the frame of English society; and as the creation of a precisely similar body in such a state of society as that of these Colonies is impossible, it has always appeared to me most unwise to attempt to supply its place by one which has no point of resemblance to it, except that of being a non-elective check on the elective branch of the legislature. The attempt to invest a few persons, distinguished from their fellow-colonists neither by birth nor hereditary property, and often only transiently connected with the country, with such a power seems only calculated to ensure jealousy and bad feelings in the first instance, and collision at last. I believe that when the necessity of relying, in Lower Canada, on the English character of the Legislative Council as a check on the national prejudices of a French Assembly shall be removed by the union, few persons in the Colonies will be found disposed in favour of its present constitution. Indeed, the very fact of union will complicate the difficulties

which have hitherto existed; because a satisfactory choice of councillors would have to be made with reference to the varied interests
of a much more numerous and extended community.

It will be necessary, therefore, for the completion of any stable
scheme of government, that Parliament should revise the constitution
of the Legislative Council, and, by adopting every practicable means
to give that institution such a character as would enable it, by its
tranquil and safe, but effective working, to act as a useful check on
the popular branch of the legislature, prevent a repetition of those
collisions which have already caused such dangerous irritation.

The plan which I have framed for the management of the public
lands being intended to promote the common advantage of the
Colonies and of the mother country, I therefore propose that the
entire administration of it should be confined to an Imperial
authority. The conclusive reasons which have induced me to recommend this course, will be found at length in the separate Report
on the subject of Public Lands and Emigration.

All the revenues of the Crown, except those derived from this
source, should at once be given up to the United Legislature, on the
concession of an adequate civil list.

The responsibility to the United Legislature of all officers of the
Government, except the Governor and his Secretary, should be
secured by every means known to the British Constitution. The
Governor, as the representative of the Crown, should be instructed
that he must carry on his government by heads of departments, in
whom the United Legislature shall repose confidence; and that he
must look for no support from home in any contest with the legislature, except on points involving strictly Imperial interests.

The independence of the Judges should be secured, by giving
them the same tenure of office and security of income as exist in
England.

No money-votes should be allowed to originate without the previous consent of the Crown.

In the same Act should be contained a repeal of past provisions
with respect to the clergy reserves, and the application of the funds
arising from them.

In order to promote emigration on the greatest possible scale,
and with the most beneficial results to all concerned, I have else-

where recommended a system of measures which has been expressly framed with that view, after full inquiry and careful deliberation. Those measures would not subject either the Colonies or the mother country to any expense whatever. In conjunction with the measures suggested for disposing of public lands, and remedying the evils occasioned by past mismanagement in that department, they form a plan of colonization to which I attach the highest importance. The objects, at least, with which the plan has been formed, are to provide large funds for emigration, and for creating and improving means of communication throughout the provinces; to guard emigrants of the labouring class against the present risks of the passage; to secure for all of them a comfortable resting-place, and employment at good wages immediately on their arrival; to encourage the investment of surplus British capital in these colonies, by rendering it as secure and as profitable as in the United States; to promote the settlement of wild lands and the general improvement of the Colonies; to add to the value of every man's property in land; to extend the demand for British manufactured goods, and the means of paying for them, in proportion to the amount of emigration and the general increase of the colonial people; and to augment the colonial revenues in the same degree.

When the details of the measure, with the particular reasons for each of them, are examined, the means proposed will, I trust, be found as simple as the ends are great; nor have they been suggested by any fanciful or merely speculative view of the subject. They are founded on the facts given in evidence by practical men; on authentic information, as to the wants and capabilities of the colonies; on an examination of the circumstances which occasion so high a degree of prosperity in the neighbouring States; on the efficient working and remarkable results of improved methods of colonization in other parts of the British Empire; in some measure on the deliberate proposals of a Committee of the House of Commons; and, lastly, on the favourable opinion of every intelligent person in the colonies whom I consulted with respect to them. They involve, no doubt, a considerable change of system, or rather the adoption of a system where there has been none; but this, considering the number and magnitude of past errors, and the present wretched economical state of the Colonies, seems rather a recommendation than an objection. I do not flatter myself that so much good can be accomplished without an effort; but in this, as in other suggestions, I have presumed that the Imperial Government and legislature will appreciate the actual crisis in the affairs of these colonies, and will not shrink from any exertion that may be necessary to preserve them to the Empire.

By the adoption of the various measures here recommended, I venture to hope that the disorders of these Colonies may be arrested, and their future well-being and connexion with the British Empire secured. Of the certain result of my suggestions, I cannot, of course, speak with entire confidence, because it seems almost too much to hope that evils of so long growth, and such extent, can be removed by the tardy application of even the boldest remedy; and because I know that as much depends upon the consistent vigour and prudence of those who may have to carry it into effect, as on the soundness of the policy suggested. The deep-rooted evils of Lower Canada will require great firmness to remove them. The disorders of Upper Canada, which appear to me to originate entirely in mere defects of its constitutional system, may, I believe, be removed by adopting a more sound and consistent mode of administering the Government. We may derive some confidence from the recollection, that very simple remedies yet remain to be resorted to for the first time. And we need not despair of governing a people who really have hitherto very imperfectly known what it is to have a Government.

I have made no mention of emigration, on an extended scale, as a cure for political disorders, because it is my opinion, that until tranquillity is restored, and a prospect of free and stable government is held out, no emigrants should be induced to go to, and that few would at any rate remain in, Canada. But if, by the means which I have suggested, or by any other, peace can be restored, confidence created, and popular and vigorous government established, I rely on the adoption of a judicious system of colonization as an effectual barrier against the recurrence of many of the existing evils. If I should have miscalculated the proportions in which the friends and the enemies of British connexion may meet in the United Legislature, one year's emigration would redress the balance. It is by a sound system of colonization that we can render these extensive regions available for the benefit of the British people. The mismanagement by which the resources of our Colonies have hitherto been wasted, has, I know, produced in the public mind too much of a disposition to regard them as mere sources of corruption and loss, and to entertain, with too much complacency, the idea of abandoning them as useless. I cannot participate in the notion that it is the part either of prudence or of honour to abandon our countrymen when our government of them has plunged them into disorder, or our territory, when we discover that we have not turned it to proper account. The experiment of keeping Colonies and governing them well, ought at least to have a trial, ere we abandon for ever the vast dominion which might supply the wants of our surplus population, and raise up millions of fresh consumers of our manufactures, and producers of a supply for our wants. The warmest admirers, and the strongest opponents of republican institutions, admit or assert that the amazing prosperity of the United States is less owing to their form of government, than to the unlimited supply of fertile land, which maintains succeeding generations in an undiminishing affluence of fertile soil. A region as large and as fertile is open to Your Majesty's subjects in Your Majesty's American dominions. The recent improvements of the means of communication will, in a short time, bring the unoccupied lands of Canada and New Brunswick within as easy a reach of the British Isles as the territories of Iowa and Wisconsin are of that incessant emigration that annually quits New England for the Far West.

I see no reason, therefore, for doubting that, by good government, and the adoption of a sound system of colonization, the British possessions in North America may thus be made the means of conferring on the suffering classes of the mother country many of the blessings which have hitherto been supposed to be peculiar to the social state of the New World.

In conclusion, I must earnestly impress on Your Majesty's advisers, and on the Imperial Parliament, the paramount necessity of a prompt and decisive settlement of this important question, not only on account of the extent and variety of interests involving the welfare and security of the British Empire, which are perilled by every hour's delay, but on account of the state of feeling which exists in the public mind throughout all Your Majesty's North American possessions, and more especially the two Canadas.

In various Dispatches addressed to Your Majesty's Secretary of State, I have given a full description of that state of feeling, as I found it evinced by all classes and all parties, in consequence of the events which occurred in the last Session of the British Parliament. I do not allude now to the French Canadians, but to the English population of both provinces. Ample evidence of their feelings will be found in the Addresses which were presented to me from all parts of the North American Colonies, and which I have inserted in an Appendix to this Report. But, strong as were the expressions of regret and disappointment at the sudden annihilation of those hopes which the English had entertained of seeing a speedy and satisfactory termination of that state of confusion and anarchy under which they had so long laboured, they sunk into insignificance when compared with the danger arising from those threats of separation and independence, the open and general utterance of which was reported to me from all quarters. I fortunately succeeded in calming this irritation for the time, by directing the public mind to the prospect of those remedies which the wisdom and beneficence of Your Majesty must naturally incline Your Majesty to sanction, whenever they are brought under Your Majesty's consideration. But the good effects thus produced by the responsibility which I took upon myself, will be destroyed; all these feelings will recur with redoubled violence; and the danger will become immeasurably greater, if such hopes are once more frustrated, and the Imperial Legislature fails to apply an immediate and final remedy to all those evils of which Your Majesty's subjects in America so loudly complain, and of which I have supplied such ample evidence.

For these reasons, I pray Your Majesty's earnest attention to this Report. It is the last act arising out of the loyal and conscientious discharge of the high duties imposed upon me by the Commission with which Your Majesty was graciously pleased to entrust me. I humbly hope that Your Majesty will receive it favourably, and believe that it has been dictated by the most devoted feeling of loyalty and attachment to Your Majesty's Person and Throne, by the

strongest sense of public duty, and by the earnest desire to perpetuate and strengthen the connexion between this Empire and the
North American Colonies, which would then form one of the
brightest ornaments in Your Majesty's Imperial Crown.

All which is humbly submitted to Your Majesty.

DURHAM.

London, 31st January 1839.

Lord Durham's Report is still important reading, both for social scientists and for those with a general or scholarly interest in politics, philosophy, and history. It is helpful to a larger public that is dealing, in a variety of vexing circumstances, with finding the appropriate way to remember a troubled past and to delineate the moral and political consequences of specific ways of interpreting historical facts and events. Deciding these questions requires entering a perennial philosophical debate, that of how to make sense of the relationship between history, memory, and politics. To show why the Durham Report is as indispensable as ever for political theorists of all stripes, I will slightly reformulate a question that is a recurrent theme in Janet Ajzenstat's introduction to this edition: Can the universalistic pull of liberal modernity be reconciled with the preservation of particular identities and cultures? In the past twenty years, this question has been a central issue in the republic of letters. It is no mere coincidence that Canadians have played leading roles in such a debate[1] and, as is apparent to readers who have read the text that precedes this essay, the pedagogical value of the Durham Report is nowhere more important than in Canada and Quebec.

In 1963, when the last edited version of the Report was published in English, Quebec was going through the political phase of its own process of late and brutal modernization, known as the "Quiet Revolution."[2] Canada as a whole, on the eve of the 1967 Centennial of Confederation, was moving equally rapidly towards establishing its own national identity at a greater distance from Britain. In 1963 the Canadian federal government led by Lester Pearson put together the Royal Commission on Bilingualism and

Biculturalism, co-chaired by Davidson Dunton and André Lauren-
deau, whose mandate was based on the idea of an equal partner-
ship between the French- and English-speaking founding peoples
of Canada.[3] It is, of course, beyond the scope of this Afterword to
address at length the political evolution of Quebec and Canada
from 1963 to the present day, although I will not completely
ignore it.[4] It is sufficient at this stage to mention that this new edition of the Report, in its own right a commemoration of Durham's
legacy, is being published at about the same time as two major historical celebrations: we are about to mark the 400th anniversary of
the founding of the City of Quebec and of Canada by Champlain
in 1608 as well as the 25th anniversary of the 1982 constitution,
the last step in Canada's adventure of quiet decolonization from
Britain and the dawn of the era of the Canadian Charter of Rights
and Freedoms. In our days as well as in 1963 and in the epoch of
Durham, the historical paths of Canada and Quebec remain inter-
twined in their joint struggle for greater political freedom and the
development of secure, distinct identities in North America.

My argument here is thus premised on the idea that the Durham
Report has both universal and particular meanings. Given how
debatable and contradictory these meanings may prove to be, I do
not pretend to be able to end the debate. But is is my hope that fifty
years from now, when the Report undergoes yet another edition,
readers will still find in this Afterword useful notes and arguments
to help them make up their own minds on these matters.

I will start logically, dealing in the first section with the fate of
the Report in French Canada and Quebec and attempting to assess
how it has been viewed by previous generations and how it is being
discussed in current historiographical debates. Variations abound,
but the basic idea remains the same: Lord Durham and his Report
are causally connected to the emergence and the development of a
specific form of national self-consciousness. I will then discuss
Janet Ajzenstat's views as presented in the Foreword to this book,
starting with the key figure of Étienne Parent. Much of what my
colleague says throughout her introduction about the meaning of
the Durham Report for Canadian history and the evolution of federalism is very enlightening; I will supplement her general view
with my particular perspective. Following some notes on Durham

as a human being and as a thinker, I will focus on two other themes: the place of the Durham Report in one of Quebec's most important ideological and intellectual aspects, "melancholy nationalism" (an expression developed by political philosopher Jocelyn Maclure) and the role of the fundamental tension between universalistic and particularistic aspects in the tribulations of modernity – a key feature of the Report – and how this tension is being played out in Canada and Quebec.[5]

COMING TO TERMS WITH LORD DURHAM'S REPORT IN FRENCH CANADA AND QUEBEC

Canada is a member of an elite G-8 group of industrialized states in the global age of the internet. Quebec is a majority French-speaking province in a federal, highly developed country that prides itself on official bilingualism. Canada and Quebec thus share two autonomous but equally interconnected public spheres, two communicational and scientific networks operating in the great languages of Western modernity, English and French. The development of this social environment from 1963 to 2006 has produced greater academic and scholarly sophistication in all fields. History, the art of understanding the past, has not been left behind in this evolution. The task of revisiting the Durham Report is made even more challenging by the complexity and vigour of historiographical debates throughout Canada, particularly in Quebec.[6] There has also been, since the last English edition of the Report, a quantum leap in the level of interest in the international academic community about Canadian affairs. To highlight the perennial importance of Lord Durham and of the constitutional blueprint that arose at least partly based on his Report, I shall start with one such foreign voice, that of Dresden Professor Ingo Kolboom: "For French Canadians, it was the genesis of a historical trauma. The repression of the Patriotes and the sanctions on French Canadians, institutionalized by the Union Act in 1840, were their true historical defeat, inasmuch as they saw these events as a traumatizing deception on the part of the British, who revealed themselves to be the Conquerors of 1763. French Canadians re-lived the defeat of 1760 through the sanctions of 1840."[7]

I believe that Kolboom's interpretation in this passage reflects the hegemonic view of Lord Durham and his influence that has affected both the history and intellectual life of French Canada and Quebec. Durham's legacy has become even more present in academia in the last decade due to a rejuvenated interest in political history and a corresponding decline in interest in more positivistic and technically oriented economic and social history.[8] With Durham, as with other matters, Quebec and other Canadian historians now engage in more frequent and energetic debates, searching for insightful ways to debunk the historical myths at work in their respective communities.[9] I want to briefly consider two questions stemming from these recent exchanges. The first arises from attempts to establish the primary cause of the 1837–38 Rebellions. Was the crisis fundamentally linked to political reasons or was it rather, as Lord Durham forcefully argued, the apotheosis of a long-standing and insurmountable ethnic conflict? University of Toronto historian Allan Greer, an expert on the Rebellions in Lower Canada, has this to say about the archival evidence on this matter:

An influential school of thought in Canadian historiography that dates back to Lord Durham and others says that all fine phrases about political rights and freedom spouted by the patriots were a cover for an essentially xenophobic movement and that what is fundamental in Lower Canada is the conflict of English and French. Everything else is secondary. I would argue that the argument is almost exactly the reverse of reality ... The conflict that came to an acute stage in 1837 and 1838 had everything to do with the breakdown of politics as usual and a crisis of the state, which called forth a mobilization of the majority of the population ... The really acute strife and conflict between English and French came after that; it followed from that fundamentally political conflict ... What seems to have resulted is something that happens in a lot of revolutionary crises in other parts of the world and other eras of history. Ethnic and linguistic minorities became quite uncomfortable, as a reaction to the revolutionary process itself.[10]

The myth that Allan Greer helps to dismantle with regard to the source of the conflict is not the only one to have survived until quite recently, bringing me to the second issue. Obsessed by Durham's scathing language throughout his Report and by the cold severity of his prescription concerning assimilation, French Canadians and Quebec thinkers have tended to portray him as a formidable figure. Fernand Dumont summarizes this trend when he characterizes Lord Durham's implacable logic and "remarquable hauteur d'esprit" as "immense."[11] Durham as a spiritual semi-God? John Ralston Saul begs to differ with this judgment:

In a way our attitudes can be summarized through our relationship to Lord Durham. We have turned his four-month visit during 1838 into the touchstone of the Canadian condition ... The words aimed at francophones have been particularly retained by part of their elite as a sore to be scratched open on a regular basis. But consider the real Durham, beyond mythology. He was neither a great figure nor a great aristocrat. He inherited money and through political activity was paid off with a title. He was of marginal junior-minister importance ... His one original idea – the union of the two provinces would provoke the assimilation of the francophones – was completely wrong ... This is the context in which Durham's gratuitous insults must be seen. It was just the sort of language you'd have expected from an immature graduate of Eton in the nineteenth century ... The combination of personal privilege, marginal success, an unstable personality and class prejudice are enough to perpetuate this sort of juvenile wilfulness in a man who cannot engage with reality.[12]

Saul certainly has a point, although I believe that there is a room for greater nuance in the assessment of Lord Durham as a human being and as a thinker. Such a careful re-examination requires a journey through current historiographical developments. McGill Professor Yvan Lamonde is Quebec's pre-eminent historian of ideas and has provided a path toward a more balanced evaluation of Lord Durham's Report through his scholarly work, particularly a masterful synthesis on the nineteenth century.[13] Aside from his impeccable bibliographical work, Lamonde's essential contributions are a precise chronicling of the mounting dissatisfaction of Lower Canadian colonial elites vis-à-vis metropolitan authorities in the 1830s, a much needed determination of the intellectual climate at the time of the Rebellions through a detailed examination of the printed sources at the disposal of Lower Canadians in order to establish their knowledge of contemporary developments and struggles in the Americas and Europe, a profound analytical and contextual analysis of the political thought of Étienne Parent and Louis-Joseph Papineau (their personal intellectual evolutions, the transition from their close collaboration to their estrangement in the camps of moderation and revolution, their opinions on Lord Durham's mission during his sojourn in the Canadas, and their reactions to his Report), and finally a lucid understanding of the complex reasons that explain the failure of the Rebellions.[14] Indispensable reading in general, Lamonde makes one key point about Lord Durham that can easily be neglected by twenty-first century readers. Durham did not belong to a neutral, fact-finding commission of the International Court in The Hague trying to assess the causes of a conflict, determine responsibilities, and draw the contours of a durable and just institutional peace that would respect the premises of human rights conventions. Rather, Lord Durham was a British imperialist first and foremost, culturally and politically biased about the matters he had to enquire into and report about. This is particularly obvious, according to Lamonde, in his lack of criticism of the Legislative Council, the one colonial institution that Lower Canadians had constantly identified, starting with Pierre Bédard in 1814, as an essentially English ethnic structure that contradicted the spirit of British constitutionalism.[15]

French Canada (rather than Lower Canada – a fundamental distinction) as a self-conscious national community begins with Lord Durham's Report and its political consequences. Starting with the nostalgic, quasi-Romantic figure of François-Xavier Garneau, a contemporary of Durham, and going from the conservative urbanity of Thomas Chapais, the ultramontane and anti-modern nationalism of Lionel Groulx, the post-1945 Montréal School (Maurice Séguin, Guy Frégault and Michel Brunet, a generation obsessed by the negative consequences of the Conquest that set the stage politically for Quebec's post-1960 independence movement) and its Laval counterpart (Fernand Ouellet, Jean Hamelin, pioneers in a more positive evaluation of the British regime and of Canadian Confederation), to arrive finally at Lamonde's generation of scholars, historians have dated the birth of an ideology or doctrine of national survival in French Canada to the early 1840s. The ideology developed at this time focused on the conservation of the cultural, linguistic, religious, and other traditional institutions of the community, a program of survival that seems to confirm Lord Durham's verdict by delineating a national life that remains largely distant from the struggles of liberal politics and the challenges of market economic practices in America. Lord Durham and his Report have played a role in all phases of this historiographic saga. For those who are curious about the centrality of Lord Durham's legacy for contemporary Quebec society, it is useful to consider the work of the late Fernand Dumont and of Gérard Bouchard, two major thinkers who, as public intellectuals, have enjoyed wide respect beyond the walls of academia.

Both Dumont and Bouchard support the project of political sovereignty for Quebec. For both thinkers, independence is the political telos of political modernity. Nations are truly normal and healthy when they are completely sovereign. Trained in anthropological philosophy, psychology, and sociology, Dumont in his master narrative, *Genèse de la société québécoise*, emphasized the role of Lord Durham in producing the key individual and collective historical consciousness pathologies in French Canada. In doing this, Dumont integrates all the elements that led Durham to prescribe forced assimilation: the spirit of contempt and disrespect for most things French Canadian and the disparaging comparisons and prophecies of inevitable doom in America. He thus makes Durham one of the most important examples of the British – later transmuted into Canadian – Other for French Canada and French Canadians. This negative discourse of necessary assimilation based on inescapable inferiority has been slowly, subtly, and systematically internalized by French Canadians in their attempts to formulate their own discourse of national self-consciousness.[16] The Durham Report led to their permanent political subordination and to the development of a profound minority complex. In the next section I will discuss some problems associated with Dumont's narrative. My point here is simply to reiterate that Dumont holds that Lord Durham is directly linked to the existence of a deep problem of false consciousness in the historical trajectory of French Canada and of Quebec, the kind of problem that can only be cured by sovereignty. Whatever one may think of the validity of its thesis, Dumont's book remains useful for its comprehensive discussion of historical materials, particularly with regard to the generation of François-Xavier Garneau, which lived in the immediate aftermath of Lord Durham's Report and had to interpret – in truth had to invent narratively – French Canada in his shadow.

Gérard Bouchard, trained in sociology and in history, provides a nice complement to Dumont's approach. Whereas the latter is fascinated by the unfolding dramas of subjective consciousness, Bouchard is more interested in the apparently more objective comparative analysis of the structural patterns at work in the evolution of modern societies. In his magnum opus, *Genèse des nations et cultures du nouveau monde: Essai d'histoire comparée*, Bouchard studies the historical trajectories of Canada and Quebec by contrasting them with movements and trends in the experiences of Australia, Latin America, the United States, and New Zealand. His excellence in the art of synthesizing intellectual doctrines is illustrated in his very useful analytical summary of the doctrine of "la survivance" for French Canada, the paradigm of survival for a national culture and a collective memory.[17] According to Bouchard, Quebec is essentially the sole exception to a pattern that saw the full political emancipation, most often through processes of radical rupture, of all New World collectivities subordinated to European empires. On this narrative, Lord Durham and his Report stand at a critical historical juncture, one that saw a definitive break in the march of Lower Canada towards full societal and political maturity.[18] There is a teleological philosophy of history at work in Bouchard's thinking that sees Quebec's sovereignty as a normal end-point – the fulfilment of the promises of its roots and destiny on the American continent.[19]

How does Lord Durham fare, ultimately, in the work of these two widely admired figures of Quebec's sovereigntist intelligentsia? In Fernand Dumont's elegant prose, Durham is respected, critically dissected without being demonized. In Gérard Bouchard's more coldly scientific but equally compelling narratives, Durham is almost completely ignored but the consequences of his thoughts and actions are omnipresent. In both cases, his name is associated with the dark side of the past.

JANET AJZENSTAT'S INTRODUCTION:
DEBATING LORD DURHAM'S INFLUENCE ON CANADA AND
ASSESSING HIM AS A HUMAN BEING AND AS A THINKER

Janet Ajzenstat is quite right to emphasize the importance of Étienne Parent, editor of the newspaper *Le Canadien* in the 1830s and arguably Quebec's first real intellectual.[20] Throughout that decade, Parent attempted to articulate the reasonable middle ground, marching in the footsteps of Bédard and thus embracing British constitutionalism while at the same time attempting to balance his support for Enlightenment liberalism with the defence of Canadian nationality ("la nationalité canadienne," as it was referred to in pre-Durham years). In April 1837, when it became clear following the Russell Resolutions that authorities in Britain would remain deaf to the grievances of Lower Canada, Parent advocated renewed prudence and warned his compatriots to take care lest they suffer a fate similar to that of Poland in 1831 at the hands of Russia. In some circumstances, writes Parent, "there is both an honourable submission and a dishonourable domination."[21] In the aftermath of Lord Durham's Report, as Ajzenstat notes, Parent had his great moment of despair, contemplating the inevitable disappearance of "la nationalité canadienne" and the assimilation of his compatriots. As Ajzenstat lucidly argues, the history of Canada would not have unfolded as it has if Parent had not found ways to reconsider this bleak judgment. She fails, however, to mention that Parent lived through his darkest hour while he was in jail. He remained in custody from late December 1838 onwards, for a period about as long as Durham's own stay in the Canadas. His imprisonment occurred during a tough colonial winter and he became deaf. Parent was jailed – not on Durham's orders, for he had gone back to Britain two months before – on the basis of an article he had written in *Le Canadien* where he argued in quasi-Lockean terms that the real conspirators, those who were primarily responsibe for the disturbance of order, were those in authority who had multiplied provocations, pushing the people from excesses to new excesses by harshness and renewed harshness.[22] Parent despaired after such repressive means were used to crush and subjugate him. Durham and his era are more than a theoretical chapter in the history of liberal doctrine. These were dark times and Parent, as Allan Greer remarks, was not the only one to suffer from the politics of terror:

There was another version of terror, the counter-revolutionary terror, that occurred after the patriots were defeated and that took very harmful forms. Houses were burned down by the dozens, possibly by the hundreds, in the wake of the fighting in 1837–38. People were killed, people by the hundreds were thrown into jail. Many were taken into custody, probably thousands, for shorter periods, although it was not well recorded. So the population in the District of Montreal, in the rural areas, was well and thoroughly frightened into submission by these tactics.[23]

Near the end of her Introduction, Ajzenstat seems to suggest that Lord Durham felt that the safeguards of the parliamentary system would overcome the potential intolerance of the French majority and the flaws of Lower Canada's colonial regime. Following this logic, she writes, "Unconstrained rule by the French majority would soon become as intolerant as unconstrained rule by Governors and their cronies."[24] However – and this question seems to me as poignantly relevant in 2006 as it was to those who first had to live with the Report in 1839 – how could Durham have been so utterly certain about that, given his studied and complete ignorance, throughout his Commission, of those such as Étienne Parent and Louis-Hyppolite LaFontaine who represented the camp of moderate Canadian patriotism and support for British constitutionalism?[25] Lord Durham, preceded by his reputation as a Liberal reformer, was greeted with sympathetic anticipation when he disembarked in Quebec City in late May 1838. The turning point in the gradual disenchantment with him and his mission was his hiring of Adam Thom, also known in Lower Canada under his pen name of "Camillus" and the author of a series of "Anti- Gallic Letters" in the *Montreal Herald*.[26] Janet Ajzenstat argues persuasively that Durham was a coherent and far-reaching liberal thinker. If his attitude toward Lower Canadians of French background – to coin a new category – gives us an accurate measure of the man, fair-mindedness (otherwise put, a respect for the key humanistic concept of *audi alteram partem*) was not one of his cherished principles.

In addition to the doctrine of responsible government, has Lord Durham left other structural legacies to the architecture of the Canadian state and the spirit of Canadian federalism? On this matter, I would like to add a couple of notes to Ajzenstat's remarkably instructive remarks. With regard to responsible government, she is trying to re-assess whether or not Lord Durham wanted to maintain "the crucial powers of control and compliance" in Great Britain at the same time that he envisaged greater political autonomy for the Canadian colonies.[27] With regard to the division of powers in Canadian federalism, she is attempting to portray him as the forefather of a coherent, overarching principle for allocation of such responsibilities: the central government would take care of general matters with representatives in the federal Parliament debating, in the language of liberal universalism, the issues of concern to all citizens without consideration of their origins, whereas provincial governments would take care of local matters, with legislative representatives embracing the language of human particularities in their debates and paying primary attention to the interests of their citizens as these pertained to their cultural or national origins.[28] On the first matter, I suspect that in 1867 the Dominion of Canada was indeed the middle of a three-tiered hierarchical structure: some crucial powers of control remained with Westminster – legislative supremacy, organization of courts and ultimate jurisdiction over judicial arbitration, determination of foreign and defence policies, and overall coordination of the political association – while the Dominion enjoyed greater autonomy than previously and thus retained substantial control of those same areas in its relationships with its provincial counterparts.[29] Provinces, while remaining subordinate in key areas, also claimed greater autonomy. If this meta-interpretation is correct, then I would certainly agree with Ajzenstat when she writes that we in Canada have forgotten both this organization and Lord Durham's role in its conception. I want to point out, however, that the idea of this principled distribution is used yet again in two recent, seminal essays, written by André Burelle and Eugénie Brouillet, that attempt to make sense of the project of federal harmony for French Canada and Quebec around 1867.[30] Thus, at least in Quebec, this particular scheme has not been forgotten, but Ajzenstat is correct that Lord Durham's role in its formulation has been completely disregarded.

What should we make in the end of Lord Durham as a human being and as a thinker? Perhaps paradoxically, I think that in the above-mentioned passages John Ralston Saul has been too harsh on him. The man who arrived here with the promise of spring in 1838, and even more the one who departed with the bitterly cold rains of November, was tired, sick, overwhelmed with sadness in his personal life, and considerably weakened as a political animal – thoroughly diminished and thus incapable of moving beyond the prejudices associated with his own complex identity as a doctrinaire liberal politician, an English aristocrat, and a self-conscious British imperialist. On a more theoretical plane the most thought-provoking evaluation of Lord Durham and his times comes, in my judgment, from Stéphane Dion. According to him, it served Durham's purposes to assert that it was French Canada that espoused the principles and practices of anti-liberalism. This apparently objective sociological assessment made it possible for him to reconcile his liberal ideas with his geo-political preoccupations. As Dion rhetorically asks himself, "Would Durham have recommended the autonomy of Lower Canada if he had considered the patriots to be sincere in their professed liberalism? We will never know, because Durham and Alexis de Tocqueville (the two pre-eminent figures of liberal colonialism in the nineteenth century) formulated their arguments in ways that allowed them to avoid choosing between empire and liberty."[31]

I have so far been preoccupied with what could be called a critical hermeneutics that privileges an understanding of the past for the sake of the past. In the next section I will put much more emphasis on considerations of the present and the future – for Lord Durham and his Report continue to be significant not only for Canada and Quebec but for humankind in general.

A CRITICAL HERMENEUTICS FOR THE PRESENT AND THE FUTURE

In a key philosophical essay on the theories and histories of identity in Quebec, Jocelyn Maclure shows that people, particularly the intelligentsia, in Quebec, a province where the majority of the population is French-speaking, are still obsessed by the spirit of Lord Durham and have failed to liberate themselves from his shadow. According to Maclure, discussions of collective identity are narrative projects. These narratives are important to the emergence and consolidation of national communities. The fundamental criteria for judging the importance of such narratives is their continued presence in the writings and minds of interpreters.[32] Beyond the contributions that Lord Durham and his Report have made to the nature of the Canadian state and Canadian federalism, described in Ajzenstat's introduction, Maclure shows that both man and report strongly influenced the dominant ideological doctrine in interpretations of the past in Quebec. Maclure characterizes this all-encompassing feature of intellectual life in Quebec as "melancholy nationalism," a meeting point of history, memory, and politics. Discussing the ramifications of melancholy nationalism allows me to begin addressing the broader significance of Lord Durham's Report, moving outside French Canada and Quebec toward the idea of an inescapable tension between particularistic and universalistic dimensions of reality. To delineate the phenomenon of melancholy nationalism as precisely as possible, I will start with two quotations: one from Maclure's essay and one from Jocelyn Létourneau's critical work on the narrative construction of memory and identity in Quebec.

There exists in Quebec a whole discourse about the fragility, the precariousness, the tragic existence, the fatigue, the modesty, the philistinism, the mediocrity, the immaturity, and the indecision of the Québécois people. Those who intone this sombre national chant are drinking from a stream with many confluents. By searching a little and by adopting a certain relationship to the past, one can indeed find in the genesis of Quebec society, as well as in its recent history, the fuel for a major depression – or more precisely, a case of collective melancholia. In Freud's terms, melancholia is experienced as a kind of mourning whose sources elude us, which we cannot ascribe to a specific, identifiable loss. That is, melancholia is an elusive, diffuse, latent feeling of grief. From generation to generation, Quebec intellectuals and writers have attempted to follow the thread of this melancholia, in the belief that they can work back to the origins of Quebec's modern-day ills.[33]

This sad view of the past was created by the great French Canadian and Québécois intellectuals, from Garneau to Dumont, loyally and in good faith – albeit with varying degrees of modulation, subtlety, and complexity ... For these pioneers of historical consciousness, the inherent fragility of the community required that they carry the country as one holds a child. Thus, for them memory had to be at the beginning of method, misery had to structure the purpose, melancholy had to set the tone, and the text had to nurture memory.[34]

According to the narrative of melancholy nationalism, the vast majority of people remain completely unconscious of their alienation because they have "internalized in their identity the belittling, traumatizing, even insulting gaze of the other."[35] Their imagination is perpetually haunted by this gaze. The highest literary expression of the perspective of melancholy nationalism can be found in the essays and novels of Hubert Aquin, who coined the famous expression "the cultural fatigue of French Canada" to describe the psychological traits that emerged, at the level of both individual and collective consciousness, as a result of Lord Durham's verdict that the French should remain permanent minors: "self-punishment, masochism, a sense of unworthiness, 'depression,' the lack of enthusiasm and vigour."[36] The highest theoretical, philosophical, and historiographical expression in the tradition of melancholy nationalism is the narrative articulated by Fernand Dumont in *Genèse de la société québécoise*. Dumont shows that internalization and appropriation of the Other's degrading contempt has led to a state of permanent mental colonization in French Canada that has both individual and collective dimensions, even in contemporary Quebec.[37] While doing research and thinking about this Afterword, I could not help but be aware that Lord Durham was, and remains to this day, the first significant Other under whose gaze the narrative of melancholy nationalism perpetually unfolds. Consider the following passages near the end of the Report, when Lord Durham vividly recapitulates the gist of his analysis:

I know of no national distinctions marking and continuing a more hopeless inferiority ... There can hardly be conceived a nationality more destitute of all that can invigorate and elevate a people, than that which is exhibited by the descendants of the French in Lower Canada, owing to their retaining their peculiar language and manners. They are a people with no history, and no literature."[38]

The fate of such a destitute nationality could only be that of permanent political subordination under the rule of law, or, in Durham's own words, obliteration through assimilation into the numerical majority of a loyal English population reinforced by a systematic policy of encouraging like-minded immigrants.[39] With these passages in mind, Lord Durham seems a good candidate for the true "Other" of melancholy nationalism. Aside from the works of Aquin and Dumont, there are two persuasive illustrations of this connection in essays written by André D'Allemagne and Jean Bouthillette in the 1960s, the period in Quebec history that witnessed the apex of French Canada's collective alienation in the context of global decolonization.[40] The fate of Lord Durham as the historical embodiment of the British or English Other is not restricted to the narratives of melancholy nationalism: "anti-Durhamism" plays a fundamental role in a number of ideological statements in support of Quebec's aspirations towards full political sovereignty. Université de Montréal political scientist Denis Monière argues that sovereignty is necessary, first and foremost, because since 1867 Canada has fulfilled Lord Durham's vision, subjecting French Canadians in Quebec to all the social and psychological consequences that result from their status as a debilitated and paralysed political minority.[41] In an attempt to rekindle support for Quebec sovereignty, Gérard Bouchard makes very explicit the link between Lord Durham's heritage, the vocabulary of melancholy nationalism, and the ideal of political independence. Bouchard advocates returning to the founding ideals of the sovereignty movement: the vision that Quebec, as a Francophone and American nation, should be master of its own destiny; the goal of granting greater status to Francophone Québécois by revaluing, nationally and internationally, all areas of collective life; and, finally, the re-making of the identity of French Canadians, to repudiate the heritage of colonialism and restore the confidence and self-respect of Québécois.[42] According to Jacques Beauchemin, the goal of sovereignty for Quebec is inseparable from a desire to redress the march of history.[43] From this perspective, achieving sovereignty would be to bury, at long last, Lord Durham and his Report.

I would now like to discuss overcoming Lord Durham's heritage, and all other similar heritages, by looking at the insights of French philosopher Paul Ricoeur on the necessity of finding an equilibrium between remembrance and forgetfulness in the search for a moral way to deal with History.

For individuals as well as for groups, the fall of historical memory into the abyss of melancholy is catastrophic. It seems to me that this is the arresting conclusion reached by Paul Ricoeur near the end of his long and remarkably productive life.[44] Whenever a community closes itself to its own sufferings, thus becoming "blind and deaf to the sufferings of other communities," history must intervene to criticize and correct the memory of the first community. According to Ricoeur, memory, with the help of a critical historical hermeneutics, is able to achieve a certain sense of justice for, as he rhetorically puts it, "How could there be a happy memory that was not, as well, a just memory?"[45] Following the triumph of melancholy, the problem for identity is a Self that suffers from its own devaluation, from its own condemnation, from the consequences of its own downgrading, resulting in depression and anxiety.

Can French Canada and Quebec, influenced by their nationalist and sovereigntist historians, be put in the category of these communities that, following Ricoeur's logic, have traced the unhappy path towards the abyss of melancholy? This is the argument propounded by Maclure and Létourneau and the view of John Ralston Saul when he portrays Lord Durham's insults as resulting in a "sore to be scratched open on a regular basis." There is undeniably an element of truth in this critical assessment. As Jean-Philippe Warren contends, it may be that in its desire to focus on a psychoanalytical approach to the understanding of history, Dumont's generation has nourished and possibly even generated an overdeveloped sense of anxiety.[46] Université Laval sociologist Simon Langlois, closely associated with Dumont's school of thought, recognizes that the author of *Genèse de la société québécoise* clearly privileged the memory of a certain French Canadian past in the history of Quebec, neglecting aspects of diversity in the past and the present of this society, and neglecting as well the duty of every nation to re-imagine the future in a new light.[47] It would be an over-simplification, however, to conclude that the dominant intellectual characteristic of modern-day Quebec is the perpetuation of a fall into the abyss of melancholy, a fall inaugurated by Lord Durham's narrative in his Report.

In the social sciences, literature, and philosophy, the last two decades have been marked by a series of debates on the pluralistic nature of Quebec's collective identity and on the need to allow much greater space to these different memories in the reconstruction of Quebec's national history.[48] It is only fair to recognize the leading role played in this enterprise by Gérard Bouchard, who has probably become Quebec's pre-eminent historian and intellectual figure since the death of Fernand Dumont in 1997.[49] As well, echoing Ricoeur's admonitions about the importance of a happy and just historical memory, Jacques Beauchemin and Daniel Jacques have argued that in Quebec the politics of conquest and re-conquest must be replaced by a politics of concord, a politics marked by processes of dialogue and reciprocal recognitions, where people steeped in their plural identities argue their way towards reasonable compromises.[50] In the politics of concord, no one vision of the collective future can claim the language of historical inevitability. Newcomers to such a society have to accept that they have climbed aboard a train or joined a movie that has started without them.[51] They should not, moreover, be over-burdened by the memory of any particular group. In Quebec as elsewhere in the world, as Daniel Jacques concludes, the wounds of the past, the duty to remember, should not be the sole guiding principle in matters of political conduct.[52]

Jocelyn Maclure, following Freud, has described melancholia as a sort of mourning "whose sources elude us." I shall now venture to identify one such possible source for this kind of mourning, rejoining Ajzenstat in her introduction when she finds at the heart of Lord Durham's Report a fundamental tension between universalistic and particularistic dimensions in the unfolding of modernity. What would have happened, in the 1840s, if Lord Durham had recommended, and British imperial authorities had implemented, a regime of Dominion-like status or responsible self-government for Lower Canada? Would the French majority have acted despotically, ruling Lower Canada in an unconstrained, intolerant, and absolutist fashion? Or would this regime have inaugurated an era of tolerance, fairness, and pluralism in the history of the modern state, establishing an edifying precedent in a world attempting to deal with the conflicting challenges of liberalism and nationalism – of universalism and particularism – in the middle of the nineteenth century? There are no guarantees either way, but in the humanities and social sciences we have known since Max Weber that it is instructive to think through such counterfactual possibilities.[53] Lower Canada stood at the crossroads of these possibilities when Lord Durham, with his Report, directed it away from the optimistic alternative. I believe that this is a major source of the mourning that can be found in the narrative of melancholy nationalism. Remember Ajzenstat's key question: is universalism implacably hostile to expressions of particularity? Political philosophers ponder such difficult questions, whereas political communities act upon them. In his seminal work, *Critique de l'Américanité: Mémoire et démocratie au Quebec*, University of Ottawa sociologist Joseph-Yvon Thériault argues that this central question that fascinates Ajzenstat has been, since the advent of Lower Canada through the Constitution of 1791, the question that dominated public debates in the colony and later in French Canada and Quebec. Thériault calls it the question of the people and then suggests that the intellectual and political configurations stemming from this question can best be understood as the "Durham moment."[54] This question has always had a double nature, with a universalistic axis – envisaging the nation as a contractual community of individuals with liberal rights – and a particularistic one – emphasizing the broad cultural heritage of the national community. Lord Durham saw the French majority in Lower Canada as too anchored in a destitute and parochial heritage to be able to reach by itself the good of universality. The general spirit of his Report follows a rather Manichean logic: either tradition or modernity; either a nation of individual citizens or a community of heritage. Durham fails to integrate into his narrative the fact that, since the first session of its Parliament in 1792, Lower Canada had been struggling, however imperfectly, to find its own balance between the good of universality and the good of particularity.[55] In the end, there is nothing mysterious about such a tension in philosophy or politics. As Ajzenstat herself remarks, the idea of the ineluctability of this tension is generally accepted by contemporary political theory.[56]

Lord Durham's Report still makes remarkable sense in contemporary Canada and Quebec not only because it affected both the nature of the emerging Canadian federal state in 1867 and the whole intellectual history of French Canada and Quebec, whether we prefer to look at it from Maclure's perspective of melancholy nationalism or from Thériault's approach insisting on a "Durham moment," but because his reductive and doctrinaire view of the conflict between universality and particularity had a great influence on the philosophical make-up of Pierre Elliott Trudeau, Canada's most important statesman in the twentieth century and the father of our 1982 constitutional revision and of our Charter of Rights and Freedoms. Having written about this extensively elsewhere, I do not want to belabour the point.[57] I shall only add that with regard to Trudeau's own understanding of the struggle between liberal universalism and national particularism in French Canada, major thinkers such as Thériault and Lamonde make an explicit connection between Lord Durham's interpretation and the one propounded by Canada's former prime minister.[58] Moreover André Burelle, a friend of Trudeau who worked for him as a speech-writer and a close collaborator in the crucial stages of his career, has just documented the triumph of doctrinaire liberalism in Trudeau's intellectual evolution that led to the ultimate exclusion of any meaningful recognition of Quebec's difference, of its particularity, in the constitution that Canada and Quebec have inherited from him.[59] If we are to believe Ajzenstat, there are ways to cope with the tension between universalism and particularism: "Politics is a matter of compromise; even fundamental principles must be bent sometimes – a little – on occasion."[60] If we are to believe André Burelle, Trudeau thought otherwise with regard to French Canada and Quebec. If the connection between Lord Durham and Trudeau holds true, then the spirit of the famous

Report belongs not only to our past but is also intimately related to the present and to the future of Canada and Quebec.

CONCLUSION

Historians should not forget that the task of making history in our liberal and democratic world belongs to citizens. Paul Ricoeur adds that although thinkers only narrate history, they remain responsible for what they say, particularly when their work applies to wounded memories.[61] Delineating the existence of a link between a sense of "wounded dignity" and manifestations of national patriotism in French Canada and Quebec is certainly not the exclusive province of the authors normally associated with melancholy nationalism. But how should we deal with these aspects of our collective memory? I am no expert on this issue. My best answer, using Lord Durham's Report as an edifying example for us and for people elsewhere, is this Afterword. More to the point, I believe, with Ricoeur, that the memory of those who actually suffered in the past must be honoured. Thus Quebec is right to honour the memory of the Patriotes, particularly the memory of the twelve who died on the scaffolds erected by colonial despotism. Once this is done, however, I believe it is appropriate to place one's historical wounds in comparative perspective, paying due respect to the wounds of the other groups and communities with whom one has shared parts of the past and with whom one hopes to share parts of the future. I am careful when discussing the future, because I believe it is open-ended. Constructing an appropriate historical memory for any community should be done without pre-judging the "normal" unfolding of history, particularly since I believe that the idea of normality is a blatant illusion. It should be recognized, as John Ralston Saul has argued, that Quebec historians of all stripes have paid greater attention to the various conflicts between francophones and anglophones than to periods of greater harmony and collaboration. A happy and just memory requires a better balance between these two poles than has been achieved so far. A happy and just memory requires that, in a complex modern society made of groups and individuals with plural identities, we should pay equal attention to what we have done together and to one another in the past, and to what we dream of accomplishing in the future.

Where does that leave us with Lord Durham and his Report? According to Ajzenstat, Lord Durham's lasting question is the problem of the relationship between universalism and particularism. In his reflections on the same question, Joseph-Yvon Thériault called it both the question of the people in French Canada and the question of Quebec. I believe that Lord Durham's question IS the question of Quebec. And dealing with this question requires not only answering it for Quebec but finding a vitally important answer for the world in the twenty-first century.

Guy Laforest
Département de science politique
Université Laval
August 2006

NOTES

1 Beiner, Ronald and Wayne Norman, eds., *Canadian Political Philosophy* (Toronto: Oxford University Press, 2001).

2 Gagnon, Alain-G., *Quebec, State and Society* (Peterborough: Broadview Press, third edition, 2003); Simard, Jean-Jacques, "Ce siècle où le Québec est venu au monde," in Côté, Roch, ed. *Québec 2000: rétrospective du XXe siècle* (Montreal: Fides, 1999),.17–78; Cook, Ramsay, *Watching Quebec: Selected Essays* (Montreal and Kingston: McGill-Queen's University Press, 2005).

3 McRoberts, Kenneth, *Misconceiving Canada: The Struggle for National Unity* (Toronto: Oxford University Press, 1997), 38–41.

4 Up-to-date political science textbooks are the right place to start addressing this question. See MacIvor, Heather, ed., *Parameters of Power: Canada's Political Institutions* (Toronto: Nelson Canada, fourth edition, 2006); and Pelletier, Réjean, and Manon Tremblay, eds., *Le parlementarisme canadien* (Quebec: Presses de l'Université Laval, third edition, 2005). For my own views, see Laforest, Guy, *Pour la liberté d'une société distincte* (Quebec: Presses de l'Université Laval, 2004), 325–55.

5 Maclure, Jocelyn, *Quebec Identity: The Challenge of Pluralism*
(Montreal and Kingston: McGill-Queen's University Press, 2003),
19–59. As Maclure acknowledges, it must be said in fairness that
Jocelyn Létourneau had previously, and critically, established a link
between misery and melancholy in Quebec's historiography. See the
essays collected in Létourneau, Jocelyn, *A History for the Future:
Rewriting Memory and Identity in Quebec* (Montreal and Kingston:
McGill-Queen's University Press, 2004), 101.

6 To grasp the basic trends in the historiography of Quebec, see
Rudin, Ronald, *Making History in Twentieth-Century Quebec*
(Toronto: University of Toronto Press, 1997); Gagnon, Serge, *Quebec and Its Historians: 1840 to 1920* (Montreal: Harvest House,
1982); Gagnon, Serge, *Quebec and Its Historians: The Twentieth
Century* (Montreal: Harvest House, 1985).

7 Kolboom, Ingo, *Pièces d'identité: signets d'une décennie allemande*
(Montreal: Presses de l'Université de Montréal, 2001), 192. I find a
clear and coherent expression of this dominant view in Dufour,
Christian, *A Canadian Challenge, Le défi québécois* (Vancouver:
Oolichan Books, 1990), chapter 3. Even those who disagree with
this paradigm agree on its centrality. See Létourneau, Jocelyn, *Le
Québec, Les Québécois: un parcours historique* (Quebec: Musée de
la civilisation and Editions Fides, 2004), 30.

8 This recent development is discussed by the editor in the introduction to his book in Kelly, Stéphane, ed., *Les idées mènent le Québec*
(Quebec: Presses de l'Université Laval, 2003), 1–11; see also Kelly,
Stéphane, and Guy Laforest, "Aux sources d'une tradition politique," in Ajzenstat, Janet, Paul Romney, Ian Gentles, and William
D. Gairdner, eds., *Débats sur la fondation du Canada, Québec*
(Presses de l'Université Laval, 2004), 527–46. The return of political
history is illustrated and discussed in a series of new journals that
have emerged in Quebec in the last decade: *Argument, Bulletin d'histoire politique, Mens: revue d'histoire intellectuelle de l'Amérique
française, Cahiers d'histoire du Québec au vingtième siècle, Les
Cahiers du 27 Juin, Globe: Revue internationale d'études québécoises*. For developments throughout Canada, see Owram, Doug,
"Narrow Circles: The Historiography of Recent Canadian Historiography," *National History: A Canadian Journal of Enquiry and
Opinion* 1, no. 1, (1997): 5–21.

9 Institute for Research on Public Policy with the collaboration of Meisel, John, Guy Rocher, and Arthur Silver, *As I Recall Si Je Me Souviens Bien: Historical Perspectives* (Montreal: IRPP, 1999).

10 These excerpts are taken from an interview with Allan Greer in Bothwell, Robert, ed., *Canada and Quebec: One Country Two Histories* (Vancouver: UBC Press, 1995), 32–3. Lengthier discussion in Greer, Allan, *The Patriots and the People* (Toronto: University of Toronto Press, 1992).

11 Dumont, Fernand, *Genèse de la société québécoise* (Montreal: Boréal, 1993),128.

12 Ralston Saul, John, *Reflections of a Siamese Twin: Canada at the End of the Twentieth Century* (Toronto: Viking, 1997), 363–5.

13 Lamonde, Yvan, *Histoire sociale des idées au Québec: 1760–1896* (Montreal: Fides, 2000). For an annotated introductory bibliography on Quebec, the reader should start with Gagnon, Alain-G., *Quebec* (Oxford: Clio Press, 1998). For a summary of Lamonde's own bibliographical progress through the history of ideas in Quebec, see Lamonde, Yvan, *Histoire sociale des idées au Québec, 1896–1929* (Montreal: Fides, 2003), 11. Étienne Parent – the learned journalist and moderate constitutionalist – and Louis-Joseph Papineau – the great Parliamentarian turned rebel and exiled radical Republican – are the most important of Durham's contemporaries in Lower Canada. Lamonde has made it much easier to arrive at a comprehensive understanding of their intellectual evolution. See Parent, Étienne, *Discours*, edition prepared by Yvan Lamonde and Claude Couture (Montreal: Presses de l'Université de Montréal, 2000); see also Lamonde, Yvan, and Claude Larin, *Louis-Joseph Papineau, un demi-siècle de combats: interventions publique,* (Montreal: Fides, 1998).

14 Lamonde, *Histoire sociale des idées au Québec: 1760–1896*, 183–282. Two enlightening recent essays attempting to further the work of Lamonde in his areas of originality are Harvey, Louis-Georges, *Le printemps de l'Amérique française: Américanité, anticolonialisme et républicanisme dans le discours politique québécois, 1805–1837* (Montreal: Boréal, 2005); and Bellavance, Marcel, *Le Québec au siècle des nationalités: essai d'histoire comparée* (Montreal, VLB éditeur, 2004).

15 Lamonde, *Histoire sociale des idées au Québec: 1760–1896*, 261.

16 Dumont, *Genèse de la société québécoise*, 123–38. For a critical yet sympathetic introduction to Dumont's project, see Beauchemin,

Jacques, "Dumont: historien de l'ambiguïté," *Recherches sociographiques* 42, no.2 (2001): 219–38. See also Warren, Jean-Philippe, "L'hiver de la mémoire," in Warren, Jean-Philippe, *Un supplément d'âme: Les intentions primordiales de Fernand Dumont (1947– 1970)* (Quebec: Presses de l'Université Laval, 1998), 159–93.

17 Bouchard, Gérard, *Genèse des nations et cultures du nouveau monde: Essai d'histoire comparée* (Montreal: Boréal, 2000), 107–10.

18 Ibid., 98–9.

19 This interpretation is shared by sympathetic and more critical readers of Bouchard as shown in, respectively, Beauchemin, Jacques, *L'histoire en trop: La mauvaise conscience des souverainistes québécois* (Montreal: Boréal, 2002), 142–3 and Létourneau, Jocelyn, *A History for the Future: Rewriting Memory and Identity in Quebec* (Montreal: McGill-Queen's University Press, 2004), 55–64. To gain a sense of Bouchard's position among Quebec historians, see Bédard, Eric, "Genèse des nations et cultures du Nouveau Monde: le magnum opus de l'historiographie moderniste," *Bulletin d'histoire politique* 9, no.2 (2001): 160–73.

20 Bergeron, Gérard, *Lire Étienne Parent: notre premier intellectuel (1802–1874)* (Quebec: Presses de l'Université du Québec, 1994).

21 Parent, Étienne, "Une soumission honorable," in Lamonde, Yvan, and Claude Corbo, eds., *Le rouge et le bleu: une anthologie de la pensée politique au Québec de la Conquête à la Révolution tranquille* (Montreal: Presses de l'Université de Montréal, 1999), 100.

22 I am trying here to render as concisely as possible a key passage; a longer excerpt can be found in Lamonde, Yvan, *Histoire sociale des idées au Québec: 1760–1896*, 267.

23 This quotation comes from Bothwell, *Canada and Quebec*, 33.

24 Ajzenstat, Janet, Introduction to this edition, xxvi.

25 Lamenting Lord Durham's failure to hear the voices of the representatives of the Lower Canadian French majority is a perennial theme. See Desrosiers, Léo-Paul, *L'accalmie: Lord Durham au Canada* (Montreal: *Le Devoir*, 1937), 123; see also Viau, Roger, *Lord Durham* (Montreal: Editions HMH, 1962), 163.

26 Bindon, Kathryn M., "Adam Thom," *Dictionary of Canadian Biography/Dictionnaire biographique du Canada, 1881–1890*, vol.

11 (Toronto and Quebec City: University of Toronto Press and Presses de l'Université Laval, 1982), 874–6.

27 Ajzenstat, Janet, Introduction to this edition, xxv.

28 Ibid., xxviii–xxviv.

29 Caron, Jean-François, Catherine Vallières-Roland, and Guy Laforest, "Le déficit fédératif au Canada," in Gagnon, Alain-G,. ed., *Le fédéralisme canadien contemporain: Fondements, traditions, institutions* (Montreal: Presses de l'Université de Montréal, 2006), 158–61.

30 Burelle, André, *Pierre Elliott Trudeau: L'intellectuel et le politique* (Montreal: Fides, 2005), 433–69; Brouillet, Eugénie, *La négation de la nation: L'identité culturelle québécoise et le fédéralisme canadien* (Quebec: Septentrion, 2005), 192–8.

31 Dion, Stéphane, "Durham et Tocqueville sur le colonialisme libéral," *Journal of Canadian Studies /Revue d'études canadiennes* 25, no.1 (1990): 75. My translation.

32 Maclure, *Quebec Identity*, 8–15.

33 Ibid., 20.

34 Létourneau, *A History for the Future*, 101–2. In the second chapter of his essay, Maclure engages critically with Létourneau's work and with my own. As he remarks, Létourneau began to focus on the centrality of this melancholical dimension in two important articles: Létourneau, Jocelyn, "'Impenser' le pays et toujours l'aimer," *Cahiers internationaux de sociologie* 105 (1998): 363; "Pour une révolution de la mémoire collective: Histoire et conscience historique chez les Québécois," *Argument* 1 (1998): 41–57.

35 Létourneau, *A History for the Future*, 101.

36 Aquin, Hubert, "La fatigue culturelle du Canada français," in Aquin, Hubert, *Blocs erratiques*, (Montreal: Quinze, 1977), 88. In English, see Aquin, Hubert, *Writing Quebec* (Edmonton: University of Alberta Press, 1988), 35. I am following here the analysis in Maclure, *Quebec Identity*, 25–8.

37 Ibid., 41–4.

38 Lord Durham's Report, this edition, 147 and 153.

39 Ibid., 153

40 D'Allemagne, André, *Le colonialisme au Québec* (Montreal: Agone, 2000), 20; Bouthillette, Jean, *Le Canadien Français et son double* (Montreal: L'Hexagone, 1972), 50–1. D'Allemagne makes a connection between the failure of the Rebellions, their demoralizing conse-

quences, and the emergence of a deep inferiority complex; Bouthillette describes how French Canadians have become strangers to themselves, how the defeat of the Patriotes remains their definitive loss, and how the fall into nostalgia has been accompanied by regret and disconsolate pain. Readers should be warned: if you believe that Marx, Hegel, Jean-Paul Sartre, and Franz Fanon are too abstract and imprecise about alienation, just read Bouthillette.

41 Monière, Denis, *Pour comprendre le nationalisme au Québec et ailleurs* (Montreal: Presses de l'Université de Montréal, 2001), 138–40.

42 Bouchard, Gérard, "Le projet de souveraineté du Québec: Sortir de l'impasse en revenant aux idées fondatrices," *Le Devoir*, 17 June 2006, B-5.

43 Beauchemin, *L'histoire en trop*, 181.

44 Ricoeur, Paul, *La Mémoire, L'Histoire, L'Oubli* (Paris: Seuil, 2000), 81.

45 Ibid., 650

46 Warren, Jean-Philippe, *Un supplément d'âme: Les intentions primordiales de Fernand Dumont (1947– 1970)*, 161.

47 Langlois, Simon, "Refondation de la nation au Québec," in Côté, Roch, and Michel Venne, eds., *L'annuaire du Québec 2003: Toute l'année politique, sociale, économique et culturelle* (Montreal: Fides, 2002), 11

48 Elbaz, Mikhaël, Andrée Fortin, and Guy Laforest, eds., *Les frontières de l'identité: Modernité et postmodernisme au Québec* (Quebec and Paris: Presses de l'Université Laval and Editions de l'Harmattan, 1996); see also Venne, Michel, ed., *Penser la nation québécoise* (Montreal: Quebec Amérique, 2000); Maclure, Jocelyn, and Alain-G. Gagnon, *Repères en mutation: Identité et citoyenneté dans le Québec contemporain* (Montreal: Québec Amérique 2001); Seymour, Michel, *La nation en question* (Montreal: L'Hexagone, 1999); Laforest, Guy, *De l'urgence* (Montreal: Boréal, 1995).

49 Bouchard, Gérard, *La nation québécoise au futur et au passé* (Montreal: VLB éditeur, 1999).

50 Jacques, Daniel, "Des 'conditions gagnantes' aux 'conditions signifiantes'," in Venne, Michel, *Penser la nation québécoise*, 71–6; Beauchemin, *L'Histoire en trop*, 182–3. These authors agree with

Maclure when he defines dialogue as a process of "reciprocal eluci-
dation"; see Maclure, *Quebec Identity*, 15.

51 Taylor, Charles, "Nation culturelle, nation politique," in Venne,
Penser la nation québécoise, 42.

52 Jacques, "Des 'conditions gagnantes' aux 'conditions signifiantes',"
in Venne, *Penser la nation québécoise*, 83.

53 Weber, Max, *Essais sur la théorie de la science* (Paris: Plon, 1965),
290–300.

54 Thériault, Joseph-Yvon, *Critique de l'américanité: Mémoire et
démocratie au Québec* (Montreal: Québec Amérique, 2002), 296–0.

55 Ibid., 294–5.

56 Ajzenstat, Janet, Introduction to this edition, xxvii. See for instance
Taylor, Charles, "Les sources de l'identité moderne," in Elbaz,
Mikhaël, Andrée Fortin, and Guy Laforest, eds., *Les frontières de
l'identité: Modernité et postmodernisme au Québec*, 357–60; and
Kymlicka, Will, "Misunderstanding Nationalism," in Kymlicka,
Will, *Politics in the Vernacular: Nationalism, Multiculturalism and
Citizenship* (Toronto: Oxford University Press, 2001), 242–53.

57 Laforest, Guy, *Trudeau and the End of a Canadian Dream* (Montreal and Kingston: McGill-Queen's University Press, 1995), 171–84.

58 Thériault, *Critique de l'américanité*, 311; see also Lamonde, Yvan,
Trajectoires de l'histoire du Québec (Quebec and Montreal: Musée
de la civilisation et Editions Fides, 2001), 14–15.

59 Burelle, André, *Pierre Elliott Trudeau: L'Intellectuel et le politique*,
68–74 and 462–44.

60 Ajzenstat, Janet, Introduction to this edition, xxvii.

61 Ricoeur, Paul, "Mémoire, histoire, oubli," *Esprit*, March-April 2006,
323.

SUGGESTIONS FOR FURTHER READING

GERALD CRAIG

Apart from the Lucas edition of the Report (Oxford: Clarendon Press, 1912), by far the most important book on Durham and his Report is Chester W. New, *Lord Durham* (Oxford, 1929), and the reader is referred to its comprehensive bibliography for items published before 1928. The Canadian portion of this volume, entitled *Lord Durham's Mission to Canada*, is available in the Carleton Library (Toronto, 1963). Two works especially, which describe political conditions in Upper Canada, should be mentioned. Aileen Dunham, *Political Unrest in Upper Canada, 1815–36* (London, 1927; also the Carleton Library, 1963), and W. Stewart Wallace, *The Family Compact* (Toronto, 1915). E.M. Wrong, *Charles Buller and Responsible Government* (Oxford, 1926) is a useful study of the colonial reformer who was Durham's principal political advisor. Attention should also be drawn to the *Report of the Public Archives*, 1923 (Ottawa, 1924), which provides a calendar of the Durham Papers at the Public Archives of Canada, and reprints several documents and dispatches.

Among several items published since the appearance of New's bibliography which bear on the Report and the Canadian background are William Smith, *Political Leaders of Upper Canada* (Toronto, 1931); D.G. Creighton, *The Commercial Empire of the St. Lawrence, 1760–1850* (New York and Toronto, 1937; reprinted as *The Empire of the St. Lawrence, 1956): The Canadian Historical Review* 20 (June, 1939) containing articles by Lord Tweedsmuir, Chester New, George W. Brown, D.C. Harvey, and

Chester Martin commemorating the centenary of the Report;
L'Abbé Arthur Maheux, "Durham et la Nationalité Canadienne-
Française," *Report* of the Canadian Historical Association, 1943,
19–24; H.T. Manning, *The Revolt of French Canada, 1800–1835*
(Toronto, 1962), and G.M. Craig, *Upper Canada, The Formative
Years, 1784–1841* (Toronto, 1963).

JANET AJZENSTAT

Two notable monographs appeared after Craig prepared his list of
readings. Ged Martin, *The Durham Report and British Policy, A
Critical Essay* (Cambridge, 1972) undertakes to deflate Durham's
reputation generally and the importance of his proposal for
responsible government in particular by arguing that Durham's
ideas were not original and had little effect on subsequent events.
The scholar will find Martin's bibliography and footnotes helpful.
By way of contrast, Janet Ajzenstat, *The Political Thought of Lord
Durham* (Montreal, 1988) approaches the Report sympathetically,
contending in the preface that the Report contains "a comprehensive statement about the conditions for political freedom and the
place of nationalities in a liberal society that can still inform and
may still convince."

Like Craig, I regard New's bibliography as indispensable; indeed
I am deeply indebted to New, Craig, and Martin. Nevertheless
there are well-known works that they do not mention, some
recent. On Canadian events of the period see William Ormsby, *The
Emergence of the Federal Concept in Canada, 1839–1845*
(Toronto, 1969); Peter Burroughs, *The Canadian Crisis and British
Colonial Policy, 1828–1841* (Toronto, 1972); and Fernand Ouellet, *Lower Canada, 1791–1840* (Toronto, 1980); Yvan Lamond,
Histoire sociale des idées du Québec: 1760–1896 (Montreal,
2000), and Gérard Bouchard, *Genèse des nations et cultures du
nouveau mond: Essai d'historie comparée* (Montreal, 2000). See
also Guy Laforest, *Trudeau and the End of a Canadian Dream*
(Montreal, 1995), chapter 8, "The Spirit of Conquest, Lord
Durham, and National Identities." On Durham's recommendation
for responsible government, consult Phillip A. Buckner, *The Transition to Responsible Government, British Policy in British North*

America, 1815–1850 (Westport, CT, 1985); but see also Janet Ajzenstat, "Modern Mixed Government: A Liberal Defence of Inequality," *Canadian Journal of Political Science* 18, no. 1 (March, 1985). On Durham's radical associates, all of whom took a lively interest in Canada, I recommend Joseph Hamburger, *Intellectuals in Politics: John Stuart Mill and the Philosophic Radicals* (New Haven, 1965). On the issue of Alexis de Tocqueville's influence on Durham, see Jacques Vallée, *Tocqueville au Bas-Canada* (Montreal, 1973), and Ajzenstat, "French Canada and the Liberal Theory of Nationality: Some Now Unpopular 19th Century Ideas," *Dalhousie Review* (Summer, 1985).

On Durham's proposal to unite Upper and Lower Canada and his views on French Canadian nationalism, see the Introduction to the translation of the report by Marcel-Pierre Hamel, *Le Rapport de Durham* (Quebec, 1948); Ramsay Cook, *Canada and the French Canadian Question* (Toronto, 1966); Jacques Monet, *The Last Cannon Shot, A Study of French-Canadian Nationalism, 1837–1850* (Toronto, 1969); Denis Bertrand and André Lavallée, "Introduction," in Denis Bertrand and Albert Desbiens, eds. and trans., *Le Rapport de Durham* (Montreal, 1969); Jean-Paul Bernard, *Les Rouges, Liberalisme, Nationalisme, et Anti-cléricalisme aux Milieux de XIXe Siècle* (Montreal, 1971). Very useful too is Guy Laforest's Afterword in this edition, which describes recent interpretations of the Report and, among other topics, explores the "return of political history" in Quebec and the historian's role in determining the political culture. A primary source not to be overlooked is Papineau's bitter outburst: Louis-Joseph Papineau, *Histoire de l'insurrection du Canada, en refutation du Rapport de Lord Durham* (Burlington and Paris, 1839; Quebec, 1968).

In 1989, Trent University held a conference to mark the 150th anniversary of the Report's publication; the presentations were collected in a special issue of the *Journal of Canadian Studies* (25, no. 1, Spring, 1990) entitled "Durham and His Ideas." Among the contributors are Alan Wilson; David R. Cameron; Janet Ajzenstat; Ged Martin; Stéphane Dion; Serge Courville, Jean-Claude Robert, and Normand Séguin; Deryck Schreuder; John Darwin; Antony Kirk-Greene; and William Westfall.

absentee proprietors,
Prince Edward
Island, 103–4,
117–18
agriculture, 9–10, 20,
149, 104
amnesty, xxxv, 87
Assembly, House of.
See Legislative
Assembly

Baillie [Thomas],
Commissioner of
Crown Lands, New
Brunswick, 113
Baldwin, Robert, xliii,
80
banks and banking,
30, 69–70, 74, 164
Bédard, Pierre, xxi,
xxii
Bermuda, xxxv
Blackstone, William,
xxii
Brock, General
[Isaac], heirs of,
115

Brougham, Lord,
xxxv
Brown, George, xxviii
Buffalo, 111, 132
Buller, Charles, xv, xli
bureaucracy: Lower
Canada, 24, 48–50,
56–61; Upper
Canada, 74–5
Burke, Edmund, xxii
Burroughs, Peter, xix

Cartier, George-
Etienne, xxvi, xxviii
casual and territorial
revenues, 47,
69–70. *See also* rev-
enue, taxation
censitaire. *See* habi-
tant
churches. *See* religion
civil list, 47–8, 170
Civil Secretary, 60
clergy reserves, xli,
75, 85, 88, 89–93,
109, 113–15; and
charitable aid and

religious instruction,
68–9
Colborne, Sir John,
90
Colonial Office, xiii,
56–8, 75, 102, 165
Commonwealth of
Nations, xix, xxxiii
communications; by
land and water, 10,
99–100, 164–6;
neglected opportu-
nities for develop-
ment of, 55, 96,
111–12
Confederation, xxvi,
xxviii.
Congress (United
States), 109, 156
Constitutional Act,
1791, xxv, 48, 168;
and clergy reserves,
68, 114
corruption and job-
bery, 54–5, 77–8,
97, 116, 143, 159;
absent in U.S.,

109–10. *See also*
bureaucracy
Craig, Gerald, viii, ix,
x, xv
Craig, James Henry,
Governor of Que-
bec, xxii
Crown, 47, 56, 59,
138–9, 142, 143,
170; and imperial
connection, 141
crown lands. *See* pub-
lic lands, casual
and territorial
revenues
Coupland, Sir Regi-
nald, xliv
currency. *See* banks
and banking
Cushing, Elmer, 115
customs duties, 47,
163–4; and con-
flicts between
Upper and Lower
Canada, 70–1,
100–1

democracy, spirit of:
in American Revo-
lution, 18; and Eng-
lish Canadian pop-
ulation, 19
despotism of the
French regime in
North America, 20
dissolution on demise
of monarch, 85
division of legislative

powers within the
empire [dyarchy],
xv, xvi, xxxix, xliii,
139–42, 156
Dunn [John Henry],
receiver general of
Upper Canada, 80
Dutch: of Niagara,
136; of New York,
156

Eastern Townships,
English minority in,
14, 25, 30, 32, 43,
63; sympathetic to
U.S., 130
Edinburgh Review,
xli
education, 27–8, 150;
and negligence of
British Govern-
ment, 21, 23, 66–7,
96–7, 107, 111;
English schools,
96–7; French
schools, seminaries,
and colleges, 22,
27–8, 55, 65–7;
and political intelli-
gence, 29
electoral frauds, 83–4
emigration: and
British policy,
118–24, 171–3;
and disposal of
public lands,
108–9, 110; to
Lower Canada, 16,

26, 32, 35, 42; re-
emigration to U.S.,
105, 112–113,
134–7; to Upper
Canada, 74–5, 79;
88–9, 93, 96
exclusion of French
Canadians from
government
employment, 23,
24, 26–7, 148
Executive Council,
xxxiv, xxxvi,
xxxvii, xxxix; and
animosities of race,
45, 56–7; collision
of with Legislative
Assembly, 11–12,
15–16, 33–4, 44–5;
and the demand for
responsibility, 76,
80–83, 88; election
of, 138–9; in Mar-
itime Provinces,
103–6; in Upper
Canada, 46, 74,
75–8. *See also*
Crown, Privy
Council, Legislative
Assembly, represen-
tative institutions
and responsible
government

Family Compact, vii,
xxxvii, 74–5, 82–3,
88
federation. *See* union

feudal tenure, xii,
20-1, 25, 32, 42-3,
149, French and
English opinion of,
17-19
fisheries disputes,
163, 166
Fitzroy, Sir Charles,
Governor of New-
foundland, 104
foreign relations,
128-9, 140-1
Fox, Charles James,
xxii

Gazette de Québec,
xxv
Governor, 6, 49-50,
56-60, 139; and
responsible govern-
ment, 151-2, 170.
See also Executive
Council, representa-
tive institutions and
responsible govern-
ment, Head, Sir
Francis Bond
grants of land: in
British North
America, 115-17;
in the United States,
116
Grey, Lord, xxxv
Grosse Isle Quaran-
tine Station,
120-1

habitant, 20-2, 25, 36

Halifax, 106, 113,
165-6
Hamel, Marcel-Pierre,
xxiv
Head, Major Charles
F., 104-5
Head, Sir Francis
Bond, xxxvii, 80-5,
95
Howe, Joseph, viii,
xiv

immigration. See emi-
gration
institutions, Old
World, in new
countries, 20-1,
64-5, 92-3, 169
intercolonial railway.
See railways
interference by home
government, 56-9,
101-2, 137,
139-41

Jessop, Henry, collec-
tor of customs,
Quebec, 120-1
Jesuit estates, 67
judiciary: administra-
tion of justice, 34,
63, 64, 164; and
Family Compact,
74, 96; judges,
independence of,
170; juries, perver-
sion of, 35; Justices
of the Peace, 61,

64-5; in Louisiana,
154; and national
hostilities, 34, 87

land policy. See public
lands
land registration. See
registry offices
Langevin, H.V., xxviii
language and litera-
ture question, 27-8,
147-8, 150; lack of
literature among
French Canadians,
149
law and legal codes,
43, 55, 64, 146
Le Canadien, xxii,
xxiv
Legislative Assembly.
142-4: attack on
Legislative Council,
76; Lower Canada,
collision of with
English popula-
tion, 30-4, 44, and
with executive,
45-50, 51-4, 158;
Maritime Provinces,
46, 102-3; New-
foundland, 46, 106;
and non-coopera-
tion with Upper
Canada, 100; and
provincial debt,
99-100; and Sir F.
Head's tenure,
80-5, 87, 95;

Upper Canada, 75–7, 96–7. *See also* Executive Council, Legislative Council, representative institutions and responsible government

Legislative Council, xxxiv, xlii, 169–70: allied with English population, 32, 33; Atlantic Provinces, 103, 106; Lower Canada, 45, 53–4; Upper Canada, 74–6

Livingstone, Mr. [Edward Livingston], 154

local government, xli, 20; and corruption, 82, 100; as foundation of self-government, 54, 61–2; in Montreal and Quebec, 63

Locke, John, xvii, xviii

Louisiana, French in, 39, 153–6

Lucas, C.P., vii, ix

Mackenzie [William Lyon], 86

MacKinnon, Frank, xiii

magistrates. *See* judiciary, justices of the peace

Maine, 163

Marine and Emigrant Hospital, 119

martial law, 124

M'Donnell [Alexander Macdonnell], Roman Catholic Bishop of Kingston, 94

Melbourne, Lord, xxxiv, xxxv, xxxvi

Militia, 34, 54, 61, 115, 116

Milnes [Sir R.S., Acting Governor of Lower Canada], 115

Missippi Emigration Society, 135

Monet, Jacques, xxiv, xxv

money bills, initiating of, 143–4, 170. *See also* Crown

Montreal Emigrant Society, 123

Morrin [Dr. Joseph], physician at Quebec, 119, 120, 122

Morris, John S., commissioner of Crown Lands, NS, 113

Mountain [Jacob], Anglican bishop of Quebec, 115

municipal institutions. *See* local government

nationality, French Canadian, 20–3, 35–8, 43–4, 145–51

Neilson, John, xxv

New, Chester, viii, x

New Brunswick, xliii, 46, 102–3, 105, 106, 109, 112–13, 163

Newfoundland, 46, 102, 106, 166

newspapers, 111, 131, 150; and national animosities, 28, 36, 74, 133; in Louisiana, 155. *See also Le Canadien, Gazette de Québec*

Nova Scotia, xliii, 46, 103, 105, 112–13, 163

officials. *See* bureaucracy

Orange Order, 94–5

Painchaud, Dr., 119

Papineau, Louis Joseph, xxii, xxiii, xxxiv, 17, 36, 48

Parent, Etienne, xxiii, xxvii

Passengers Acts, 120–2

patronage, 24, 45, 50, 55, 74–5, 141; and human ambition, 162

Poole, Dr., 121, 122

post offices, 71, 163

prerogative of the Crown. See Crown

Prince Edward's Island, 46, 103–4, 105, 166

Privy Council, 59

Proclamation of 1763, 41

Protestant clergy. See religion

public lands: disposal of, xxxix, 69, 104–18, 163, 171; and the Family Compact, 74, 97–8; and imperial interests, 140; in the U.S., 109–10. See also public works, settlement

public works, 31, 55–6, 77–8, 99–100, 159

quarantine, 120–2

Quebec Act, 1774, xxv, 64

Quebec Emigrants Society, 120, 123

racial conflict: Louisiana, 155–6;

Lower Canada, xxxvi, xxxvii, 13–17, 19, 26–32, 33–4, 37–40, 124–5; and U.S opinion of, 39, 128–32

railways, 111, 165–6

rebellions, 1837–38, xxii, xxxiv, xxxvii: Lower Canada, 11, 15, 33, 38, 127–8; Upper Canada, 85–6, 91, 129; and U.S. involvement with, 39, 85, 128–33

rectories, 88, 90

reformers, xxxvii, xlii, and the Legislative Council, 76, 90; as political opposition in Upper Canada, 75–6, 79; and rebellion, 86, 87–8, 125–6; on responsible government, 60, 76–7. See also Head, Sir Francis Bond

registry offices, 17–18, 32

religion: Church of England, 74–5, 89–92, 94; Church of Scotland, or Presbyterians, 89, 91, 93; and educa-

tion, 22, 66–8; and endowments, 159, 169; intolerance in Upper Canada, 94–95; Protestants and Protestant clergy, 42, 43, 67–9, 89–91, 94–5; Roman Catholic Church and Roman Catholics, 20, 35, 43, 54, 93–4; tolerance in Lower Canada, 27, 37, 67

representative institutions and responsible government, xii, xiii, xxxvii–xli, 46–7, 48–51, 54, 125–6, 137–8, 170; in Maritime Provinces, 103–4; and reformers of Upper Canada, 76–7, 87–8

revenue, 47, 70, 110, 170; and disputes between the Canadas, 70–1, 78, 100, 159; and federal union, 157; in New Brunswick, 103; and the prerogative of the Crown, 143, 170. See also casual and territorial revenues, customs duties, taxation

Roebuck, John Arthur, xxii, xxiii

Rolph, Dr., 80

Russell, Lord John, xii, xxxv, xli

St. Lawrence River, 20, 31, 41, 98–9

Secretary of State for the Colonies, 56–8, 90, 104, 109, 141

seigneurial tenure. *See* feudal tenure

settlement, 40–1, 108–9, 115–16, 118, 144, 171–3; and policy in U.S., 109–13

sherrifs, 61, 96

Skey, Dr. Joseph, 120

Smith, Adam, 162

speaker, election of, 51

Stuart, Andrew, 149

Talbot, Colonel Thomas, 115

taxation, 31, 71–2, 100, 121–2; and local assessment, 78, 144

territorial revenues. *See* casual and territorial revenues

Tory party: Upper Canada, xlii. *See also* Family Compact

Townships. *See* Eastern Townships

uncertainty of policy, evil of, 7–8, 38, 45, 58, 101, 108–9

union: British North America, 142–3, 157–8; and inclusion of Atlantic provinces, 106, 196; and legislative union, 160–7; Upper and Lower Canada, 30, 71, 101, 158–9, 168

United Empire Loyalists, 115, 116

United States and British North America: American settlers in British North America, 39, 105, 115, 116, 146; and British North American emigration to the U.S., 112–13, 130, 134–5; British North American envy, 77, 81, 101, 126–7, 160–2; cultural similarities, 132–3; and differences, 61, 92, 105, 111–12, 116, 143–4; and threat of annexation, 37–9, 130–3, 147, 151

Wakefield, Edward Gibbon, xv, xxxvii, xli